T0068534

FAR FROM
THE TREE

FAR FROM THE TREE

HOW CHILDREN AND THEIR PARENTS LEARN
TO ACCEPT ONE ANOTHER ... OUR DIFFERENCES UNITE US

YOUNG ADULT EDITION

Andrew Solomon
adapted by Laurie Calkhoven

SIMON & SCHUSTER BFYR

NEW YORK   LONDON   TORONTO   SYDNEY   NEW DELHI

SIMON & SCHUSTER BFYR

An imprint of Simon & Schuster Children's Publishing Division
1230 Avenue of the Americas, New York, New York 10020
Text copyright © 2012 by Andrew Solomon
Young Reader's Edition adaptation copyright © 2017 by Simon & Schuster, Inc.
Jacket illustration copyright © 2017 by Maricor/Maricar
SIMON & SCHUSTER BFYR is a trademark of Simon & Schuster, Inc.
For information about special discounts for bulk purchases, please contact
Simon & Schuster Special Sales at 1-866-506-1949 or business@simonandschuster.com.
The Simon & Schuster Speakers Bureau can bring authors to your live event.
For more information or to book an event, contact the Simon & Schuster Speakers Bureau at
1-866-248-3049 or visit our website at www.simonspeakers.com.
Andrew Solomon is represented as a speaker by the Tuesday Agency. For more information or
to book an event, contact the agency at 1-319-338-7080. Further information may be found on
Andrew Solomon's website at www.andrewsolomon.com.
Jaclet design by Chloë Foglia
Interior design by Hilary Zarycky
The text for this book was set in Perpetua Std.
Manufactured in the United States of America
First Edition
2 4 6 8 10 9 7 5 3 1
Library of Congress Cataloging-in-Publication Data
Names: Solomon, Andrew, 1963– author. | Calkhoven, Laurie.
Title: Far from the tree / Andrew Solomon ; adapted by Laurie Calkhoven.
Description: How Children and Their Parents Learn to Accept One Another . . . Our
Differences Unite Us —Young Adult edition. | New York : Simon & Schuster
Books for Young Readers, [2017]
Identifiers: LCCN 2016027697 (print) |
| ISBN 9781481440905 (hardcover) | ISBN 9781481440929 (eBook)
Subjects: LCSH: Children with disabilities—United States—Psychology—Juvenile literature.
| Exceptional children—United States—Psychology—Juvenile literature. | Parents of
children with disabilities—United States—Juvenile literature. | Parents of exceptional
children—United States—Juvenile literature. | Identity (Psychology)—United States—
Juvenile literature. | Parent and child—United States—Psychological aspects—
Juvenile literature.
Classification: LCC HV888.5 .S652 2017 (print) | LCC HV888.5 (eBook)
| DDC 362.4083/0973—dc23
LC record available at https://lccn.loc.gov/2016027697

For John,
for the sake of whose difference
I would gladly give up all the sameness in the world

Contents

Will it come like a change in the weather?
Will its greeting be courteous or rough?
Will it alter my life altogether?
O tell me the truth about love.

—W. H. Auden,
"O Tell Me the Truth About Love"

Son

I HAD DYSLEXIA AS A CHILD; indeed, I have it now. I still cannot write by hand without focusing on each letter as I form it, and even then, some letters are out of order, or left out entirely. My mother saw this early on and began to work on reading with me when I was two. I spent long afternoons on her lap, learning to sound out words. We practiced letters as though no shapes could ever be lovelier than theirs. To keep my attention, she gave me a notebook with a yellow felt cover on which Winnie-the-Pooh and Tigger were sewn. We made flash cards and played games with them. I loved the attention, and my mother brought a sense of fun to her teaching.

When I was six, my parents applied to eleven schools in New York City, and all eleven turned me down. Despite my advanced reading skills, my test scores said I would never learn to read and write. Only a year later did the principal of one school overrule the exam results so that I could be enrolled.

That early victory over dyslexia taught my family that with patience, love, intelligence, and will, we could defeat a neurological abnormality. Unfortunately, it also set the stage for our later struggle. It made it hard to believe that we couldn't correct something else that was perceived as abnormal—my being gay.

People ask when I knew I was gay, and I wonder what that means. Recent studies have shown that as early as age two, many boys who will grow up to be gay avoid some rough-and-tumble play. By age six, a good number behave in some ways that aren't typical "boy." I knew that many things I liked were unmasculine: I never traded a baseball card, but instead shared the plots of operas on the school bus, which did not make me popular.

I was popular at home, but I was also corrected. Once, when I was about seven, I was leaving a shoe store with my mother and brother, and the salesman asked us what color balloons we'd like to take home. My brother wanted a red balloon. I wanted a pink one. My mother said that I did *not* want a pink balloon. She announced, over my protests, that my favorite color was blue, so I ended up taking a blue balloon. The fact that in adulthood my favorite color is blue stands as evidence of my mother's influence; the fact that I am still gay is evidence of its limits.

Though it was supposed to be integrated, my gradeschool class actually included only a few black and Latino kids, and they mostly socialized with one another. My first year at school was second grade, and when Debbie Camacho had a birthday party in Spanish Harlem, my mother made me go. I was one of only two white kids who went, out of a class of forty; none of my friends was there and I was terrified. Debbie's cousins tried to get me to dance. Everyone spoke Spanish, the food was unfamiliar, and I had a kind of panic attack and went home in tears.

I didn't see the parallels between everyone else's avoidance of Debbie's party and my own unpopularity. It never occurred to me that she and I had anything in common. It was only years later that I understood why my mother had made me go, and recognized that it was a moral issue. Then I was glad to have been there: It was the right thing to do. Debbie's party was the beginning of my tolerance toward people who were different from me, and that attitude ultimately helped me understand that I was okay even though I was different.

A few months after Debbie's party, Bobby Finkel had a birthday and invited everyone in the class but me. My mother called his mother, sure that there had been a mistake. Mrs. Finkel said that Bobby didn't like me and didn't want me there. My mother picked me up after school on the day of the party and took me to the zoo and out for a hot fudge sundae. Now I can see how hurt my mother must have been for me—more hurt than I was, or let myself notice I was. She knew that being different had sad consequences, and she wanted to protect me.

Making me choose the blue balloon had been partly an effort to shelter me and partly an act of aggression. In many ways, my mother encouraged me to be myself, and she made me believe I could be loved for who I was rather than for who the larger world suggested I should be. But at the same time, she wanted to change me in ways that I couldn't be changed. That made me angry; it still does. The hardest thing to make sense of was the fact that the love was real even though it coincided with the rejection of a central part of me.

I floundered in the tricky waters of elementary school, but at home, away from the cruelty, my quirks were mostly humored. When I was ten, I became fascinated by the tiny European country of Liechtenstein. A year later my father took us along on a business trip to Switzerland, and one morning my mother announced that she'd arranged for us all to drive to Liechtenstein. The same mother who forbade the pink balloon took us to lunch in a charming café, on a tour of the art museum, and to visit the printing office where they made the country's gorgeous postage stamps, just to indulge my weird fascination.

Still, there were limits, and pink balloons fell on the wrong side of them. My parents' rule was to be interested in others from within a pact of sameness. I wanted to do more than just be interested in the whole world: I wanted to be a part of it. I wanted to dive for pearls, memorize Shakespeare, break the sound barrier. Maybe I wanted to transform myself because I wanted to break away from my family's way of being. Maybe I was already trying to get closer to who I wanted to become.

In 1993, I was assigned to investigate Deaf culture for the *New York Times*. I thought of deafness as a defect. Most deaf children are born to hearing parents—parents who often think deafness is a tragedy, and throw themselves into making sure their deaf children learn to speak and read lips. Teaching those skills usually takes so much time and energy that parents neglect other areas of their children's education. Some deaf people become very good at speech and lip-reading over time, but at the expense of learning history and math, and they end up fairly uneducated.

Some kids stumble upon Deaf identity as teenagers, and

it makes them feel free and powerful. They move into a world that uses Sign as a language and they become proud of the same things about themselves that used to embarrass their parents. Some hearing parents accept this confident new identity, but others struggle against it.

I understood this complex process of self-discovery because I am gay. Gay people usually grow up with straight parents, who often believe that their children would be better off straight. Frequently, they pressure their kids to be or act straight. These kids discover gay identity as teenagers or later, and it comes as a huge relief. So the line between illness (the negative way of looking at a condition) and identity (the positive way of looking at it) is never clear. Something you start out considering as an illness can become a cornerstone of your identity. Also, what some people think of as an illness, others think of as an identity. And the same attribute can be defined as an illness at one time, then in a different historical time it can change to an identity. Sometimes, it can be an identity and an illness at the same time, even for the person who has the condition.

When I started writing about the deaf, the surgical insertion of a device called a cochlear implant, which can offer something similar to hearing, was a recent innovation. Its supporters said it was a miracle cure for a terrible defect. The Deaf community saw it as an attack on their culture. The issue is complicated by the fact that cochlear implants are most successful when they are introduced in infants, meaning that the decision is made by parents before the child can possibly weigh in with an opinion.

My parents would have said yes to a childhood operation

that would have made me straight. If such a process is ever invented, I think most of gay culture would be wiped out within a generation. That thought makes me terribly sad.

But it has taken time for me to value my own life. I, too, once wished to be straight. While I have come to understand the richness of Deaf culture, I know that before I did this research, I would have assumed that the only thing to do for a deaf child would be to fix the abnormality.

A few years after I began spending time in the Deaf community, a friend gave birth to a daughter who was a dwarf, and she had a lot of questions. Should she raise her daughter to believe that she was just like everyone else, only shorter? Or should she make sure that her daughter had dwarf role models and developed a dwarf identity? Or should she consider surgery to lengthen her daughter's limbs? I saw a pattern that was becoming familiar.

First I had found common ground with the Deaf, and now I felt the same way about a dwarf. Who else was out there waiting to join us kids who were different, and whose parents had a hard time figuring out what to do about it?

Because genes and cultural habits get passed down from one generation to the next, most of us share at least some traits with our parents. These are *vertical* identities, like the trunk of the family tree. Ethnicity, for example, is a vertical identity. Children of color are born to parents of color. Language is usually vertical, since people who speak Greek as a first language usually raise their children to speak Greek too, even if those children also speak another language some of the time.

Nationality is vertical, except for immigrants. Nearsightedness and blond hair are often passed from parent to child, but neither one is an important basis for identity—nearsightedness because it is easily corrected, and blond hair because what's in style shifts all the time, and besides, you can change your hair color easily, many times over.

But what happens when something about you is so completely alien to your parents that you have to learn your identity outside of your family? This is a *horizontal* identity, one that does not show up on the intergenerational family tree. These identities can come from a recessive gene, a random genetic mutation, or values and preferences that you don't share with your parents. Being gay is a horizontal identity because most gay kids are not born to gay parents. They need to learn about being gay by observing and taking part in a subculture. Physical disabilities and genius are both usually horizontal identities. Mental illness is also usually horizontal. So are conditions such as autism and intellectual disabilities. Even being a psychopath is a horizontal identity. Most criminals weren't raised by gang members; they have to invent their own identity outside of their families.

In the twenty-first-century United States, it is sometimes still hard to be black or Asian or Jewish or female, but no one suggests that all people should try to turn themselves into white Christian men. Many vertical identities make people uncomfortable, and yet we don't try to eliminate them. Instead, over time, we recognize the flaws in our society that have made these conditions difficult for the people who have them. We try to fix the society, not to change the Asians or Jews or women or African-Americans. Parents teach these children a sense of pride about who they are, even when the larger society is divided by prejudice.

The disadvantages of being gay are no greater than those of believing in a minority religion, but many parents have long tried to turn their gay children straight. Many parents also rush to make certain kinds of physical differences "normal." Some children's minds are labeled as diseased—with autism, intellectual disabilities, or transgenderism—in part because those minds make their parents uncomfortable. Things get corrected that would be better left alone.

My parents misunderstood who I was, and I have come to believe that all parents sometimes misunderstand the core nature of their own children. Many parents see a child's horizontal identity as an insult. Those same children are also different from most of their peers. They're not accepted at home *or* in the world. Families tend to support and encourage vertical identities. Horizontal ones, however, are often treated as failings.

We use the word *illness* to criticize a way of being, and *identity* to validate a way of being. Many conditions can be viewed as both an illness and an identity. Just as in physics, where we've learned that energy is sometimes a wave and sometimes a particle, we need to come up with a new vocabulary for conditions that can be both illness and identity.

I thought that if the identity of being gay could grow out of homosexuality, which used to be considered an illness; and if the identity of Deafness could grow out of deafness, which has been widely considered a disability; and if the identity of dwarfism could emerge from what was considered an apparent deformity, then there must be other categories in this awkward in-between territory. Instead of being in a marginal minority, I was suddenly in vast company. Each of these experiences—deafness, gayness, and dwarfism, among many others—can isolate those who are affected, but together our struggles and differences connect us. Everybody is different in one way or another. It's the one thing we all have in common.

The children I describe in this book have horizontal conditions that their parents find strange and alien. They are deaf or dwarfs; they have Down syndrome, autism, schizophrenia, or severe disabilities; they are prodigies; they are people born out of rape, or people who commit crimes; they are transgender.

There's an old saying that the apple doesn't fall far from the tree, meaning children tend to be like their parents. The children in this book are apples that have fallen elsewhere—some a couple of orchards away, some on the other side of the world. Yet many of these children learn to embrace their horizontal identities, and help their families to tolerate, accept, and even celebrate them.

All children are startling to their parents. I have yet to meet any parent who doesn't sometimes look at his or her child and think, "What planet did you come from?" I've yet to meet a child who hasn't sometimes wondered the same thing about his or her parents. So these dramatic situations expand on a theme. By learning more about exceptional cases, we can start to understand the universal phenomenon of difference within families.

You need three levels of acceptance: self-acceptance, family acceptance, and acceptance by the larger society. It's important to know how autistic people feel about autism, or dwarfs about dwarfism. Self-acceptance is critical. But compassion and empathy begin at home. Most of the parents and children I have written about love one another across the divide of their differences. When they look deep into their child's eyes, parents can see both a reflection of themselves and someone entirely strange, and still love their child completely. Children can look back and feel the same combination of reassuring sameness, confusing differences, and overpowering love. The society at large will often take its cues from the family and the self. There is more imagination in the world than one might think.

Most kids want to be like other kids. That was never true for me. Even in kindergarten, I spent recess talking to my teachers because other children didn't get what I was about. By seventh grade I was eating lunch in the office of the principal's secretary. I graduated from high school without once visiting the cafeteria, where I would have sat with the girls and been laughed at for doing so, or sat with the boys and been laughed at for being the kind of boy who should really sit with the girls. I liked being different, so when I began to realize my sexual desires were even more forbidden than most kids', I was thrilled by my own exotic nature. I was also horrified by it; I thought if anyone found out I was gay, I would have to die.

At the top of my list of people I didn't want to find out were my parents—who had communicated a clear message to me about "being a boy" ever since the time of the pink balloon. As an adult, I can understand that my mother didn't want me to be gay partly because she thought it wouldn't be a happy kind of life for me. She also didn't like to think of herself as the mother of a gay son. The problem wasn't that she wanted to control *my* life, but that she wanted to control *her* life. But there was no way for her to fix *her* problem of having a gay son without involving me.

Although being gay was a horizontal identity, my discomfort with myself was an inclination I inherited from my mother. My mother was Jewish (a vertical identity) but initially at least, she didn't want to be. She had learned that attitude from her own father, who kept his religion a secret so he could hold a job at a company and belong to a country club where Jews were not allowed. In her early twenties, my mother was briefly engaged to a man who broke it off when his family threatened to disinherit him if he married a Jew. Five years later my mother chose to marry my Jewish father and live in a mostly Jewish world, but she carried her lifelong experience of anti-Semitism within her. When she saw people who fit certain Jewish stereotypes, she would say, "Those are the people who give us a bad name." She once said that a girl in my ninth-grade class who was considered a beauty looked "very Jewish." It wasn't intended as a compliment.

Like my mother, I carried a need to deny my own identity. Long after childhood, I hung onto childish things. I was immature and prudish as a means to obliterate my sexual desires. I had an idea that I could be Christopher Robin forever in the Hundred-Acre Wood. The last book in the Winnie-the-Pooh series, *The House at Pooh Corner*, ends, "Wherever they go, and whatever happens to them on the way, in that enchanted place on the top of the Forest, a little boy and his Bear will always be playing."

I decided I would be that boy with the bear, because what growing up meant for me was humiliating. At thirteen I bought a copy of *Playboy* and studied it for hours. I wanted to be more comfortable with women's bodies, but it was much harder than my homework. I wanted a normal life and a family one day, and by the time I reached high school I knew that to achieve that, I'd have to have sex with a woman. I didn't think I could bring myself to do so. I thought often about dying. The half of me that wasn't planning to be Christopher Robin was planning to throw myself in front of a train.

When I was in eighth grade at the Horace Mann School in New York, an older kid nicknamed me Percy. This was long before Percy Jackson came along and made the name *Percy* cool; at the time, it sounded both feminine and weirdly old-fashioned. That guy and I were on the same school-bus route, and each day when I boarded, he and his friends would chant, "Percy! Percy! Percy!" Sometimes everyone on the bus chanted at the top of their lungs for the entire forty-five minutes. I sat there pretending that it wasn't happening.

Four months after it began, I came home one day and my mother asked if anything had been happening on the school bus. A boy had told his mother, who had called mine. When I admitted it, my mother hugged me for a long time and asked me why I hadn't told her. That had never occurred to me, partly because talking about something so embarrassing would only make it more real, partly because I thought there was nothing to be done about it, and partly because I felt that the things the other kids found so disgusting about me would also be disgusting to her.

A chaperone rode the school bus after that, and the chanting stopped. Instead I was called "faggot" on the bus and at school, often within hearing of teachers who said nothing. Homophobia was everywhere when I was growing up, and my school delivered a sharply polished version of it.

In June of 2012, the *New York Times Magazine* published an article about some male faculty members who had sexually abused boys at the school while I was student there. The article quoted students who later developed addictions and other self-destructive behavior, which they believed was a result of the abuse. One had committed suicide. When I was in ninth grade, the art teacher, who was also a football coach, kept trying to talk to me about masturbation. I thought it might be a trick, and that if I responded, he'd tell everyone I was gay. No other faculty member ever made a move on me—perhaps because I was a skinny, awkward kid with glasses and braces, perhaps because my parents had a reputation of being fiercely protective, perhaps because of the false arrogance with which I tried to protect myself from everyone else.

The article made me sad and confused. Some of the teachers accused of the abuse had been especially kind to me. My eighth-grade history teacher had taken me out to dinner, given me a copy of the *Jerusalem Bible*, and talked with me during free periods. The music teacher had awarded me concert solos, let me call him by his first name and hang out in his office, and led the glee-club trips that were among my happiest adventures. These men seemed to recognize who I was and thought well of me anyway. Their unspoken acknowledgment of my sexuality helped me avoid becoming an addict or a suicide. But their behavior toward others had been horribly destructive.

The art teacher was fired soon after my conversations with him. The history teacher was let go and committed suicide a year later. The music teacher, who was married, survived when many gay teachers were fired, only to have his reputation destroyed after he died. Other gay teachers, innocent ones, were fired because the school was trying to root out pedophilia, which they falsely equated with homosexuality. The larger school community supported prejudice against gay people in the mistaken belief that gay people were child abusers. It was a terrifying place to be as a gay teen; if anyone found out, I thought, I would be not only a social outcast, but also unemployable for the rest of my life.

The head of the theater department, Anne MacKay, was a lesbian who survived the firings, which targeted gay men. Twenty years after I graduated, we started to e-mail each other. When I learned that she was dying, I went to visit her. Miss MacKay had been the wise teacher who once explained gently that I was teased because of how I walked, and tried to show me a more confident and masculine stride. I had come to thank her. But she had invited me so she could apologize. She felt as if she had failed the gay students to whom she might have been a beacon. We both knew, though, that if she had been more open back then, she would have lost her job.

When I was in high school, I knew she was gay, and she

knew I was gay, yet we were never able to talk about it. Seeing her after so many years stirred up an old loneliness. It reminded me of how isolating an exceptional characteristic can be unless we find a way to turn it into a horizontal identity through solidarity with other people like us.

There are a lot of sexual opportunities available to young people, especially in New York, where I grew up. One of my chores was to walk our dog before bedtime. When I was fourteen, I discovered two gay bars near our apartment. I would walk Martha, our Kerry Blue Terrier, on a circuit that included both of those bars, watching the guys spill out onto the street while Martha tugged on her leash. When I eventually had sex with a man, at seventeen, I felt that I was cutting myself off forever from the normal world. I went home and boiled my clothes, then took a scalding hour-long shower.

When I was nineteen, I read an ad in the back of *New York* magazine that offered therapy for people who had issues with sex. I knew the back of a magazine wasn't a good place to find treatment, but I was too embarrassed to reveal my problem to anyone who knew me.

So I took my savings to an office in the Hell's Kitchen neighborhood and had long conversations about my sexual anxieties without telling the so-called therapist that I wasn't interested in women. I also didn't mention the busy sexual life I had by that time with men. I began "counseling" with people I was told to call "doctors," who prescribed "exercises" with women. These women weren't exactly prostitutes, but they weren't exactly anything else.

I wasn't cured of being gay, but I did eventually recover from the idea that I had an illness. That office on West 45th Street still shows up in my dreams. My treatment took only two hours a week for about six months, and it made it possible for me to have heterosexual experiences that I'm glad to have had. I've truly loved some of the women with whom I've had relationships, but I was never able to forget that the "cure" that helped me be with them was all about hating myself. The pressure that led me to make the effort to turn myself straight made romantic love almost impossible for me during my early adulthood. I was either inauthentic with women, or self-loathing with men.

My interest in the differences between parents and children grew out of my need to understand the central despair that cast such a long shadow over my otherwise-happy life. While I'd like to blame my parents, I have come to believe that a lot of my pain came from the world around me, and some of it even came from me. In the heat of an argument, my mother once told me, "Someday you can go to a therapist and tell him all about how your terrible mother ruined your life. But it will be *your* ruined life you're talking about. So make a life for yourself in which you can feel happy, and in which you can love and be loved, because that's what's actually important."

You can love someone but not accept that person. You can accept someone but not love him or her. I wrongly saw the flaws in my parents' acceptance of me as proof that they didn't love me enough. Now I think their experience felt like having a child who spoke a language they'd never thought of studying. Love is ideally there from the second a child is born. Most parents love their children. Acceptance, however, is a process, and it takes time. It always takes time, even when your child doesn't have a particularly challenging, alien identity. My parents didn't immediately accept me, but they always loved me. I can see that now. But until they accepted me, I didn't know if or when they would do so, and that caused me a lot of anguish. It made it much harder for me to accept myself.

How are parents to know whether to erase or celebrate one of their child's characteristics? When I was born, homosexual activity was a crime. During my childhood, it was also defined as a symptom of illness. It was certainly not something to be encouraged. Now that I'm an adult, being gay is an identity, and I'm pretty happy. The tragic life my parents feared I might have when I asked for the pink balloon turned out not to be the only possibility. Yet, the view of homosexuality as a crime, an illness, and a sin is still held by millions of people. Working on this book, I sometimes felt it was easier for me to ask people about their disabled children, their children conceived in rape, and their children who committed crimes, than it would have been to look at how many parents still respond negatively to having gay children.

If we develop prenatal tests for homosexuality, how many couples will choose to abort their gay children? If we develop a drug that can be used to prevent homosexuality in unborn children, how many parents will be willing to try it? Ten years ago, in a *New Yorker* poll of parents, one out of three said they would rather have an unhappy straight child than a happy gay one. You can't hate a horizontal identity much more explicitly than to wish unhappiness for your children as a reasonable price of being sure they won't be different from you. Self-acceptance is only part of the struggle. So is acceptance by the larger society. Family is the one in the middle, the one that translates between the individual and the society, and for that reason it is especially powerful. All three goals can feel very elusive. So what do we do with the kind of feelings revealed in the *New Yorker* poll?

I would hate to see my horizontal identity vanish. I would hate it for those who share my identity, and for those who don't. I hate the loss of diversity in the world, even though I sometimes get tired of embodying that diversity. I don't wish for anyone in particular to be gay, but the idea of no one being gay makes me miss myself already.

While I might have had an easier life if I had been straight, without my struggles I wouldn't be me, and I like being myself better than I like the idea of being someone else. I have wondered whether I could have stopped hating my sexual orientation earlier without the over-the-top aspects of Gay Pride: the "dykes on bikes" and drag queens who I used to think gave us a bad name. A friend who thought Gay Pride was getting a bit carried away with itself once suggested we organize Gay Humility Week. It's a good idea, but its time has not yet come. Nonetheless being able to celebrate myself within gay culture makes up for all the years of self-loathing. Someday I hope being gay will turn into a neutral fact, but that's some way off. Neutrality, which appears to lie halfway between shame and rejoicing, is the endgame. We'll know we've reached it when activism becomes unnecessary.

It is a surprise to me to like myself. Among all the possibilities I contemplated for my future, that one never came up. In the Gnostic *Gospel of Thomas*, Jesus says, "If you bring forth what is within you, what is within you will save you. If you do not bring forth what is within you, what is within you will destroy you." Jesus's words embrace those of us with horizontal identities. Keeping my gayness locked away nearly destroyed me. Bringing it forth has helped save me.

Modern love comes with more and more options. For most of history, people married members of the opposite sex, and only from their own class, race, religion, and community. People were also supposed to accept the children born to them because one could do little to choose or change them. Physical and social mobility have altered that logic. Birth control introduced greater choice into having children. So did modern fertility treatments. Now, parents can decide whether to initiate, continue, or terminate a pregnancy based on embryo analysis and prenatal testing.

Reports of infants thrown away in dumpsters or abandoned to foster care show that humans have the ability to detach themselves emotionally. Oddly, this abandonment seems to have as much to do with an infant's appearance as with its health or character. Parents will usually take home a child with a life-threatening *internal* defect, but often enough, not one with a minor *visible* defect. Obvious disabilities can offend parents' pride and their need for privacy. Everyone can see that this child isn't the one you wanted. Parents expect doctors to fix all kind of problems that aren't life-threatening. Short kids are given human growth hormones. Cleft palates are repaired. We are eliminating some of the variety within mankind.

Yet, while modern medicine can make us more uniform in trivial ways, we have become more far-flung in our desires and our ways of realizing them. The Internet allows anyone to find others who share his or her quirks or differences. Twenty-five years ago, if your child had primordial dwarfism, you might have had trouble finding anyone else who shared that rare condition; today, you can type the words into Google and find a worldwide community. These online support systems are vital as the lines between illness and identity are challenged and we allow our true selves to emerge.

Modern life is lonely in many ways, but everyone with access to a computer can find like-minded people. Vertical families are breaking down, especially in divorce, but horizontal ones are flourishing. If you can figure out who you are, you can find other people who are the same. Social progress is making disabling conditions easier to live with.

Some vertical identities, such as schizophrenia and Down syndrome, are thought to be entirely genetic. Others, such as being transgender, are thought to be largely a result of the environment in which the fetus develops or the child is raised. Nature and nurture are believed to be opposing forces, but more often it is nature *via* nurture, not nature *versus* nurture. Environmental factors can alter the brain. Conversely, brain chemistry and structure partly determine how we are affected by the world around us.

Even though nature and nurture are intertwined, it is easier for parents to tolerate syndromes assigned to nature. If your child has dwarfism, no one will accuse you of bad behavior for having produced such a child. However, a child's success in accepting his or her dwarfism and valuing his or her own life may be mainly a function of nurture. If you have a child who has committed serious crimes, it is often assumed that you did something wrong as a parent. But there is increasing evidence that some criminality may be hardwired in the brain, and that even the most nurturing parents cannot necessarily sway a child who is predisposed to gruesome acts.

The social perception of whether any supposed deficit is the parents' fault is a critical factor in the experience of both children and parents. Blaming the parents stems from ignorance, but it also reflects our belief that we control our own destinies and those of our children. Unfortunately, that belief does not save anyone's children; it only destroys some parents, who crumble under society's criticism or blame themselves. There is no contradiction between loving someone and feeling burdened by that person. No one loves without reservation. We would all be better off if we could stop disapproving of parental ambivalence. All that children can require of their parents is that they neither insist on perfect happiness nor lapse into the brutality of giving up. These parents need space to feel ambivalent. For those who love, there should be no shame in being exhausted—even in imagining another life than the one they have.

My study is of families who accept their children, and how that acceptance relates to those children's self-identity. In turn, it looks at how the acceptance of the larger society affects both these children and their families. Our parents are metaphors for ourselves: we struggle for their acceptance as a displaced way of struggling to accept ourselves. Our society is likewise a metaphor for our parents: Our quest for esteem in the larger world is a manifestation of our wish for parental love.

Social movements have come in sequence. First came religious freedom, followed by women's suffrage and minority race rights. Gay liberation and disability rights ensued. The women's movement and the civil rights movement were focused on vertical identities, so they gained traction before the movements on behalf of those with horizontal identities. Each movement borrows from the ones that came before.

Preindustrial societies could be cruel to people who were different, but they did not hide them away. Postindustrial societies put the disabled in institutions. That set the stage for eugenics, the belief in scientifically "improving" the human population by preventing "defective" people from reproducing. Hitler murdered more than 270,000 people with disabilities on the grounds that they were "travesties of human form and spirit." Hitler wasn't alone. Laws to permit involuntary sterilization and abortion were passed in Finland, Denmark, Switzerland, and Japan, as well as in twenty-five American states.

The disability rights movement, at the most basic level, seeks to accommodate difference rather than erase it. One of its successes is to understand that the interests of children, parents, and society are not the same, and that disabled children are the least able to defend themselves. In spite of persisting challenges, the disability rights movement has made tremendous strides: social progress. At the same time, scientific advances allow parents to avoid having certain kinds of disabled

children: medical progress. Some disabilities might be elimi-
nated completely.

It's not easy to know where to draw the line. There are
treatments for many of the conditions I investigated that can
erase them to some degree. Most deaf children can get implants
that let them hear, more or less. A drug to block the action of
the gene that causes most dwarfism is being tested. Is selective
abortion the first step in a campaign to eliminate people with
disabilities? That might not be the aim of parents, but medical
advances could reduce the disabled population by great numbers. I believe in social progress and medical progress, but I
wish they were more awake to each other. Sometimes scientists
don't understand that there are people who would prefer no
to be cured—just as I wouldn't want, at this point, to be cur
of being gay.

Repairing people's bodies and repairing social prejud
are goals that sometimes get tangled up in troubling
A repaired body may have been achieved through su
trauma. A partially repaired prejudice can eliminate th
for civil rights that its existence called into being by
people question the special protections that victims
dice often enjoy. If you have the disability of dwarfis
accommodations need to be made; if you're just sho
own problem. Disabled people are protected by fra
they are judged to have an identity rather than an
may lose those protections.

Although we have moved in recent years aw
models and toward identity models, such a shif
good thing. After I had come to see Deafness

autism and transgenderism as identities worthy of appreciation, I came upon the pro-ana and pro-mia movements, which seek to remove the negative associations around the eating disorders of anorexia and bulimia. Anorexia has the highest mortality rate of any mental illness. To propose that anorexics and bulimics are simply pursuing an identity is as morally questionable as accepting the belief that gang members are merely pursuing an identity that happens to include killing people. It's clear that there are boundaries to the concept of identity. It's not clear where those boundaries lie.

Over ten years I interviewed more than three hundred families for this book. A child's traumatic origins (rape) or traumatic acts (crime) can have surprising parallels to the conditions of the mind (autism, schizophrenia) or of the body (dwarfism, deafness, multiple severe disabilities), or of both (Down syndrome, transgenderism). I wanted to show that raising and/or being a child with extraordinary abilities (prodigies) is in some ways like raising and/or being a child with reduced capacities.

Each of these chapters poses a particular set of questions, and taken together, they show us the issues faced by children with horizontal identities and their families.

I had to learn a great deal to be able to hear these children and their mothers and fathers. On my first day at my first dwarf convention, I went over to a teenage girl who was sobbing. "This is what I look like," she blurted, half laughing and half crying. "These people look like me." Her mother, who was standing nearby, said, "You don't know what this means to my

daughter. But it also means a lot to me, to meet these other parents who will know what I'm talking about."

Many of the worlds I visited had such a rewarding sense of community that I felt a startling desire to belong to them. I remember walking into a meeting of the National Association of the Deaf and thinking, "I wish I were Deaf." That's not to say that I wished I couldn't hear. I make use of my hearing all the time and I'm very attached to it. But I saw the intimacy and humor shared by all these men and women who had conversations flying from their moving hands, and I wanted to be part of the excitement among them. I do not want to make light of the difficulty of these horizontal identities, but I knew about that going in. What I did not know about or expect was all the joy.

Many of the people I interviewed said that they would never exchange their experiences for any other life. Having a severe challenge intensifies life for both children and parents. The lows are almost always very low; the highs are sometimes very high. Those who believe their suffering has been valuable are able to love more freely than those who see no meaning in their pain.

The world is made more interesting by having every sort of person in it. That is a social vision. We should alleviate the suffering of each individual to the outer limits of our abilities. That is a humanist vision with medical overtones. Some people think that without suffering, the world would be boring. Some think that without *their own* suffering, the world would be boring. Life is enriched by difficulty. But it is not suffering that is precious. The advantages are achieved in the ways we think about that suffering. Suffering will never be in short supply. The trick is making something exalted out of it.

The question I was most frequently asked about this project was which of these conditions was the worst. Difference and disability seem to invite people to step back and judge. Parents judge which lives are worth living, and worth their living with; activists judge those parents for doing so; doctors judge which lives to save; politicians judge how much accommodation people with special needs deserve.

The tendency to make negative judgments is not confined to people in the mainstream. Almost everyone I interviewed for any chapter in this book was put off by some of the other chapters. Deaf people didn't want to be compared to schizophrenics. Criminals couldn't stand the idea that they might have something in common with transgender people. Prodigies and their families objected to being in a book with the severely disabled.

One mother who spoke freely to me about her teenager's autism only reluctantly told me that he was also transgender. The mother of a transman admitted that her son was on the autism spectrum only after I knew her very well. Where people feel pride and where they feel shame can be surprisingly variable.

We needed the multiculturalism that all the different identities claimed as an antidote to the melting pot of assimilation, where everyone had to conform to a single ideal. Now it's time for the little provinces of multiculturalism to find their collective strength. Our differences unite us. *Intersectionality* is the theory that various kinds of oppression feed on one another—that you cannot eliminate sexism, for example, without addressing racism. If we tolerate prejudice toward any group, we tolerate it toward all groups.

In 2011, gay marriage became legal in New York State after several Republicans in the State Senate agreed to support it. One of them, Roy J. McDonald, said that he had changed his stance on gay marriage because he had two autistic grandchildren, which had caused him "to rethink several issues." Each piece of the battle for broader recognition of one identity strengthens the others. The American poet Emma Lazarus said, "Until we are all free, we are none of us free." This book is about how we work together for that collective freedom. I encountered activists of every stripe while I did this research. The changes they sought seemed, individually, restricted to their own experiences with horizontal identities, but as a group they represent a rethinking of all humanity.

Some parents want to spur social change. Others use activism to distract themselves from grief, or because it gets them out of the house. Just as belief can result in action, action can result in belief. Parents can gradually fall in love with their children and with their children's disabilities, and by extension with all the world's disadvantages. Many of the activists I met were determined to help other people because they could not initially help themselves. By teaching the optimism or strength they had learned to families who were reeling from a recent diagnosis, they strengthened their own families.

I know that the child I was appalled my mother and concerned my father. I used to be furious at them for not embracing this horizontal part of me, for not embracing the early evidence of it. I wish I'd been accepted sooner and better. Acceptance was always easier for my father than it was for my mother, who died when I was twenty-seven and still grappling to define my identity. My father accepts himself more readily than my mother did herself. In her own mind, she always fell short. In my father's own mind, he is victorious. The inner daring of becoming myself was my mother's gift to me, while the outer audacity to express that self came from my father.

Writing this book addressed a sadness within me and—somewhat to my surprise—has largely cured it. In the wake of these stories about horizontal identities, I recast my own story. I have a horizontal experience of being gay and a vertical one of the family that produced me. The fact that they are not fully integrated no longer seems to undermine either one. I realized that I had demanded that my parents accept me, even while I had resisted accepting them. I set off to understand myself and ended up understanding my parents. Their love ultimately forgave me; mine came to forgive them, too.

For some parents of children with horizontal identities, acceptance comes when parents realize that they have slowly been falling in love with someone they didn't know enough to want. As these parents look back, they see how every stage of loving their child has enriched them in ways they never would have imagined.

For the children with horizontal identities, self-acceptance often comes when they find their horizontal communities. Sometimes they are led to these communities by their parents. Sometimes they have to drag their families kicking and screaming into these new worlds. Like mine, their horizontal and vertical identities may never be fully integrated.

This book's surprising discovery is that most of the families described here have ended up grateful for experiences they would have done anything to avoid.

Deaf

SCHOOLS PLAY AN UNUSUALLY IMPORTANT PART in the lives of deaf children. More than 90 percent of deaf children have two hearing parents. They enter families that do not understand their situation. They are first exposed to Deaf ways in schools. The Lexington Center for the Deaf is New York City's leading institution of Deaf culture and the largest school for the deaf in New York State, with three hundred and fifty students from preschool through high school. My introduction to the Lexington Center for the Deaf came when it was at the center of a controversy.

On Friday, April 22, 1994, I received a phone call from a man who had read my writing for the *New York Times* and heard I was planning to write on the Deaf. "There's a situation brewing at Lexington," he said. "If it's not resolved, we're going to see something happening in front of the center on Monday." I got some further details, and then he said, "You never heard from me. And I've never heard of you." And he hung up.

The school had just announced the hiring of a new CEO. A hearing board member, R. Max Gould, had been elected to the post by the center's board of directors. Deaf activists, Lexington student leaders, faculty representatives, and alumni organized within minutes and requested a meeting with the chairman of the board to demand Gould's resignation. They wanted a Deaf CEO. They were brushed off.

When I arrived at Lexington on Monday, crowds of students were marching outside the school. Some wore sandwich boards that read THE BOARD CAN HEAR BUT THEY ARE DEAF TO US. Others wore DEAF PRIDE T-shirts. MAX RESIGN signs could be seen everywhere.

Groups of students climbed onto a low wall so their cheers would be visible to the crowd. Others chanted back silently, many hands moving together in repeating words. I asked the sixteen-year-old African-American student-body president whether she had also demonstrated for race rights. "I'm too busy being Deaf right now," she signed. "My brothers aren't deaf, so they're taking care of being black." A deaf woman standing nearby threw in another question: "If you could change being deaf or black, which would you do?" The student was suddenly shy. "Both are hard," she signed. Another student interceded. "I am black and Deaf and proud, and I don't want to be white or hearing or different in any way from who I am." Her signs were big and clear. The first student repeated the sign for *proud*—her thumb rose up her chest—and then suddenly they were overcome with giggles and returned to the picket line.

For many deaf students, schools such as Lexington are the end of terrible loneliness. "I didn't know that there were other people like me until I got here," one deaf girl said to me at Lexington. "I thought everyone in the world would rather talk to someone else, someone hearing." A deaf person's school is a primary mode of self-identification and his or her introduction to Deaf culture.

When capitalized, *Deaf* refers to a culture, as distinct from *deaf*, which is a medical term. This distinction echoes that between *gay* and *homosexual*. An increasing number of deaf people maintain they would not choose to be hearing. To them, *cure*—deafness as a medical condition—is objectionable. *Accommodation*—deafness as disability—is more agreeable. *Celebration*—Deafness as culture—trumps all.

St. Paul's declaration in his letter to the Romans that "faith comes by hearing" was long misinterpreted to mean that those who could not hear were incapable of faith. Rome allowed no one to inherit property or title who could not give confession. For this reason, starting in the fifteenth century, some noble families, where deafness was common as a result of inbreeding, undertook oral education for their deaf children— education to teach them to speak and read lips. Most of the deaf, however, had to rely on sign languages. Their signs were often very primitive, though in urban settings, they evolved into coherent systems.

In mid-eighteenth-century Paris, the Abbé de l'Épée learned Sign. He was one of the first hearing people ever to do so. He then taught the deaf to read and write. It was the dawn of emancipation: You did not need speech to learn the languages of the speaking world. He went on to found the Institute for the Instruction of Deaf-Mutes in 1755.

In the early nineteenth century, the Reverend Thomas Gallaudet of Connecticut set off for England to get information about deaf education. The English told him that their oral method was secret, so Gallaudet traveled to France, where he was warmly received at the Institute. A young deaf man, Laurent Clerc, accompanied him back to America to establish a school for deaf children. In 1817 they set up the American Asylum for the Education and Instruction of the Deaf in Hartford, Connecticut.

The fifty years that followed were a golden age for the American deaf. French sign language mixed with homespun American signs as well as the sign dialect on Martha's Vineyard (where there was a strain of hereditary deafness) to form American Sign Language (ASL). Deaf people wrote books, entered public life, and achieved widely. Gallaudet College was founded in 1857 in Washington, D.C., to provide advanced education of the deaf.

Once the deaf became high-functioning, however, they were once more asked to use their voices to accommodate the hearing world. Alexander Graham Bell led the nineteenth century oralist movement, which culminated with the first international meeting of educators of the deaf, the Congress of Milan in 1880. There, an edict was passed to ban the use of manualism—a disparaging word for Sign—so that children might learn to speak instead. Bell, who had a deaf mother and a deaf wife, was appalled by the idea of "a Deaf variety of the human race," and founded the American Association to Promote the Teaching of Speech to the Deaf. Among other things, it sought to forbid deaf people to marry one another, and to keep deaf students from mixing with other deaf students. He went as far as to ask that deaf adults undergo sterilization and persuaded some hearing parents to sterilize their deaf children.

When Lexington was founded, the oralists' aim was to

teach the deaf to speak and read lips so they could function in the "real world." How that dream went horribly wrong is the grand tragedy around which modern Deaf culture has constructed itself. By World War I, some 80 percent of deaf children were being educated without Sign. Deaf teachers who had signed were suddenly unemployed. Pupils who signed had their hands struck with a ruler. Oralism has been compared to the conversion therapies used to "normalize" gay people. Despite this, schools remained the cradle of Deaf culture, because they were the primary place where deaf people met one another. Few non-deaf people studied Sign. In fact, the notion that Sign might be a full language eluded scholars until the linguist William Stokoe published his groundbreaking book *Sign Language Structure* in 1960. He demonstrated that Sign had a complex and deep grammar of its own, with logical rules and systems. Sign employs the same mental faculties as English, French, or Chinese.

In hearing children, the critical period for connecting meaning to sounds is between eighteen and thirty-six months. Language-acquisition capacity tails off at about age twelve, though some exceptional people have acquired language much later. Language can be learned only through exposure. In a vacuum, the language centers of the brain atrophy. In the language-acquisition period, most children can learn any language. Once they have language itself, they can learn additional languages later on.

Deaf children acquire Sign exactly as hearing children acquire a first spoken language. Most deaf children can learn spoken languages such as English or Spanish in their written form as second languages. For many, however, speech is a mystical gymnastics of the tongue and throat, while lip-reading is a guessing game. Some deaf children acquire these skills gradually, but making speech and lip-reading the only communication available to deaf children results in permanent confusion. If they bypass the key age for language acquisition without fully acquiring any language, they cannot develop adequate cognitive skills and will suffer from a preventable form of intellectual disability. Forbidding Sign does not turn deaf children toward speech, but away from language.

The 1990 Individuals with Disabilities Education Act (IDEA) has sometimes been interpreted to mean that separate is never equal, and that everyone should attend mainstream schools. For wheelchair users provided with ramps, this is splendid. For the deaf, who are unable to learn the basic means of communication used by hearing people, mainstreaming is the worst disaster since the Congress of Milan. Oralism destroyed the quality of the deaf residential schools, but mainstreaming killed the schools themselves. At the remaining deaf schools, the standard of education is often low. At mainstream schools, much of the education is inaccessible to deaf students. In neither instance are deaf people getting optimal learning. Only a third of deaf children complete high school. Of those who attend college, only a fifth graduate. Deaf adults earn about a third less than their hearing peers.

The deaf children of deaf parents frequently have a higher level of achievement than the deaf children of hearing parents. Deaf of Deaf, as they are called, learn Sign as a first language at home. They usually don't start learning English until they go to school. Nonetheless, they are more likely to develop fluent written English than are children of hearing parents who use English at home and go to mainstream schools. They have started their lives by gaining fluency in language, and fluency in an additional language therefore comes more readily to them.

Communicating in Sign is more meaningful to many deaf people than being unable to hear. Those who sign love their language. Those who understand signing can see the finest shade of meaning in a gesture. "Like the pleasure some hearing people take in the distinctions between words like 'dry,' 'arid,' 'parched,' 'desiccated,' or 'dehydrated,' so the deaf can enjoy distinctions in the gestures of sign language," one fluent signer explained.

It is estimated that one in a thousand newborns is profoundly deaf, and that twice as many have a less severe hearing impairment. Another two or three per thousand will lose hearing before age ten. Deaf culture allows them to think of themselves not as unfinished hearing people, but as cultural and linguistic beings in a world with one another.

After a week of protests outside the Lexington Center, the demonstrators went to the Queens borough president's office. Greg Hlibok, perhaps Lexington's most famous alumnus, was going to speak.

Six years earlier, Gallaudet University had announced the appointment of a new president. Students rallied for a Deaf CEO, but a hearing candidate was selected. In the week that followed, the Deaf community as a political force came into its own. Hlibok was the Deaf Rosa Parks, leading the Deaf

President Now movement with other student activists. Demonstrations closed down the university and received national media coverage.

They won. The board chairman resigned, and her place was taken by a Deaf man, Phil Bravin. Bravin immediately named Gallaudet's first Deaf president.

At the borough president's office, Greg Hlibok was electrifying. An articulate signer can create a picture by using signs and gesture. Hlibok compared the Lexington board to adults playing with a dollhouse, moving around the deaf students like little toys. He seemed to be building the house in the air. The students cheered, waving their hands over their heads, fingers splayed, in Deaf applause.

A week later an emergency board meeting was scheduled, but the day before it was to take place, R. Max Gould resigned. The chairman of the board followed suit.

At Lexington graduation the following week, Greg Hlibok said, "From the time God made Earth until today, this is probably the best time to be deaf."

Most hearing people assume that to be deaf is to lack hearing. Many Deaf people experience deafness not as an absence, but as a presence. Deafness is a culture and a life, a language and an aesthetic, a physicality and an intimacy different from all others.

And yet the battle between oralism and sign language continues.

Parents fear losing their children to the Deaf world. This is more than a dark fantasy. I met many Deaf people who thought of the previous generation of Deaf people as their parents. The higher achievement levels of Deaf of Deaf were used as an argument that deaf children should be adopted by deaf adults.

The Deaf psychologist Neil Glickman has spoken of four stages of Deaf identity. People start out pretending to be hearing, with a discomfort similar to that of the only Jew at the country club or the only black family in the suburb. They progress to marginality, feeling they are a not a part of either deaf or hearing life. Then they immerse themselves in Deaf culture, fall in love with it, and disparage hearing culture. Finally, they achieve a balanced view that there are strengths in both the deaf and the hearing experience.

Shortly after Lexington's graduation in 1994, I attended the National Association of the Deaf (NAD) convention in Knoxville, Tennessee, with almost two thousand deaf participants. During the Lexington protests, I had visited deaf households. I had learned how deaf telecommunications work; I had met dogs who understood Sign; I had discussed mainstreaming and oralism; I had become accustomed to doorbells that flashed lights instead of ringing. I had observed differences between British and American Deaf culture. I had stayed in a dorm at Gallaudet. Yet I was unprepared for the Deaf world of the NAD.

The NAD has been at the center of Deaf self-realization and power since it was founded in 1880, and the convention is where the most committed Deaf gather for political focus and social exchange. At the president's reception the lights were turned up high because deaf people lapse into speechlessness in semidarkness. Across the room, it seemed almost as though some strange human sea were breaking into waves and glinting in the light, as thousands of hands moved at stunning speed.

The NAD is the host of the Miss Deaf America pageant, and Friday night featured the competition. The young beauties, dressed to the nines and sporting state sashes, were the objects of considerable attention. Genie Gertz, Miss Deaf New York, the daughter of Russian Jewish parents who emigrated when she was eight, delivered an eloquent monologue about finding freedom in the United States—which included, for her, the move from being a social misfit in a country that is not easy on disability to being Deaf and proud. It seemed like a striking idea that one might be deaf and glamorous: an American dream.

Disconcerting though it may sound, it was impossible, at the NAD convention, not to wish you were Deaf, part of the society you were inhabiting. I had known that Deaf culture existed, but I had not known how heady it is.

How to reconcile this Deaf experience with the rest of the world? Today a bilingual and bicultural educational approach, commonly referred to as Bi-Bi, is used at both the elementary and secondary model schools on the Gallaudet campus. In a Bi-Bi curriculum, students are taught in Sign and then learn English as a second language. Written English is given a high priority; many students perform on par with their hearing counterparts. On average, schools employing a solely oral approach graduate students at eighteen who read at a fourth-grade level; students from Bi-Bi schools often read at grade level. Spoken English is taught as a useful tool, but is not a primary focus.

Some Deaf activists argue that being deaf is not a disability.

The danger of this line of reasoning is that if deafness is not a disability, deaf people should not be protected under the Americans with Disabilities Act (ADA) and should not have the right to various accommodations: translators in hospitals and courtrooms, relay interpreters on telephone exchanges, captions on television programs. None of these services is automatically available to people in the US who, for example, speak only Japanese. If deafness is not a disability, then on what basis does the state provide for separate schools, and on what basis does it provide Social Security disability insurance? Deaf people have to subscribe to the disability definition in order to gain access, but that can undermine their struggle for other rights, those that come of being seen as their own "normal."

When parents choose Sign for their deaf children, they surrender them in some ways to Deaf culture. Whereas oral communication places strain on the deaf member of the family, the decision to sign places the greater strain of understanding on the hearing members. I met many deaf individuals who said that being deaf is of course a disability. I also met deaf people who subscribed to the old deaf self-hatred, who were ashamed and saddened when they gave birth to deaf children, who felt they could never be anything more than second-class. In some ways, it doesn't matter whether their ears are cured or their self-image is cured, but they are out there and they need validation.

Bridget O'Hara did not grow up at the best time to be deaf. Luke and Mary O'Hara, both hearing, married young, moved to a farm in Iowa, and started to have children. Their first,

Bridget, was born with Mondini malformation, a syndrome in which an essential part of the inner ear is not fully formed. It is associated with degenerative deafness and other neurological impairments, including migraine headaches and poor balance. Bridget's hearing loss was diagnosed when she was two; the Mondini diagnosis came many years later.

Luke and Mary were advised to raise her just like any other child, and Bridget desperately tried to figure out speech and lip-reading without special education. "My mom labeled everything in the house so I could see what words went with what things, and she made me use full sentences, so I have good spoken English compared to other deaf people," Bridget said. "But I could never find confidence in myself. I never said anything that didn't get corrected."

Bridget had three younger sisters. "My sisters would go 'Duh! You're so stupid!' My parents' body language made it clear they thought the same thing. At some point I just stopped asking questions." Bridget was so roundly teased for her errors that she came to suspect even her most powerful intuitions, which left her profoundly vulnerable. The only person Bridget trusted unconditionally was her sister Matilda, two years younger than she was.

Bridget was the first deaf person to attend her school. She had to lip-read all day. She would come home from school exhausted from it, and because she was a good reader, would curl up with a book. She didn't have any friends. "I didn't realize that there was a Deaf culture out there. I just thought I was the stupidest person in the world."

Bridget and her sisters were subject to their father's

violent temper. He would whip the girls with a belt. Bridget preferred outdoor chores to indoor ones, and she often helped her father in the yard. One day they came in from raking, and Bridget went upstairs to take a shower. A minute later her father, naked, stepped into the shower with her. "I was naive in many ways because I didn't really have communication with anyone," she recalled. "But I somehow knew this was not right. But I was afraid."

In the months that followed, Luke began to touch her, then forced her into submissive sexual acts. "At the beginning, I would question my father. He would escalate the physical abuse, and I would get whipped. I blame my mother almost more, for not doing anything." About that time, Bridget walked in on her mother in the bathroom holding a bottle of pills. When Mary saw Bridget, she poured the pills down the toilet. "After I got older," Bridget said, "I realized she was *that* close to killing herself."

When Bridget was in ninth grade, her grandparents took all the grandkids except her to Disney World; she had gone previously and it was the others' turn. Bridget's mother went along, so Bridget was left home with her father. "I now have no memory whatsoever of that week," Bridget said. "But I apparently told Matilda about it when she got back from Disney World, and she later said she couldn't have anything to do with Dad, because of what he did to me." I wondered whether the abuse was linked with her deafness. "I was the easier mark," Bridget said.

Bridget's grades started to slip in her sophomore year of high school. More and more material was in lectures rather than in reading. She couldn't follow what was going on and was being tortured by classmates. Every time she went to the bathroom, she'd get beaten up by a gang of girls; she came home one day with a gash on her face that required stitches. Soon the girls started dragging her to the janitor's closet between classes, where boys would take advantage of her sexually.

"What angered me the most was adults," she said. "I tried to tell them. They wouldn't believe me." When she came home with her shin cut open and needed stitches again, her father called the school. Bridget couldn't hear what he said and no one told her.

Bridget began having attacks of vertigo. "I now know that is a symptom of Mondini malformation. But I can't help wondering how much was also because of all the fear." Someone asked Bridget if she wished she were hearing, and she said she really didn't; she wished she were dead. Finally, she came home from school one day and announced that she was never going back. That night her parents told her there was a deaf school just forty-five minutes away, which they had never mentioned because they wanted her to be part of "the real world." Bridget enrolled at fifteen.

"I learned to sign fluently in a month," she said. "I started blossoming." Like many other deaf schools, this one had a low standard of education, and Bridget was academically ahead of her peers. She had been unpopular at her previous school because she was seen as an idiot. She was unpopular at this one because of her academic prowess. "Nonetheless, I became outgoing and made friends for the first time," she recalled. "I started caring about myself and taking care of myself."

Bridget had tried to get her mother to leave her father, but the family was Catholic and her mother had always "played the Catholic card." But after Bridget went off to college at NYU, her parents announced plans to divorce. "My mother had felt that I needed to have both of them," Bridget said. "Once I left, I guess she felt free."

In the years that followed, Bridget's headaches escalated; several times she blacked out and collapsed. When she finally went to a doctor, he told her she needed immediate surgery for her malformation. She told him her symptoms were probably psychosomatic, and he was the first person to say to her, "Don't be so hard on yourself."

Bridget eventually finished her degree and got a job in finance, but five years later the episodes intensified again. Her neurologist told her not to work more than twenty hours a week. Eventually she was told it was too dangerous to continue working at all.

In her thirties, Bridget began having vision problems. She was wearing extremely powerful hearing aids, and they were amplifying the sound so much that they were stimulating her ocular nerve, causing her vision to blur. Her doctor recommended a cochlear implant. This is a mechanical device that is placed surgically in the brain and connected to a transmitter. Sound reaches the transmitter and is conveyed to the implant, which stimulates the parts of the brain involved with hearing. In this way, sound information bypasses the ear and goes straight to the brain.

Bridget is now able to understand some speech. "I love my implant," she told me. Her daily headaches became weekly. Her vision returned to normal. But she still has unreliable and sometimes paralyzing symptoms. She has taken volunteer jobs, but employers want consistency, and her symptoms are unpredictable.

In 1997, Bridget's mother was dying of cancer. She was too sick to be alone. The three hearing sisters had families and couldn't deal with her, so Mary came to New York, to Bridget's small apartment. She lived another eighteen months. The burden of what was unsaid became intolerable. "I didn't get into the sexual, but I did talk about the physical abuse," Bridget said. "She started crying, but she wasn't ready to admit her part." When the care got to be more than Bridget could handle, Matilda moved in to help. "Matilda and I would talk at night, and Matilda talked about the sexual abuse," Bridget recalled. "It had a real impact on her, even though it happened to me and not to her." Matilda's anger was terrifying to Bridget.

Shortly before Mary died, Bridget's aunt called Matilda, saying that Mary was imagining crazy things in the hospital, weeping desperately about how Bridget had been sexually abused by her father and Mary hadn't done anything about it. "So my mother never apologized to me," Bridget said. "But she knew what happened, and she apologized to someone."

A year later, Matilda seemed to be struggling; she kept talking about what had happened to Bridget, and she still seemed very, very angry. Then she got divorced and she disappeared. "I didn't hear from her for almost two months," Bridget said. "Then she came to town, and I knew she was depressed. She said, 'I should have been the one who died.'" A few weeks later, Bridget learned that Matilda had hanged herself. Bridget explained to me, "I feel that I let her down. That my problems and my deafness and my sexual abuse were a burden on her."

Bridget's two remaining sisters have both learned Sign and taught it to their children; they now have videophones so everyone can be in touch. When one lost her husband to leukemia, she made sure there were interpreters at the funeral. They organize a family trip every year, which includes Bridget's father and Bridget. I wondered how Bridget could tolerate those vacations. "He's old now," she said, "and harmless. What he did to me is a long time ago." Then she began to weep quietly. "If I didn't go, my sisters would want to know why. They have no idea what happened; they were much younger than Matilda and me. What would happen if I told my sisters?" She stared out the window for a long, long time. "What happened when I told Matilda?" she finally asked me. She shrugged her narrow shoulders. "A week in Disneyland every year—it's really a small price to pay."

The story of deaf children being abused is much too common. Bridget was rare only in being willing to tell me about it. It's an open secret that deaf kids have trouble telling their stories. When a Deaf theater group did a piece in Seattle about incest and sexual abuse, they sold out an eight-hundred-seat auditorium, and they hired counselors to wait outside the theater. Many women and men broke down in tears and ran out during the performance. "By the end of the show, half the audience was sobbing in the arms of those therapists," one person who attended said.

The story of Spencer Montan lies at the other end of the spectrum. "I had never met a deaf person," his mother, Barb, said of the time when she learned her son lacked hearing, "so I can only describe it as free-falling." Her husband, Chris, is president of Walt Disney Music, and his whole life has been about sound. When Spencer was diagnosed, Chris was "rocked, devastated." Barb contacted Tripod, a California school for both deaf and hearing children started by the parents of another deaf child.

The Montans decided almost immediately that they would learn to sign. "Spencer would take speech therapy, but we would learn his language and culture," Barb said. "I've got to go where he's going. I can't let any cognitive delay happen." Chris worried that the language gap would undermine his ability to be a good father. He said to Barb, "We can't have Spencer feel like he grew up in a hearing household and got left out."

Deaf students from Cal State came over to instruct Spencer and his family in ASL. Barb and Chris created such a strong signing environment that Spencer didn't know he had a disability until he was four or five. Spencer could understand his parents' amateurish signing as well as full-fledged ASL. Because public education does not begin until age five, they enrolled their son in a privately funded Montessori preschool program for deaf and hearing children, which was part of the Tripod system. Spencer's development in ASL was rapid; the hearing kids in the class learned nearly as fast.

The Montans did consider cochlear implants. At that time, a large part of the Deaf community opposed the implants. They claimed that they were taking away the next generation of Deaf children by making them effectively hearing. This point of view was shocking to most hearing people, who generally assumed deaf people wanted to hear—that deafness was an illness rather than an identity. They had no idea about Deaf culture, poetry, clubs, lives. Of course, most hearing people wouldn't want to lose their hearing, but for Deaf people, being deaf is not a loss, but a way of being. As one Deaf woman said to me, "There are ways that life is easier for men than for women, but I don't experience being a woman as a *loss*. It's who I am and a valued part of me. My deafness is the same." To many people with this identity, the idea of the cochlear implant seemed like an assault on their culture, and they felt insulted by the device and by the question of "curing" the deafness they so cherish.

Chris said, "In 1991, I wasn't sure what way the technology was going to advance. If Spencer were newly diagnosed and thirteen months old today, I would implant him, and I say that knowing all the great Deaf people we've met, and as a strong supporter of Deaf culture. It's a different question today, medically and politically." Implants given early allow many children to learn speech as fluently as they would if they had hearing, but those children usually need some coaching to learn how to process the sounds that reach their brains. Implants given later take a lot more training, because the brain is not used to processing sound and doesn't know how to interpret it. If Spencer were to get an implant as a young adult, he would have to lose a year of high school to do auditory training to interpret the data it would produce. He doesn't feel it would be worth that disruption.

Barb has been frustrated by the antispeech sentiment in the Deaf world. "Spencer is fine signing with me the way I sign, with Chris the way he signs, with his deaf friends in fluent ASL. He is fully bilingual between written English and Sign." At the same time, she recognizes the importance of Deaf society.

"Every culture, you want critical mass, and he's got it with his deaf friends. We all need our people."

"Parents of deaf kids should know not to be afraid, not to let their kids be afraid," Spencer told me. "My parents made sure I was never afraid."

Spencer was refreshingly open about language. "I know that my voice is useful, and I am glad to develop it. Mom and Dad went to take ASL classes so we could communicate. If they could learn ASL, I can do this, too. My main language is ASL. But by practicing and practicing, I don't need tutors to help me with my English. I work on my voice, and the kids at my school and in my baseball league work on signing. We want to live in one world."

That one world never became a reality for Jacob Shamberg, whose parents founded Tripod a decade before Spencer was born. They wanted to make sure that Jacob got a good education that included both hearing and deaf children. I met Jacob shortly after he graduated from the School of Visual Arts at twenty-eight. Despite extensive speech therapy, he is unable to speak in a way that is consistently comprehensible. "I've been sorry for myself for a long time, for being deaf," Jacob said. "Last year I tried to kill myself. It was not that I wanted to die, but I felt like I had no control over my life."

I wondered why Jacob's sense of struggle persisted in the face of the acceptance and love he experienced at home and at school. Jacob said, "Three nights ago, I went out for drinks with the other people in a class I'm taking, and all of them are hearing, and we just wrote back and forth. But there's a point where they're all chatting, and I'm like, 'What's going on?' I'm lucky that they're open to being with me, but I'm still left out. I have a lot of hearing acquaintances. But good friends? No. Deaf culture teaches me how to see the world, but it would make surviving the world a lot easier if I could hear. If I were going to have a Down syndrome child, I think I would abort. But what if my mom had found out I was deaf when she was pregnant and aborted me? I don't want to be racist, but walking alone at night, I see an unknown black person approaching, and I feel uncomfortable, even though I have black friends. I hate it. So it's the same when I make people uncomfortable because I'm deaf: I understand it, and I hate it. I just hate it."

It is not possible to create in America the one world of acceptance that Spencer spoke of, but many hearing parents of deaf children work hard to enter into the Deaf community. It requires an openness on the part of the parents and a willingness for the whole family to be comfortable in both the Deaf and non-Deaf worlds.

In 1790, Alessandro Volta discovered that electrical stimulation to the auditory system could mimic sound. In 1957, André Djourno and Charles Eyriès used an electric wire to stimulate the auditory nerve of a patient undergoing brain surgery. During the 1960s, researchers began placing multiple electrodes in the cochlea. These devices, instead of amplifying sound as a hearing aid would, actually stimulated the brain areas where sound would be received by hearing people. This technology was gradually refined, and in 1984, the FDA approved a device for use by late-deafened adults. Because it transmitted on a single channel, it gave information on the loudness and timing of sounds, but did not convey the content of those sounds. Today, some devices operate on twenty-four channels.

Today's cochlear implant does not allow you to hear. It allows you to do something that resembles hearing. Implanted early, it can provide a basis for the development of oral language. It makes the hearing world easier. After the device has been surgically implanted, an audiologist works on mapping it, making a series of adjustments to ensure that it is tuned to the brain of the recipient.

Deafness, which often used to go undetected until age three, is now regularly diagnosed within hours of birth, and almost always before three months. Though the cochlear implant is approved only for children over the age of two, children under a year old have been implanted.

The device remains controversial. Opponents point to the complications that can arise from surgery and to the fact that the devices produce only a crude approximation of sound. Parents of children who have been implanted can be careless about language acquisition. One study showed that less than half of the implanted children had greater than 70 percent speech discrimination, or the ability consistently to hear which word is which without seeing the speaker. Parents believe, however, that if children can understand most words, they are a lot better off than they would be with no hearing.

Nancy and Dan Hessey have fallen on both sides of this debate since their daughter Emma became deaf. On June 29, 1998, Dan and Nancy arrived in Vietnam to adopt a child. The orphanage told them that their daughter was very sick with pneumonia and they immediately rushed her to the hospital. Emma had an allergic reaction to medication and nearly died. It was two months before they were able to bring Emma home. A virus had caused her hearing to degenerate until it was nearly gone.

At first they were against the idea of a cochlear implant and moved more than once looking for good schools and communities to raise a deaf child. Neither of them was good at ASL, however, and they worried that they couldn't communicate well with their own child, so when Emma was four, she had one ear implanted. Complications followed. Even after she was well, Emma was caught between two cultures and two languages. Eventually, she was implanted in her other ear. This time, it all went smoothly. By the time I met Emma, she was nine. Her grammar and usage were not quite at age level, but she was speaking fluidly and unselfconsciously. She had a 75 percent success rate at word recognition.

Dan and Nancy tried to keep Emma in a bicultural environment, but they noticed that when she could sign or speak, Emma always spoke. Gradually, they allowed her signing to stop. Today, Emma communicates with speech and hearing only.

Medical insurance will now often cover the implant, the surgery, and the audiological training that follows. For most hearing parents, the choice seems straightforward. One mother said, "If your child needs glasses, you get glasses. If your child needs a leg, you get a prosthetic. It's the same thing." Those with the implants who are reclassed as hearing do not receive the accommodations they would get as disabled people. The problem is that those who do not get implants may be seen as having "chosen" their condition in the face of a "cure," at which point they do not "deserve" the "charity" of taxpayers. The existence of implants may, therefore, take disability status from other deaf people.

Rory Osbrink was born hearing, an eager and athletic child. One December Friday in 1981, soon after his third birthday, Rory came down with what appeared to be the flu. On Sunday he suddenly seemed much worse and his parents rushed him to the hospital. Rory had meningitis and went into a coma. He was in an oxygen tent for the next five days and in and out of the hospital for forty days.

In the hospital, Rory stopped reacting to sound. His parents soon learned his deafness was permanent. The cochlear implant had not yet been approved for children, but after Rory was nearly hit by a fire truck with its sirens blaring, his parents decided to try giving him one anyway. Rory was the second child ever to receive one. But the sound that he got was extremely primitive and ultimately not very useful.

Rory was enrolled in mainstream schools and played on the schools' sports teams. Rory was a star baseball player at his school, had begun to sign, and had joined a deaf baseball team, too. He was also adept at reading lips.

In junior high, Rory began working seriously on ASL, and in high school, he learned about Deaf identity. He got a baseball scholarship to the University of Arizona, but when he went to meet the coach, the coach was patronizing, and wrote notes instead of looking into Rory's face and allowing him to read his lips. "I can't play for you," Rory said. He drove out that night and soon enrolled at Gallaudet.

Rory never really came back to the hearing world. At Gallaudet, he majored in Deaf studies and philosophy and played on the baseball team. The Dodgers offered him a tryout. He got in touch with Curtis Pride, who played pro baseball and is hard of hearing and who said no one in the pro sports world was going to help "the deaf guy." Rory got a master's in education instead.

Rory later married a woman who was fifth-generation deaf. He turned off his implant and has never used it again; he said that with it he felt like "a duck in a world of chickens." The Deaf world became his home. Today he's a teacher and a baseball coach who protests parents implanting their children. "As for pediatric cochlear implant, it should not be tolerated since it ignores the children's right to choice," he wrote.

I wondered whether the child must always win in these debates. Should the parents rise to the occasion of having a deaf child, and allow that child simply to be? Hearing parents are thrown back on their own dichotomy: Do they have a deaf child, or do they lack a hearing one?

It will be some time before implanted people can discern the voice of a single turtledove in a forest full of crows, but implant developers are closing in on enabling the perception of sufficient auditory information for the development of verbal fluency. Many Deaf activists believe that cochlear implants are part of an attempt to destroy and eliminate the Deaf community. One British Deaf activist compares implants to Hitler's "Final

Solution" plan to rid the world of Jews. Another activist wrote, "Could you imagine if somebody stood up and said, 'In a few years we're going to be able to eliminate black culture'?" He went on: "If hearing people saw the Deaf community as an ethnic group with its own language, as opposed to someone who is handicapped, then you wouldn't have such a deep misunderstanding."

Is the underlying hearing person being liberated by the implant, or is the authentic Deaf person being obliterated?

Some opponents of implants have proposed that people make their own choice when they turn eighteen. That's an impractical idea from both a medical and cultural point of view. By eighteen, if your experience of the world has been defined by being deaf, to give it up is a rejection of who you have become.

Children with implants have experienced social difficulties. Some become "culturally homeless." They are neither hearing nor deaf. The population at large does not like threats to the status quo. Unease drives homophobia and racism and xenophobia—the constant impulse to define an *us* and a *them*. It happens here too, even though the wall between hearing and deaf is being broken down by a broad range of technology: hearing aids and implants.

Though some implanted children disconnect their implants in their teen years, most see them as extremely useful. In one study, two-thirds of parents reported that their children had never refused to use the implant.

Barbara Matusky rejected the idea of cochlear implants when first her son, Nick, and later her daughter, Brittany, were diagnosed with deafness. Both were educated at the Maryland School for the Deaf. The school day took place in Sign, but students also received oral education.

Both children made strong showings in written English. Nick makes little use of spoken language, but Brittany decided in college that she was going back to speech therapy and has been thinking about getting a cochlear implant. She wants to work in film production, and she wants to be comfortable in the hearing world.

Brittany has been concerned about how her Deaf friends would react to her getting an implant. "So what does she do?" her mother asked. "Does she give up her dreams and settle? Or does she get this implant if it will make it easier to get her dream job? They're deaf in a hearing world, that's the reality."

Deaf people in the hearing world are always going to be at a disadvantage. So the question is whether people prefer to be marginal in a mainstream world, or mainstream in a marginal, Deaf world. Many people prefer the latter. At the same time, those who oppose cochlear implants—and who, in some cases, oppose hearing aids—are a noisy bunch. Their concern is not unfounded. By 2010, up to 40 percent of American children diagnosed before they turned three years old received a cochlear implant. Parents who do not implant their children today are choosing a shrinking world. The insularity of the deaf has gone out of fashion.

While the debate rages, assistive devices for hearing loss continue to be refined and developed. Technologies now in the works include the implantation of electrodes that stimulate hearing nerve fibers, the miniaturization of implant technology, fully implantable cochlear devices, and implantable hearing aids.

At the same time, research into biological cures for deafness has blossomed. More than a hundred genes for deafness at birth have been identified, and another one seems to be picked up every month. Much deafness that occurs later in life is also genetic. Some kinds of deafness are caused by the interaction of multiple genes rather than by a single one. At least 10 percent of our genes can affect hearing or ear structure, and other genes and environmental factors can determine how profound the deafness will be. Scientists continue to make strides toward developing gene therapies to cure or reduce hearing loss. Genetic research into deafness angers the Deaf community in part because of its relevance to selective abortion, when expectant parents could choose to terminate a pregnancy that would result in a deaf baby. Many see it as a threat to Deaf culture.

In the early 1960s, a rubella epidemic in the United States resulted in a high incidence of deaf children, because rubella during pregnancy frequently results in a deaf newborn. This generation is called the Rubella Bulge. Vaccines now protect most expectant American mothers from rubella, and most children from rubella and meningitis. The deaf population grows smaller.

Meanwhile, cochlear implants mean that a large proportion of children born deaf are functioning in the hearing world.

"From the time God made Earth until today, this is probably the best time to be deaf," Greg Hlibok said at the

Lexington graduation. This is also the moment when the deaf population is dwindling. As it gets better and better to be deaf, it also gets rarer and rarer.

Vertical identities are deemed natural. Horizontal ones are deemed unnatural. Implants can easily come to seem more "natural" than deafness to hearing people, most of whom cannot imagine choosing against an implant, given a choice for themselves or their children. So more people get implanted, leaving fewer to make up the marginal culture, creating more pressure to get implants, and so on, until few people are left to populate the Deaf world.

Jacob Shamberg wrote to me, "While I'm pretty comfortable with my disability and don't see C.I. as an evil force intent on destroying the Deaf culture, I do get a sense of impending extinction. There'll always be deaf people worldwide, but there is a real possibility that it'll be near-eradicated in developed countries within fifty to one hundred years. I say 'near' because there'll always be immigrants, untreatable conditions, cultural holdouts, and so on. But no more people like me." I thought that was one of the loneliest things I'd ever read from anyone: "No more people like me." Think how you would feel if there were no more people like you. I imagine a world stripped of people like me, and it makes me sad.

The loss of Deaf culture would be a great tragedy; preventing any individual child from getting implants could be considered cruel. By narrowing a child's options, parents define that child as an extension of themselves, rather than a person of his or her own. Yet implants may compromise the option of being content in the Deaf world.

For many years, the defining means of Deaf life was in-person socializing at Deaf social clubs—now largely vanished as deaf people are able to communicate online. The Deaf used to congregate at the Deaf theater—but with the advent of captioned television and film, that has faded as well. Is Deaf culture to be defined simply as a function of shared language used for in-person interactions?

We will never have a society in which children are routinely taken from their parents and given to another group of people to raise. The 90 percent or so of deaf children who are born to hearing parents will continue to be brought up as those parents see fit. If the cochlear implant is improved, if gene therapies advance, then cures will triumph. Vertical identities will go on forever. Horizontal ones won't.

Yet just as Deaf culture is being forced to assimilate to the mainstream, mainstream culture is assimilating the Deaf world. As many as two million Americans know ASL and the numbers are on the rise. It is one of the most-taught languages on college campuses. More hearing people are applying to Gallaudet. Deaf people are ambivalent about all this. They note that the language has separated from the culture, and that many of the students learning it know nothing about Deafhood.

I am fully persuaded that there is a rich Deaf culture. What then are our social obligations? Can we confer on it a societal equivalent to the landmark status with which we mark buildings that are never to be destroyed? The cochlear implant debate is really a holding mechanism for a larger debate about assimilation versus alienation. A race is going on. One team consists of doctors who will make the deaf hear. They are humanitarian miracle workers. On the other team are the champions of Deaf culture. They are visionary idealists. Yet each would render the other irrelevant. As Deaf culture grows stronger, it is dying.

If Deaf culture can be made as visible, powerful, and proud as gay culture is now, *before* the cure is perfected, then perhaps the accomplishments of the activists born in the Rubella Bulge who led the Gallaudet and Lexington protests will allow for a long history of Deaf culture. If the cure comes before that happens, then Deaf culture will come to an end.

Would the world be better with more cultures in it? I believe it would. In the same way that we mourn the loss of species as they become extinct, and fear that reduced biodiversity could have catastrophic effects on the planet, we should fear the loss of cultures. Diversity of thought and language and opinion is part of what makes the world vibrant. And yet what is happening to the Deaf has happened to the Quakers, to Native Americans, to whole tribes and countries. It is estimated that by the end of this century, fully half of the six thousand languages currently spoken on Earth will have vanished. With those tongues will go many traditional ways of life. The Deaf may vanish along with many ethnicities, their languages along with many languages.

I think the only locus for hope is to recognize that new cultures are being born all the time. This book chronicles numerous communities that would never have emerged without the Internet. Some of those communities are cultures. Historic preservation is noble, but it should not prevent invention.

My own father's culture was impoverished; he grew up in a tenement in the Bronx, made his way into the professional class, and raised my brother and me with many advantages. He has sometimes expressed nostalgia for the world he left and has tried to explain it to us. The world to which he was born, of recent Jewish immigrants from Eastern Europe doing manual labor and speaking Yiddish, has vanished. There is no question that something has been lost. Yet I prefer the prosperous, American way I grew up. Every bit of progress kills something, but also encodes its origins. I do not wish for the life my father left behind, but I know that some spirit forged in that adversity made me possible.

Deaf culture has been a heroic enterprise, and now it is slipping out of relevance. Some aspects of it will be carried forward, but as a way of life, it is not likely to last for long. You can admire Deaf culture and still choose not to consign your children to it. The loss of diversity is terrible, but diversity for the sake of diversity is a lie. A Deaf culture kept pure when hearing is available to all is the equivalent of those historical towns where everyone lives as though it were the eighteenth century.

Will those born without hearing continue to have things in common? Will their language remain in use? Of course—just as candles have remained in the age of electricity, just as people read books despite television. We will not lose what Deaf culture has given us. But vertical demand for medical progress will outflank any horizontal social agenda.

Dwarfs

UNTIL I ATTENDED MY FIRST DWARF convention—the 2003 Little People of America (LPA) meeting—I had no clue how many kinds of dwarfism there are. Dwarfism is a low-incidence condition, usually occurring because of a random genetic mutation. Since most dwarfs are born to average-height parents, they do not have vertical community. The national LPA gatherings are, for some participants, the annual exception to a certain kind of loneliness. One dwarf I met told me she was "happy for one week a year," although others emphasized that they loved both their lives—the one in the larger world, and the one among their LPA friends.

I was struck by how the concentration of little people (LPs) at LPA changed my perception of them. Instead of seeing primarily short stature, I saw that one was exceptionally beautiful, that one was unusually short even for a dwarf, that one laughed uproariously and often, and that one had an intelligent face. I began to see how generically I had responded to little people until then. I understood what a relief it had to be for them that, at LPA, no one was focused on their height.

It would be difficult for an outsider to express this view of Latinos or Muslims, for instance. To say that a person's ethnicity or religion overwhelmed one's ability to see other characteristics would come across as bigoted. But dwarfism has been the exception to these social rules, even in PC America.

Many of the attendees I met on my first day at LPA could identify instantly conditions that I had never heard of and certainly had never seen. When I went down to the conference mixer the first night, I saw a brother and sister who had primordial dwarfism; they were full-grown, perfectly proportioned, and only about twenty-nine inches high. Their parents stood with them to make sure they weren't trampled—a danger even at a dwarf convention. The conference featured athletic competitions, a marathon-length talent show, and a fashion show. The conference also provided an eagerly awaited opportunity for dating. A dwarf comedian cracked, "You know you're a teenager at LPA if you've had more boyfriends this week than you've had in the last year."

Leslie Parks's parents were not pleased when she began hanging out with Chris Kelly during her senior year in high school in Huntsville, Alabama. The future they imagined for their daughter did not include a romance with a dwarf, even one who was a DJ with his own radio show. "I was your typical middle kid, nothing special about me," Leslie said. "I sort of fell into it with him. I was in student government, and he would DJ parties." Chris, several years older than Leslie, was divorced, he had kids, and he was a dwarf. Leslie felt she was dating a star, but her parents didn't see it that way, and they threw her out of the house during her senior year. Within a few months, Leslie and Chris were married.

When Chris was young, his parents had tried every new

"treatment" on the market, including injections of growth hormone made from the pituitary glands of monkeys. Because of or in spite of the shots, Chris was four feet ten inches, which is tall for a person with achondroplasia, the most common form of dwarfism. Chris's two children from his previous relationship were both of average height. When Leslie became pregnant, she had no thought that she might be carrying a dwarf. At seven months she went for an ultrasound. "They said, 'His head is too big for seven months. But his femur is much too short for seven months. What's going on here?'" Leslie knew exactly what was going on. "I was devastated. I'm glad I found out ahead of time, because I had time to get the mourning over with by the time he was born." Leslie could not talk to her husband about her despair at the prospect of a child who looked like him. She felt totally alone. Her parents were horrified to have a dwarf grandson, though over time their attitude has softened.

Chris and Leslie divorced when Jake was two. As a child, Jake would sometimes weep, saying, "I don't want to be little." Leslie wanted to cry too. "You don't want your child to perceive that you think his situation is hopeless, but also you don't want to deny his experience. A few times I've said, 'Have you talked to your daddy about this?' He'd say, 'No, I'm crying 'cause I don't want to be like me, which means I don't want to be like him. That would hurt his feelings.'"

Leslie and Chris have very different takes on parenting. "Dad is the fear side," Jake told me. "Mom's like, 'Hell, yeah, you're gonna play T-ball; you're gonna play baseball; you're just like everybody else.'"

"I don't look at myself as a little person until somebody

brings it to my attention. Normally, people do," Jake said. Eventually the typical problems of adolescence set in. Jake was popular and had a strong sense of self-esteem, but he was coming to the age where he wanted girlfriends.

Leslie took Jake to an LPA convention when he was thirteen. They were both overwhelmed. Later Jake said to me, "In regular life, I use my stature to start conversations with people to make friends. At that first conference, all I had was myself." Jake befriended only tall people that week, most of them siblings of dwarfs. He wasn't ready to make little friends. The next year was different. "He became a real teenager," Leslie said. She even caught him lying about his age to a much older girl. Jake adores LPA, but it's important to him and to Leslie that he's happy in his own world as well. As Jake said to me, "It's not like it's the only thing about me."

The visibility of dwarfs is intensified by their iconic place in fairy tales as supernatural beings. This isn't a burden shared by any other disability or special-needs group. Filmmaker Woody Allen once quipped that *dwarf* was one of the four funniest words in the English language. When I described the other categories in this book, my listeners were hushed by the seriousness of the enterprise. At the mention of dwarfs, friends burst into laughter. Dwarfs still appear in freak shows, in dwarf-tossing competitions, and in specialized pornography. There is callousness toward dwarfs beyond that shown to any other disabled group.

More than 80 percent of people with skeletal dysplasias—the primary dwarfing conditions—are born to average parents with no history of dwarfism, either because of a genetic mutation or because both parents carry a recessive gene.

Dwarfism is also outside the experience of the vast majority of doctors, who can be insensitive in talking about the condition with parents. One set of parents was told, "You have given birth to a circus dwarf." Another doctor recommended that a child he had diagnosed should "be sent to live with a dwarf troupe in Florida."

Such behavior is not simply rude. The way news of a dwarfing condition is communicated to parents may have a lasting effect on their ability to love and care for their child. Organizations such as LPA have fact-filled websites and sponsor online chat groups and local support groups to give average-size parents of dwarf children opportunities to meet dwarfs who are living positive, fulfilling lives. Still, many parents begin in sadness, denial, and shock.

Parents can establish a relationship with dwarfism as an acknowledged fact and a valuable identity: put light switches where they are easily reached, refit the kitchen to make it convenient for a little person, travel to dwarf conferences, involve dwarfs in their child's life. These moves are generally positive. Like all children, dwarf children want to be seen and want to be loved for who they are. Teaching them to feel acceptance of and then pride in their form of difference is absolutely critical, and it begins with these accommodations. Even so, a young dwarf will ultimately have to face the identity's limitation: The world is built for average-size people. There aren't enough dwarfs to make an all-dwarf life practical.

Parents may prefer to mainstream completely: to persuade their child that being short is not so different from being tall, to encourage him or her to make friends with other children regardless of their height. Such parents say that the tall world is the real world and tell their children that they will just have to get used to it. But this tough love can backfire. It can be a strain to be told constantly that you don't really have a disability. And avoidance of the LP world can come at the cost of isolation. In childhood, it works out fine, but life can get tough in middle school and high school; few teenagers of average height will date someone who is three foot six.

Most families combine various approaches—providing some access to the LP world, trying to put their child at ease in the non-LP world, and availing themselves of medical treatments that respond to their child's specific needs. The exact nature of the balance differs from household to household. It is not relaxing for parents to figure this out, but they succeed surprisingly often. Research indicates that short-statured people generally outscore their parents on measures of overall contentedness, which is to say that parenting a dwarf seems to be emotionally harder than being a dwarf.

We still fit people into the binary world of *disabled* or *nondisabled*; we grant those who are officially disabled social assistance, legal protections, and special parking spaces. It's difficult, though, to delineate where *disability* sets in. A man who is five foot six might prefer to be six feet tall, but he is not disabled. A man who is under four feet tall faces significant challenges. Many dwarfs experience serious additional physical challenges, with bones and joints that can be compromised, but even putting aside such medical problems, being short has a price. Dwarfism is recognized under the Americans

depression, as well as lower levels of self-esteem, when compared with their average-height siblings. Levels of depression
seem to be higher for LPs with average parents than for LPs
with LP parents. LP parents know firsthand the trials of being
an LP, and this is essentially the difference between growing
up with a vertical identity and growing up with a horizontal
one. LPA and similar organizations can be a blessing, though
they can, equally, be a trial, especially for people who have
resisted the imperative to grapple with dwarfism as an identity.
Within the social hierarchy at LPA, one is very much exposed.
Furthermore, attending LPA can traumatize people who have
blamed all their problems on their dwarfism, and who must
now come to terms with personal flaws.

Dwarfs are stared at more and more as they mature
and stop looking simply younger than they are. One recent
study observed that adults with achondroplasia have "lower
self-esteem, less education, lower annual incomes, and are
less likely to have a spouse." The great majority of college-age
LPA members attend college, but outside LPA, the numbers
are probably much lower. Michael Ain, who has achondroplasia and is now a pediatric orthopedic surgeon at Johns
Hopkins Hospital, recalled his experience as a medical school
applicant: "In the one field where you'd think people would
be most understanding, they were the most bigoted. Doctors
told me, 'You can't be a doctor. Don't even apply.' The first
guy I interviewed with told me I couldn't hold the respect of
my patients, because of my stature." The level of prejudice
can be truly astonishing.

In New England in the late 1950s, dwarfism was considered shameful. When Leslye Sneider's mother learned she had given birth to a dwarf, she had a nervous breakdown and spent three years in a psychiatric hospital. "She just could not accept it," Leslye said. "So she never saw me, never held me." Leslye's father didn't do much better. "He moved back in with his parents, and I was raised all around the state of Maine, by my maternal grandmother and a couple of my aunts."

When Leslye's mother came home from the hospital, "She did her best with what she had," Leslye remembered. "But my mother never got to grips with my being a little person. When we would go out shopping, and somebody would make a comment or stare, my mother would say, 'Oh, God! Why do I have to deal with this?'" Leslye's father remained distant; her closest relationships were with French Canadian babysitters who had migrated to Maine. "They were from really wonderful, loving French Catholic families. I used to go to church with them, even though my parents were Orthodox Jews. I hate to think what my life would have been without them."

When Leslye was eleven, her mother became aware of LPA and took Leslye to a regional conference. It was the first time Leslye saw another LP. When she was sixteen, she attended her first national conference. Leslye fell in with the "in" crowd of active and involved teens. Leslye had been miserable in high school. "I think LPA was what high school would have been had I been average-size." She dated for the first time.

For a long time, Leslye was aware that her mother had spent years in a psychiatric hospital, but she wasn't told what had pushed her over the edge. But at some level she always knew. Her understanding that she had caused her mother to go crazy weighed heavily on her. As a result, "I have no children. I have a lot of unresolved anger instead."

Many of Leslye's closest LPA friends were from California, so she applied to UCLA and was accepted. She found a therapist and went on anti-depressant medication, which she has taken ever since. "I sometimes wonder which has had a bigger effect on my life—my dwarfism or my depression and all the other depression around me," Leslye said. "The dwarfism was easier to overcome than the sadness."

Today she's at peace with her life. Happily married to an LP husband who is an accomplished artist, she said, "I wouldn't be with Bruce if I weren't little. How can I regret being an LP when it led me here? I always come back to feeling that I wouldn't have wanted it different."

Many dwarfs have protested against dwarf-tossing, a "sport" in which a dwarf is put into a harness and a person of average height, often drunk, hurls him as far as possible onto a padded surface. So far, laws against dwarf-tossing exist only in France, Florida, Michigan, New York, and the city of Springfield, Illinois. In February 2008, a "dwarf bowling" meet planned by a New York bar was canceled after a local newspaper reported that this variant on dwarf-tossing (in which a dwarf on a skateboard is rolled down an alley to knock over pins) was also illegal. In 2005, it was discovered that dwarf-tossing was among the festivities featured at a lavish $160,000 stag party financed by Fidelity Investments.

That such things still take place today is shocking, but the practice seems especially demonic give the skeletal problems that dwarfs commonly suffer. Dwarfs who participate are often in difficult financial circumstances. Some have protested that they should be allowed to earn their living this way if they choose, and point out that pro football also leads to damage to the body. Others believe that tolerating activities such as dwarf-tossing injures not only the dwarfs who are tossed, but also the rest of the dwarf community. They point out that woman-tossing or even dog-tossing would not be allowed.

Some within LPA argue that it's also humiliating for a dwarf to play an elf in the Radio City Christmas Spectacular. For many, however, Radio City and similar venues are easy money. Dwarf actors point out that they are seldom hired for mainstream roles. Stereotypes are persistent.

When the skeletons of what appeared to be a race of dwarfs were found on the island of Flores in Indonesia, the media referred to them in dismissive tones. The reports described these ancient dwarfs as belonging to the human species, but also referred to them as "things" and "creatures." Today, the Aka, Efé, and Mbuti of central Africa generally grow no taller than four feet ten inches. The word *Pygmies*, often used to describe them, is considered an insult, but that's the least of their problems: African Pygmies are often worked to death as slaves, have been the targets of attempted genocide, and have even been cannibalized by aggressors seeking "magical powers."

Anna Adelson was born in New York in 1974, and her parents were overjoyed to see her. Her mother, Betty, was able to hold Anna for a few minutes before she was taken away to be cleaned up. The next morning and afternoon, Betty couldn't understand why the nurses wouldn't bring the baby to her. Finally one did, but grudgingly.

Just before Betty and Saul took Anna home, the hospital neonatologist told them that Anna had achondroplasia. He said only that Anna would be short and gave no further information about the potential complications. Betty went to the NYU medical library and read. A cousin told her about LPA.

"I wanted to meet another family with a dwarf child, and I wanted to meet a happy adult. I kept in constant motion until I found them," Betty said. When Anna was four months old they found their way to Johns Hopkins and to Dr. Steven Kopits. "He would pick up the baby and exclaim in his Hungarian accent, 'What a beautiful baby you have!' He told you everything you needed to know and what you should look out for. He would write a long letter to your pediatrician at home and make an appointment for you to come back for a follow-up. When we went to Johns Hopkins, I knew the medical part could be dealt with."

Betty experienced some initial struggle in finding a preschool that would accept Anna, but Anna prospered. She was lively and sociable. She has been a vegetarian since the age of twelve; she's marched for reproductive rights; and she's traveled to Pennsylvania to ring doorbells for presidential candidates. In junior high, when her school didn't want her to go on a ski trip, Anna organized friends to picket the headmaster's office.

During her teen years, Anna found it hard to concentrate on her studies. Then she announced that she was gay. "She came out by calling me from college," Betty said. "The next day I wrote her a long letter. I told her that what was most important to me was not whether she loved a man or a woman, but that she loved and was loved well—that she experience passion, and the wonderful surprise of finding that someone feels about you as strongly as you do about them: lucky and full-hearted."

Anna's acceptance of her dwarfism took longer than her grappling with her sexuality. She had stopped going to LPA events early in her teen years, feeling that the world of her average-size family and friends was enough. She returned with some hesitancy at twenty-five. She soon became president of her local chapter and organized a "Difference within Difference" workshop at national conferences for those who are set apart from the majority of LPs by race, religion, disability, or sexual preference.

Today, Anna lives with her girlfriend a few blocks from Betty and Saul. "She loves and is loved well, as I hoped," Betty said. "If Anna had been average, would my world have been narrower? Yes. I recognize the gift that's been given. If someone said to me, 'Betty, how'd you like to give birth to a lesbian dwarf?' I wouldn't have checked that box. But she is Anna, cornerstone of the family. I wish the road had not been so steep for her, but I'm so glad she managed to climb it with grace."

Taylor van Putten has spondylometaphyseal dysplasia, Kozlowski type, a disease that affects slightly fewer than one in a million people. He is relatively tall for a dwarf, and until his second birthday he was in the ninetieth percentile for height. But he had other problems. He screamed when his mother moved his legs to change his diapers. When he started to walk, he was clearly in pain. Doctors couldn't find anything wrong until he was two and a half, when the family was referred to a dwarfism specialist at UCLA.

When I met Taylor at sixteen, he had had four limb-straightening surgeries, he suffered from severe back problems, his rib cage was pressing on his lungs, and doctors suggested that both his hips be replaced. "I've been in casts for a total of forty weeks, so that's almost a year of my life," he said. He knew that he would be in some measure of pain for as long as he lived.

Carlton van Putten's family history prepared him to be a father to Taylor. Carlton's mother was one of eleven children in a Cherokee family. Her family was rejected by the Cherokee people because they chose not to live on the reservation. They were also ostracized by the white community. Carlton's father was a black man from the Caribbean. When they were first married, hotels would not allow them to stay in the same room because he was black and she wasn't. "My mom walks into this hotel, and to the hotel guy, she's white," Carlton said. "But in her mind, she's black, since she belongs to the stigmatized minority of Native Americans. Sometimes there's a big discrepancy between how we see ourselves and how the world sees us."

Carlton and Tracey van Putten did everything they could to build Taylor's self-esteem. "We probably went a little overboard, because he's borderline cocky," his mother said. "Wherever he went, he would make friends that would really look out for him, like bodyguards. I'd imagined him being stuffed into lockers or garbage cans. It never materialized." Taylor laughed when he heard that. "The only time I was put in a locker was when I got paid ten dollars to do it," he said, "and it was worth it."

Taylor attended elementary school in the Boston area. He was, in his own words, "school-famous." His proportions were not noticeably dwarflike until he was ten or so. "That's when the staring began," he said. "It's the same natural curiosity that makes someone slow down to look at a traffic accident and see if anyone died. Is there blood? We just have to glance."

The van Putten family moved near San Diego just as Taylor was finishing fifth grade. The transition to middle school wasn't so bad, but when the family moved a few miles away, to Poway, they had to switch school districts again. "That was my angry, socially retarded period," Taylor said. "Everybody's made their friends by seventh grade. I was just like, 'Why should I even try *again*?' That's when I started looking in the mirror and saying, 'I really don't like that. Legs: short, stocky, curved, out of proportion. Everything: arms, hands, toenails.'"

After one of his surgeries, Taylor was prescribed strong painkillers. "I realized that I was getting high and I enjoyed it," he said. "I smoked a lot of weed, took a lot of ecstasy, acid, mushrooms." Tracey was upset but not surprised. "He was angry and he decided he was going to punish us," she said.

The spiritual has always been emphasized in Taylor's life. He explained, "I've been going to church since I was born; still do. In the middle of my angry period, I recognized that I don't fit with Christianity. I don't think there could be any kind of puppet master that could be both a hundred percent love and power and still allow civilizations to rot and fester, and individuals to be born with this kind of pain." Over time, though, his anger began to resolve. "You can't solve what I have, but you can come to accept it. I quit drugs, and after that, in eleventh grade, last year, surrounded by all the coolest people I could ever want, I enrolled in four AP classes."

Taylor later said that he always managed to get what he really wanted. "But it required a step or two more than most people need. It's pretty painful physically, most intensely in my legs and ankles. I use weights and swim because I care about being healthy and how I look. Going to hike with friends, my back is breaking, my hips are about to fall off. I have to take a break. 'Taylor, dude, what's up? Let's go.' I'm dying. I don't think most people realize. I have to purposely laugh if someone makes a midget joke. I don't find it funny, but they're not trying to hurt my feelings, and I'm not going to go on a jihad against Comedy Central. I did the class-clown thing in elementary school, the quiet-in-the-corner thing in middle school, and now I try to balance it. Other people have no idea what it's like to be me. But then, I have no concept of what it's like to be normal."

Taylor used to want to be alone for the rest of his life, but now he wants to find someone. As he reimagines his future, his grandfather is his inspiration. "Look at the racism he faced and stood up to," Taylor said. "So my enlightenment—I kind of like to think of it as my enlightenment—is that I can have dwarfism be a factor in everything I do, but not hate it, not have it limit more than what it limits."

Genes have been found for the primary forms of dwarfism, including achondroplasia, the most common. A different muta-tion of the same gene causes hypochondroplasia, a milder form of dwarfism. Another mutation causes a lethal form of dwarfism, and finding that gene has allowed prenatal diagnosis of the condition, giving parents the option to terminate pregnancies that were certain to end in tragedy. Genetic research on Dwarfism also, however, has allowed people to select against healthy achondroplastic children.

A quarter of respondents in a recent survey would choose abortion if they found out they were expecting a dwarf. Even more striking, more than 50 percent of medical professionals surveyed would make that choice. The question of testing has since been hotly debated among little people, with some couples expressing the desire to screen out average-size fetuses and ensure a dwarf child.

LPA has responded to the issue of genetic testing with a statement that reads in part, "We as short-statured individuals are productive members of society who must inform the world that, though we face challenges, most of them are environmental (as with people with other disabilities), and we value the opportunity to contribute a unique perspective to the diversity of our society. For LPA members there is a common feeling of self-acceptance, pride, community, and culture."

Writing in the *New York Times*, Virginia Heffernan described dwarfism as a "cherished inheritance—a trait, like deafness, that is simultaneously a stigma, a handicap, a source of pride, and a prerequisite for membership in a complex, charismatic, and highly exclusive culture."

The shape of dwarfs' bodies determines their physical capabilities. Dwarfs decry two issues: the problem of how they look to other people, and the problem of how the world is not set up for people of their size. There are authentic inconveniences to being short in a world built for taller people; there is also a lot of pain attached to being laughed at, to being considered "cute" when one wants to be taken seriously in a business context, to being either considered too strange-looking to be sexually attractive or considered sexually attractive as an exotic fetish.

Nowhere are those issues more confused than in the debate around extended limb-lengthening, or ELL. Treatment begins at the growth-spurt age, usually around eight or nine. The child is sedated, and metal screws are inserted into the lower leg bones at one-and-a-half-inch intervals, so that they stick out through the flesh of the leg. Each leg is then broken in about ten places. Because there is no longer a functional bone in the lower leg, a large brace is affixed to the outside of the leg and attached to the screws. In a month or so, the bone begins to heal—the fragments reach toward one another. When they are nearly connected, the brace is adjusted to pull them apart again and stretch the leg. This is repeated regularly for about two years, with the bone kept broken, the ligaments and muscles and nerves all constantly stretched. When the lower legs have fully healed the process is repeated on the lower arms, then the upper legs, then the upper arms. Limb-lengthening surgery means spending the end of childhood and most of adolescence in considerable pain. It means spending those years with enormous metal braces covering your body and metal screws projecting from your arms and legs. But it does work. It can add fourteen inches to a person's height—which can be the difference between being seen as freakish and being seen as normal.

The process costs between $80,000 and $130,000.

Skeptics contend that ELL is complicated and painful, and that the procedure is needless given that little people can function quite well in society without it. Like those who speak out against cochlear implants, ELL opponents object to the surgery's implication that their condition needs to be corrected.

The political position is tied up with the medical one. People who have had ELL tend to speak well of it, and studies show that the procedure boosts self-esteem. The people who choose it are often those who disliked being dwarfs, and the procedure gives them a new start, with the social rewards given to people whose appearance fits mainstream standards. But the surgery can turn out badly, with nerve damage and heavy scarring. People who have experienced complications are among the loudest voices speaking out against it.

Some children seem to move easily toward a celebration of their difference. For others, difference is almost insufferable. Likewise, some parents can tolerate having a child who is different, and some can't. At nine, I'd have given anything not to be gay and would have gone through a procedure like this had there been one. Now that I'm forty-eight I'm glad that I didn't compromise my body. The trick is knowing which prejudices of a nine-year-old will change with time and which ones are true readings of the heart that will last into adulthood.

Human growth hormone (HGH) does not confer greater height on people with skeletal dysplasias, but its use has long been approved for people with pituitary dwarfism. Nowadays, HGH is increasingly used for average-size young people who are not tall and wish to be so. Like ELL, such hormone therapy must be undertaken during the growth years, usually in the early teens. Whether it works in people with adequately functioning pituitary systems is debatable, but some studies indicate that it can add up to four inches of additional height. The cost of treating people with HGH is between $12,000 and $40,000. Some wealthy parents have sought it for their children of average height because they believe that making their children tall is a favor to them.

It may be a high calling to make the world more welcoming of dwarfs; it is easier for the mainstream to make dwarfs fit the world. Do dwarfs who accommodate the world through medical procedures make it easier for the social injustices to continue? And do they therefore have a moral obligation to refuse such procedures and keep pressure on society to accept them as they are? That's a lot to ask of an LP is who is trying to live a life of personal satisfaction.

The advantages of height are proven. Tall people win more votes in elections, and studies show that men over six feet earn, on average, a salary 12 percent higher than shorter men. Tall people are icons of beauty in films, in advertisements, and on the fashion runways. Our language is full of expressions like *stand tall and proud* and disparaging terms like *fall short of*, *comes up short*, and *puny*. The use of *dwarf* as a verb—a disparaging one in most instances—does not help matters.

Dwarfs have created dating sites such as datealittle.com, littlepeoplemeet.com, and shortpassions.com. "Much of the dwarf population missed the years the basic dating ground rules were learned," one LP said. "We're naive." There are additional problems. John Wolin, an LP sportswriter at the *Miami Herald*, elaborated. "Many of us have trouble coupling. Our limbs may be too short or too rigid to bend around our partner's. Because of the spinal-cord damage many of us suffer, we may have trouble with erections." Dwarfs must also decide how they feel about being involved with average people (APs) rather than LPs.

For many little people, the question of whether to partner with another little person or one of average height is political. Some believe that dwarfs who marry people of average height fail to accept themselves as dwarfs. Rates of depression seem to be slightly higher among little people in mixed-height marriages. Most dwarfs who marry still marry other dwarfs.

Childbearing presents other medical challenges. LP couples who decide to have children both celebrate their own lives and take a leap of faith about the lives they may expect for their children. Many little people, some with biological children and some without, adopt dwarf children given up for adoption by average-size parents.

Yet many average-size parents do not give up such children. When Clinton Brown III was born, doctors whisked him away. A doctor explained to Clinton II and Cheryl that their son had diastrophic dysplasia, and was therefore terribly deformed and likely to die. He offered to have the baby placed in an institution and told Cheryl she would never have to see him. "That's my baby," Cheryl said. "I want to see my baby."

Clinton was in an incubator when Cheryl finally saw him, and she was allowed only to touch his toe, but when she did, his eyes opened and she saw that they were blue and beautiful. She also saw what she would come to know were signposts of diastrophic dwarfism: the unjointed hitchhiker's thumb that springs from the bottom of the palm, the flat nose, the cauliflower ears, and the cleft palate. He had scoliosis and clubfeet, and his legs were bunched up under him like airplane landing gear. His head was gigantic. "Some kids have a mild version of this, but he had every symptom possible," Cheryl said. "I think of it as the deluxe package." Clinton had his first surgery when he was two weeks old. When he was eleven months old, Cheryl found Steven Kopits at Johns Hopkins. After all the doctors who had described the problems Clinton would face, Kopits picked Clinton up, held him in the air, and said, "Let me tell you. That's going to be a handsome young man one day."

When Clinton was almost three, after six months of constant surgery, he began to walk. Kopits worked on Clinton's clubfeet, his tibiae, his fibulae, his knees, his hips. Clinton had eleven back surgeries, cleft palate surgery, surgery to correct a hernia. He spent six months in a full-body cast, flat on his back, with a circle of metal with four pins fixed in his skull to immobilize his head and spine.

Clinton said, "When I was a kid, I was bitter toward the fact that I was little. Angry that I didn't have the same opportunities as everybody else. You either face the war, or you falter. It was everyone else's problem that they didn't know how to handle it, and it was my problem that I didn't know how to teach them how.

"I was such a sports fan, and I wanted to be an athlete," Clinton said. "We used to play hockey in the street, but everybody started getting huge and running me over, so I couldn't play. It's just a big piece of childhood that I missed out on." During the long periods of immobility and surgery, Clinton was homeschooled. He worked hard. "I figured I had nothing else to do, so I got ahead of my class on most things. I decided to do really well academically, 'cause I just had to be the best at *something*." When he graduated, Clinton was accepted to Hofstra—the first member of his family to enroll in college. He decided to major in banking and finance, volunteered to be a peer counselor, and helped run orientation week for new students. "I wish all life was college. I'm in the big, macho fraternity; I'm friends with all the girls on campus; I've dated here and there. I have fun."

With his unjointed fingers, Clinton still needed help buttoning a shirt, but he became increasingly independent in other ways. He got a driver's license and a specially fitted car. His parents were amazed. "When he first went to Hofstra, he met this group of guys that he's been hanging out with for the last four years," Cheryl said. "They would go out to bars and stuff." She worries about him drinking and driving, but, she observed wryly, "If you'd told me when he was born that my worry would be that he'd go out driving after drinking with his college buddies, I'd have been overjoyed."

Clinton has learned to set boundaries with the public. "I used to become really upset," he said. "I would cry. Now I just go right up to the person. My mom's always 'Be nice, be nice.' But sometimes you can't be nice. I walked by this guy's table, and he goes to his friend, 'Oh my god, look at that midget.' I said, 'Don't *ever* do that,' and I knocked his beer into his lap. You can't yell at kids. They don't know any better. So I go up to the parent: 'Listen. Why don't you teach your kids some manners and have some class about you?' And it's no better in classy places."

At eighteen, Clinton found his first summer job in finance; five days a week, he made the solo commute by scooter, train, and subway, an hour and a half each way, to the Manhattan offices of Merrill Lynch. Clinton has gone on to win promotions, get better jobs, and—after having trouble with access to the subway—speak to the Metropolitan Transportation Authority on behalf of Americans with disabilities.

"My parents worry about me too much, and my way for them to let that go is for me to be financially and physically independent. I was in the hospital so much, so my parents were my best friends. Now I have no boundaries; I have no inhibitions; I want to do so much. God didn't give me legs to run or arms to throw a football, but He gave me a brain, and He gave me a heart, and I try to use both of those to the best of my ability."

Down Syndrome

ANYONE INVOLVED IN ANY WAY WITH disability has come across "Welcome to Holland," a modern fable written by Emily Perl Kingsley in 1987. Here is the piece in its entirety:

I am often asked to describe the experience of raising a child with a disability—to try to help people who have not shared that unique experience to understand it, to imagine how it would feel. It's like this. . . .

When you're going to have a baby, it's like planning a fabulous vacation trip—to Italy. You buy a bunch of guidebooks and make your wonderful plans. The Coliseum. The Michelangelo *David*. The gondolas in Venice. You may learn some handy phrases in Italian. It's all very exciting.

After months of eager anticipation, the day finally arrives. You pack your bags and off you go. Several hours later, the plane lands. The stewardess comes in and says, "Welcome to Holland."

"Holland?!?" you say. "What do you mean Holland?? I signed up for Italy! I'm supposed to be in Italy. All my life I've dreamed of going to Italy."

But there's been a change in the flight plan. They've landed in Holland and there you must stay.

The important thing is that they haven't taken you to a horrible, disgusting, filthy place, full of pestilence, famine, and disease. It's just a different place.

So you must go out and buy new guidebooks. And you must learn a whole new language. And you will meet a whole new group of people you would never have met.

It's just a different place. It's slower-paced than Italy, less flashy than Italy. But after you've been there for a while and you catch your breath, you look around . . . and you begin to notice that Holland has windmills . . . and Holland has tulips. Holland even has Rembrandts.

But everyone you know is busy coming and going from Italy . . . and they're all bragging about what a wonderful time they had there. And for the rest of your life, you will say, "Yes, that's where I was supposed to go. That's what I had planned."

And the pain of that will never, ever, ever, ever go away . . . because the loss of that dream is a very, very significant loss.

But . . . if you spend your life mourning the fact that you didn't get to Italy, you may never be free to enjoy the very special, the very lovely things . . . about Holland.

Seven to eight million Americans have intellectual disabilities, and one in ten American families is directly affected by such conditions. Down syndrome, the result of a triplication of the twenty-first chromosome, is the most common form of intellectual disability, occurring in about one of every eight hundred births in the United States, for a total American population of more than four hundred thousand people. In addition to intellectual disability, Down syndrome can entail a host of other problems, ranging from heart defects and a malformed digestive tract to hearing and vision problems. Poor muscle tone affects coordination and speech. People with DS have smaller brains and are at increased risk for depression, psychosis, disruptive behavior disorders, and autism. Down syndrome appears to have existed in all human populations across the span of human history; it has been found in chimpanzees and gorillas as well.

Prenatal testing, including amniocentesis, can identify DS, giving parents the ability to terminate if they are so inclined. But Down syndrome can be more or less acute, and none of these tests can establish how severely challenged the child will be.

At the time Emily Perl Kingsley and her husband, Charles, were expecting, they decided to forego amniocentesis because the risk of injuring the fetus seemed too great. "And if I had had amnio," Emily said, "I would have terminated, and I would have missed out on what has been not only the most difficult but also the most enriching experience of my life."

Jason Kingsley was born in 1974. The doctor told Charles that such a child belonged in an institution and discouraged the Kingsleys from seeing their baby. He said that "this mongoloid" would never learn to speak, think, walk, or talk.

This was soon after a television news exposé of the horrific conditions at Willowbrook, a New York State facility for people with intellectual disabilities, and Emily and Charles couldn't bear the idea of institutionalization. It was also a time when many people argued that *nurture* was more important than *nature*. Though other doctors at the hospital made further grim predictions, a social worker there mentioned that a new, experimental program called *early intervention* might help kids with DS to learn some basic skills.

When Jason was ten days old, Emily and Charles took him to the Mental Retardation Institute to investigate early intervention. The doctor there said almost the opposite of what they had been told at the hospital. They had to start with stimulation of every kind, especially of Jason's senses, because no one knew what might be possible for a child with DS who received enough positive input. Charles and Emily painted Jason's room blinding red with green and purple flowers. They hung things from the ceiling on springs, so they were always moving and bobbing. There was music all the time, and they talked to Jason day and night. They moved his limbs through stretches and exercises to improve his muscle tone.

One day when he was four months old, Emily was saying, "See the flower?" for the eight hundredth time, and Jason reached out and pointed to the flower. "He could have been stretching," she said. "But I experienced it as him saying, 'O-*kay*, Mom, I *got* it.' It was a message to me: I am not a lump of mashed potatoes. I am a person." Emily called Charles immediately. "He's in there!" she cheered. Emily and Charles tried to come up with new experiences for Jason almost daily. Emily sewed a quilt that had a different fabric every few inches—terrycloth, velvet,

Astroturf—so that every time Jason moved he would experience a new sensation. When he was six months old, they took a giant roasting pan and filled it with Jell-O, forty packages worth, and lowered him into it so he could writhe around and experience the strange texture, and eat some of it too.

Jason learned better than Emily and Charles could have hoped. His speech was slightly slurred, but he could communicate. Emily taught him the alphabet. He picked up numbers; he learned words in Spanish from watching *Sesame Street*, where Emily had been a writer since 1970.

Jason started reading at four, ahead of many typical peers. At six, he had a fourth-grade reading level and could do basic math. By the time Jason was seven, he could count to ten in twelve languages. He had learned Sign as well as English and could tell Bach from Mozart. Emily took Jason on the road and they addressed obstetricians, nurses, and psychologists, as well as parents of children with DS. Emily felt that she had licked DS; she lived in triumph.

Emily arranged for Jason to appear as a regular guest on *Sesame Street*, and he made tolerance normal for a new generation. She wrote a screenplay based on their experience and insisted that the producers cast children with DS, a radically new idea at that time. A television news program did a special about Jason and a friend who also had Down syndrome and had received early intervention. The two boys eventually wrote a book, *Count Us In*. "Give a baby with a disability a chance to grow a full life, to experience a half-full glass instead of a half-empty glass," Jason wrote. "Think of your abilities, not your disability." Jason became the first DS celebrity. His fame marked the emergence of Down syndrome as a horizontal identity.

Emily had been told that her child was subhuman. When this proved to be untrue, it was logical to question every belief about DS. Emily began to think that maybe no one knew what these kids were capable of. Yet while Jason learned more than anyone with DS had ever learned, he had limitations. He could read better than he could understand what he was reading. "Then around the time he turned eight, the rest of the world caught up and went past, and I began to realize all the things he couldn't do and would never be able to do. All the trained-seal stuff was fantastic, but in the real world, the intelligence to count in many languages is not as important as social intelligence, and he didn't have it. I had not made the Down syndrome go away."

Jason would hug strangers and didn't understand that they weren't friends. He wanted to attend sleepaway camp, but after he had been there a week, Emily got a call saying that the other kids didn't like him and didn't like how he kept hugging everyone. Some parents had said that if Jason didn't leave, they were going to pull their own kids. When he played soccer, he would forget which team he was on. The typical kids who had been his friends began to snigger. Jason could be a TV star, but he could not function in everyday settings. It was a horrible readjustment for both Emily and Jason. It was around this time that Emily wrote "Welcome to Holland."

As Jason reached his teen years, his classmates began having parties, but he wasn't invited. Emily called other parents of teens with Down syndrome, and began to host a monthly party at her home. "They felt so normal," Emily said. "They loved it." When I met her, the monthly parties had been going on for fifteen years. Jason and his friends were still having a good time.

Jason had been in a special-needs classroom, but nonetheless passed the required exams for a high school diploma and attended a post–high school program where he learned money management, time management, cooking, and housekeeping in addition to job-related skills.

Other things remained elusive. Jason wanted to drive. "It's fun for boys and sexy for girls," he wrote in *Count Us In*. "You can get girls if you drive." He wanted a red Saab turbo convertible. Emily had to tell him he couldn't drive because his reaction time was slower than other people's. "I made it something physical," she said. "He's no dope. He shouldn't drive because he doesn't have the judgment, but how to say so?"

Charles set Jason up in an apartment of his own, but Jason lost first one job and then another because he wanted to do things his own way. He is too bright for most others with Down syndrome; they can't keep up with his verbal abilities, Emily explained. But he is not bright enough for people without disabilities. It's a lonely place to be. He has a sort-of girlfriend, who also has DS. Emily took him for a vasectomy, afraid of leaving the responsibility of birth control to a girl whose capacity she was unclear of.

When Jason was twenty, his father was diagnosed with cancer, and he died three years later. Jason became deeply depressed. Emily realized that Jason needed structure and supervision and decided that a group home was the answer. The waiting list for a local facility was an impossible eight years.

One day, Emily spotted a house for sale in Hartsdale, New York, and realized it would be a perfect group home. It had three bedrooms, enough for Jason and two friends; it was near the main bus stop and across the street from a supermarket, a bank, and a pharmacy. Emily bought the house and then asked Westchester Arc (the organization's name was originally an acronym for Association of Retarded Citizens) to run it. Jason moved in with two best friends he had met at the parties Emily had been throwing. The three receive Social Security disability checks that go straight to Arc, which spends the money to maintain and staff the house.

"They love one another," Emily said. "They call themselves The Three Musketeers." Jason has a job working for the local radio station, where he is very happy. "I'm stepping back a little," she said. "The ultimate job is to appreciate him for who he is—and who he is is really terrific. Anything he's accomplished, he's accomplished because he really stuck to it. Nothing comes easy to him." She paused, then said, "He's kept a lot of dignity in the face of that. I really, really admire him tremendously. I'm also sad for him, because he's smart enough to know that almost everybody is accomplishing things that he's not, smart enough to realize that his life is different." The loneliness that comes along with being such a high-functioning adult with DS continues.

I went to a reading at Barnes & Noble that Jason and his friend did when their book was reissued. Jason answered questions with fluency and poise. Emily was aglow and Jason was aglow. The parents of children with DS who had come to hear him were aglow too—with hope. During the book signing, people approached Jason reverently. He and Emily were heroes, and Jason loved being a hero. I could understand his loneliness, but I could not miss his pride.

For most of history, Down syndrome had not been compared to a holiday among windmills and tulips. The first person to describe Down syndrome was John Langdon Down, in 1866. He referred to his subjects as *Mongoloids* or *Mongoloid idiots* on the basis that their faces, with slightly slanted eyes, resembled those of people from Mongolia. Down proposed that human evolution had gone from black people to Asians to white people, and that white people born with Mongolism were actually a throwback to their primitive Asian antecedents—a position then considered rather progressive insofar as it acknowledged evolution.

French physician Édouard Séguin was the first to recognize the merits of early treatment. Séguin emigrated to the US in the middle of the nineteenth century and established institutions for the care and education of the disabled, whom he trained to take on manual labor jobs.

By 1900 the jobs that had been done by Séguin's trained individuals were being claimed by the great influx of immigrants. The rising theory of genetics suggested that intellectually disabled people were untreatable. Medical texts delineated how to classify someone an "idiot," an "imbecile," or a "moron." Eugenicists linked intellectual disability and criminality, and laws favoring sterilization were passed. They were not repealed for nearly fifty years.

Many people who had a child with DS institutionalized him or her immediately and often told no one, not even their other children, that the child existed. In 1968 the ethicist Joseph Fletcher wrote in the *Atlantic Monthly* that there was "no reason to feel guilty about putting a Down's syndrome baby away, whether it's 'put away' in the sense of hidden in a sanatorium or in a more responsible lethal sense. It is sad, yes. Dreadful. But it carries no guilt. True guilt arises only from an offense against a person, and a Down's is not a person." Some parents who had been persuaded that their intellectually disabled children were not persons left them in repugnant conditions, as at Willowbrook.

Yet even as prejudice against those with intellectual disabilities was growing, a new movement to help the disabled was also unfolding. The argument that the disabled deserved caring treatment coincided with a larger shift in our conception of early education. The first kindergartens were founded in Germany in the early nineteenth century. By the end of the nineteenth century, nursery schools began to crop up in Europe and the United States. New Deal teaching jobs and the push of mothers into the work force during the Second World War led to even more. The new science of behaviorism rose up in opposition to eugenics and suggested that people are made, not born, and can be educated and shaped into anything. Advocates of the new field of psychoanalysis also began to question whether the shortcomings of the disabled might be the result of early deprivation rather than genetic inadequacy.

In 1935, the federal government began matching state funds for treating the disabled. At the same time, investigators began to look at how a stimulating and enriching environment allowed poor children to succeed. It was also demonstrated that good maternal care was crucial to the development of a healthy child. This is accepted today. Sixty years ago, it was a radical idea.

Eugenics was finally discredited when the world learned of the Holocaust. At the same time, the influx of handicapped veterans at the end of World War II softened prejudice against disabled people in general. Better education programs were established for children with special needs.

When John F. Kennedy became president, he established a commission to study intellectual disability and its possible prevention. His sister, Eunice Kennedy Shriver, worked to reintegrate the disabled into the larger society. Her vision took meaningful form in the wake of the civil rights movement. When black people rose up against the characterization that they were inferior, they opened the door for other marginalized people to do the same. Head Start, founded in 1963, was dedicated to the idea that people lived in poverty not because of inherent deficits, but because they had not received appropriate early stimulus.

By the end of the 1960s, insights from Head Start were being applied to people with intellectual disabilities, and in particular to children with Down syndrome. Early intervention was a better value for the money than institutionalization. In 1973, Congress passed, over President Richard Nixon's veto, the Rehabilitation Act, which prohibited discrimination on the basis of disability in federal programs and employment. Even with the budget cuts of the Reagan years, programs for disabled children remained in force.

The passage of the Americans with Disabilities Act of 1990 extended the 1973 protections and was a major triumph. Parents, with support from disabled people themselves, had capitalized on changing ideas about humanity. They validated lives long considered worthless.

Early intervention (EI) is now a federal program for infants with any of a broad range of challenges, including Down syndrome. EI is the full expression of the nurture-over-nature argument—the ultimate triumph of psychoanalysis, civil rights, and empathy over eugenics, sterilization, and segregation. It reflects changing understandings of nondisabled children and new theories of early education. It continues to evolve today.

Disabled children, like nondisabled children, thrive on attention, engagement, stimulation, and hope.

Betsy Goodwin didn't expect complications before her daughter, Carson, was born with Down syndrome in 1978 in New York. But her obstetrician said, "Why don't you have a healthy baby, and we'll forget about this one?" She called her childhood friend Arden Moulton, a social worker, and asked for advice. Arden said that institutionalizing Carson was the last thing Betsy should do. The lack of resources for DS babies and their families quickly became apparent. A few months later Betsy decided to start an organization for parents in her situation and asked Arden to help. This is how, in 1979, the National Down Syndrome Society (NDSS) was established.

The first project of the NDSS was to organize a conference for scientists working on any aspect of the condition. There had never before been such a gathering. Betsy went to Washington to meet with the head of the National Institutes of Health (NIH), who told her that with amniocentesis, there would soon not be anyone born with Down syndrome. "I don't know whether he'd met anyone Catholic," she said drily, twenty-five years later.

Betsy became pregnant again when Carson was two, and

she considered amniocentesis. Finally, she decided against it. Betsy's son was born typical, as was another son three years later. "My three kids get along great," Betsy said. The obstetrician had warned her that keeping Carson would ruin her marriage and cause suffering in siblings. Like his other predictions, both of these turned out to be untrue.

Carson has a warm personality and is socially comfortable. When her brothers were in high school, she loved to dance. "I used to see this arm come out of her bedroom, and she'd grab one of her brothers' friends and make them dance with her," Betsy said.

When I met Carson, she had recently lost her job at Whole Foods because she always seemed to put the tomatoes in the bottom of the bag. "She's never been a tomato fan," Betsy said. "I assure you that the doughnuts would be on top." Carson has trouble understanding that other people think or feel differently— her mother's preference for John Coltrane over Britney Spears, for example, baffles her. She knows that her Down syndrome makes her different, even though she doesn't grasp exactly how. That's why, Betsy explained, her dancing gives her so much joy: "She loves anything that makes her an equal."

The two key movements in educating disabled children after they have graduated from EI are *mainstreaming* and *inclusion*. In the 1970s and 1980s parents advocated for mainstreaming, so that disabled students could be taught mostly in dedicated classrooms within ordinary public schools. The 1990s brought a shift to inclusion, which entails educating disabled children in the same classrooms as their nondisabled peers, often with a special assistant. This integrating of disabled children into regular schools has changed the appearance of the American classroom.

There are two essential questions in the debate about these philosophies: What is better for the child with a diagnosis, and what is better for typical children? Some parents complain that disabled children in the classroom are a distraction. Others argue that inclusion benefits everyone, both by making typical children more open and humane and by giving children with disabilities good role models.

The pitfall is that people with DS who are in inclusion programs are often cut off from their peers, and people without DS are willing to go only a certain distance in building relationships with people who have the condition. The teen years are hard enough without the loneliness that comes from being left out and friendless.

Adam Delli-Bovi's mother, Susan Arnsten, was twenty-two and living in Ithaca, New York, when Adam was born. "I started looking, too quickly, at how I could use this challenge for something good," Susan said. "I didn't give myself time to grieve. My parents thought it was a tragedy, so I had to make it into just the opposite." Susan applied for federal supplementary security income (SSI) for Adam. When the first check came, she used it to enroll in a course called Learning and Children.

Susan's research and learning were critical. "A regular kid will initiate. They'll learn in spite of anything you do," Susan said. "But with Adam you had to kind of bring it to him and he'd meet you maybe a quarter of the way."

Adam had persistent upper respiratory infections, and was

moments. Somehow Adam had learned the moves, and with only minimal prompting from Susan, he did the whole thing, a little awkwardly but with charm. Watching this private cabaret, I thought that what the whole household had achieved was intimacy. Susan's genuine belief that happiness was a fluid concept seemed to fill the room with love.

Until Ronald Reagan signed the Baby Doe Amendment in 1984, which said that to neglect or withhold treatment for disabled infants was child abuse, parents and physicians could legally let such infants die. The Princeton ethicist Peter Singer has supported the right of women to choose abortion to the end of pregnancy and to commit infanticide on disabled newborns. His extreme position reflects the ongoing devaluation of people with Down syndrome, which has contributed to the politicization of the disability community.

By 2000, the resistance to prenatal screening from the disability rights camp had crystallized. In their seminal discussion of the problem, disability scholars Adrienne Asch and Erik Parens wrote, "Prenatal diagnosis reinforces the medical model that disability itself, not societal discrimination against people with disabilities, is the problem to be solved. Prenatal genetic testing followed by selective abortion is morally problematic and it is driven by misinformation."

Preventing births of any subclass of people devalues them. A society in which fetuses with Down syndrome are routinely aborted clearly believes that DS is a grave misfortune. This does not mean that many people hate or want to slaughter people with DS; indeed, many people who would choose to terminate a DS pregnancy would also go out of their way to be kind to a person living with the syndrome. But I know from personal experience how kind sympathy can be a noxious prejudice; I do not care to spend time with people who pity me for being gay, even if their sympathy reflects a generous heart and is offered with egregious politesse.

Asch claims that women abort disabled fetuses because of the woeful lives that would come of their pregnancies; that such woe is the product of chauvinism; that such chauvinism could be resolved. Janice McLaughlin, at the University of Newcastle, wrote, "Mourning the choice the woman is compelled to make is not the same as saying she is wrong or an active participant in discrimination. Instead it points to the ways in which she, too, is a victim." But the acts of those women do not merely reflect the society; they create it. The more such pregnancies are terminated, the greater the chance that more will be terminated. Accommodations are contingent on population; only the ubiquity of disability keeps the disability rights conversation alive at all. A dwindling population means dwindling accommodation.

Down syndrome has been at the center of the abortion debate for two reasons: DS was among the first major genetic anomalies for which prenatal testing existed, and it is the most common of the genetic anomalies that can be detected in utero. At present, about 70 percent of expectant mothers who receive a prenatal diagnosis of Down syndrome choose to abort. Ironically, outcomes for people with DS have improved more radically in the last forty years than outcomes for almost any other anomaly. People who would have languished in institutions and died at ten are now reading and writing and working. The life expectancy for people with DS in the United States is around fifty, double the 1983 figure.

In about 95 percent of cases, Down syndrome is the result of spontaneous mutation rather than a transmissible gene, and people who have DS seldom reproduce. Targeted abortion had been expected to eliminate most of the population with Down syndrome, but the proportion of babies born with the condition in any given year has increased or remained constant. Eighty percent of Down syndrome births are to women under thirty-five who have not had testing. As people with DS live longer, the number of people on the planet with DS is increasing; the number in the United States may double between 2000 and 2025, to as many as eight hundred thousand.

The American College of Obstetricians and Gynecologists recommended in 2007 that all pregnant women undergo an ultrasound that helps identify possible chromosomal anomalies in the first trimester, with the option of genetic counseling and further testing in the second trimester for those at risk of having DS babies. Disability rights groups oppose this. One columnist who has a son with DS called it a "search and destroy mission." Moderates have asked that people be better informed about the experience of having a DS child. Activists worry that women who wish to keep a DS pregnancy may feel pressured to terminate as prenatal diagnosis gets easier. Others worry that women who decide to keep such a pregnancy may lose out on social and financial aid afterward.

As the techniques for prenatal diagnosis of DS have become more available, funding for research about the condition has diminished. This seems particularly tragic because treatment for the major symptoms of DS is now a field full of promise.

As with the deaf and their implants, and dwarfs and their ELL, this is another scramble—not so much for identity, this time, as for science. If people with DS can be normalized, should we think more carefully about terminating DS pregnancies? It's as if the scientists are in a race against the people who are promoting early-screening methods. If science isn't quick enough to offer alternatives, the entire field might collapse.

Deirdre Featherstone didn't want children, so she was delighted to learn she was infertile. When she became pregnant in 1998, however, she decided to let things unfold. Her husband, Wilson Madden, wanted to do amniocentesis, but said that if they found out something was wrong, it wouldn't make a difference. Deirdre said to him, "Well, if I find out there's something wrong, this kid's out of here, because, as you well know, I don't want to be anyone's mother. I don't even have the courage to be the parent of a regular kid. I'm perfectly ready to have an abortion if there's anything wrong. You aren't. So you'd better stop pushing the amnio."

They didn't have the test. "Thank God, because it would have been the biggest mistake of my life," Deirdre said. "You can't assess what you don't know." A midwife delivered baby Catherine at home and told her parents to see a pediatrician right away. The pediatrician confirmed that Catherine had Down syndrome. "I already knew that Catherine was the nicest person I was ever going to meet," Deirdre said.

Catherine was born into a very different world from the

pre-EI one Carson Goodwin had entered. Deirdre said, "One of the things that made the early period difficult was that she would have therapy three times a week for speech, then occupational therapy, then physical therapy, and also craniosacral therapy. Her schedule was so full, it was hard for me to leave the house. That was probably the only difficulty, besides adjusting to the fact that somebody else is depending on you to live."

Deirdre surprised even herself with how much joy she found in parenting. "I started off knowing she was flawed, and all the surprises since then have been good ones. She's one of the nicest, kindest, most thoughtful, sensitive people that I've ever met. She's funny. She always highlights the positive; I don't know how much of that is personality or if that's Down syndrome. When she makes up her mind that she's not doing something, that is that, which is also typical of Down syndrome."

The mother of a child with special needs inevitably becomes a soothsayer. "Somebody I know called me in tears, saying, 'I just found out my kid has DS; what should I do?' I said, 'What do you want to do?' She said, 'It's my baby, and I want to have it.' I said, 'I'll tell you what, it's the best thing that has ever happened to me. And had I had the information, I would have made this big, big mistake by not having her. You've met my kid, we have a really good time.'"

Deirdre never had to make her way through the gauntlet of prejudice that determined Emily Perl Kingsley's early experiences. "People still give up their child. People still have abortions when they find out," Deirdre said. "I'm not here to judge it. You hate lima beans, I love lima beans. There's a lot of political correctness that I find ridiculous. But I'll take whatever's made it unacceptable to make fun of a child because she's different." She described being at Catherine's public school in New York City one day when a five-year-old girl said, "I heard that when Catherine was inside you, you broke your egg, and that's why she came out funny." Deirdre said, "If you break your egg, then you don't have a baby at all." The little girl said, "You mean she's not broken?" Deirdre said, "No, she's not broken. She's a little different." Deirdre looked around the play area and said, "See that little girl over there? She has red, curly hair, and you have blond hair. This little boy, he's black and his mom and dad are white, and they're Italian, and his sister is his sister, but they're not really related biologically." One of the parents nearby said, "I'm Korean and my husband's white." Another said, "I didn't marry a man, but my partner is a lady, so my child is also different."

Catherine was just another variation on the idea that the only normality is nonnormality. "Sometimes I see somebody with a child with Down's, and I'll say, 'My daughter's in the same situation, she's eight,'" Deirdre said. "Nine times out of ten, people will say, 'Congratulations. Welcome to the club.' I think a lot of us feel lucky."

It is easy to focus on the tales of people with DS who are triumphantly high-functioning, whose parents take great pleasure in how smart and successful they are within the parameters of the syndrome. Given how much less these children are likely to attain than typical children, however, to universalize intelligence and achievement as a measure of worth is in some ways to deny who they are. They are not intellectually brilliant and can't accomplish so much by general standards, but have real virtues and are capable of personal fulfillment. Many parents of people with DS began their conversations with me by saying how super-high-functioning their children were, and I began to wonder how it was that I only saw parents of such high-functioning kids. When I began talking to their children, I found that some of them were extraordinarily intelligent and advanced given their condition, and that many others had a few things at which they excelled, from which their parents cheerily generalized. The parents' perceptions of high-functioning frequently outstripped the children's actual level of accomplishment.

Without exception, these parents reported that their children tried hard to please them. Stubborn, intractable when stuck on an idea, the children nonetheless had an eagerness, not as typical of the other disorders examined in this book, that was infinitely moving to their parents. Down syndrome kids are famously sweet-natured, but their less advertised characteristic is that they are troupers.

People born with DS develop slowly and stop short of typical intellectual maturity. They are often warm and sociable, eager to please, and free of cynicism. Larger studies indicate that many people with DS are also stubborn, defiant, aggressive, and sometimes disturbed. Those with milder cases tend toward depression and anxiety. Both children and adults with DS are at heightened risk for physical and sexual abuse.

Many treatments exist for the symptoms of DS. The extra chromosome cannot be suppressed or removed, though there is preliminary work on gene therapy to achieve this. Plastic surgery can normalize the appearance of people with DS. Procedures include a shortening of the tongue—which is said to reduce drooling, improve speech, and help people with DS to breathe better—and a wide range of cosmetic changes such as nose jobs, removing excess fat from the neck, and reshaping the eyes to remove the slant. The National Down Syndrome Society and other groups object to these measures as unnecessarily painful and even cruel, the DS version of limb-lengthening. They would like to use public education to change responses to DS faces rather than change the faces of people with DS.

Until the late 1960s, no one with DS had ever achieved prominence of any kind, but since that time, actors, activists, writers, and artists with the condition have emerged. The first major publication by someone with DS was *The World of Nigel Hunt: The Diary of a Mongoloid Youth*, published in the UK in 1967. Hunt was the son of a school headmaster who, with his wife, attempted to educate Nigel like any other child and included him in the regular classes at his school. Nigel's book recounts his day-to-day life, with touching references to his mother's illness and death. Jason Kingsley and Mitchell Levitz's *Count Us In* is an often joyful and occasionally humorous account of their lives, including knowing descriptions of the particular challenges they've faced. In 2000, Windy Smith, who has DS, addressed the Republican National Convention in Philadelphia, reading aloud a letter she had sent to George W. Bush; she went on to serve on the President's Committee for People with Intellectual Disabilities within the Department of Health and Human Services. Many debated whether this represented exploitative manipulation by the Bush campaign.

The highest-profile person with Down syndrome for a long time was the actor Chris Burke, who starred in the TV program *Life Goes On*, but there have been several others, including Luke Zimmerman, a young actor in the TV series *The Secret Life of the American Teenager*, who was also a football player in Beverly Hills High. Lauren Potter appears on the Fox hit *Glee* as a cheerleader with DS and has her own Facebook fan page.

Some three-quarters of intellectually disabled people in the United States live with their parents. The proportion of children and youth in institutions has gone down by about three-quarters, but the total number of people in institutions has gone up, because life spans have lengthened. Many people with DS are placed when they are between eighteen and twenty-one, at the age when typical children are moving out of their family houses. Whereas families used to separate themselves emotionally from the children they placed, many now remain deeply involved; placement out of the home is not placement out of the family. Many parents want to be present to effect a progressive transition from family home to group home to avoid "transfer trauma."

Though big state institutions still exist in thirty-nine states, they have mostly given way to a vast array of smaller, more intimate, community-based care facilities. More than half of parents visit only one facility and place their child there, sometimes for geographic reasons, but often without regard to the range of quality at such facilities. In 2011 the *New York Times* reported hideous abuses at residential facilities throughout New York State. "Employees who sexually abused, beat or taunted residents were rarely fired, even after repeated offenses," the paper stated. "State records show that of some thirteen thousand allegations of abuse in 2009 within state-operated and licensed homes, fewer than 5 percent were referred to law enforcement. One obstacle complicated any effort to take action against employees accused of abusing those in their care: The victims often cannot talk or have extreme cognitive impairment. Local law enforcement officials point to this to explain a lack of prosecution of cases. But another factor seems to be at work. In many cases, the developmentally disabled do not have families actively involved in their lives, and, hence, no advocates."

Some people with DS thrive at home and others thrive away from home, which reflects the personalities of the people with DS and the nature of their families. Living at home means a familiar environment, and, ideally, more love. Adults with DS who live with their parents may suffer a lack of contact with peers and considerable loneliness. After high school, such people have fewer things to do outside the house and they tend not to learn skills for building friendships. Residential facilities make it easier for people with DS to find friendship and even romantic love.

People with DS have romantic and sexual feelings. Many men with Down syndrome are sterile, but women with DS are as fertile as those without disabilities. Parents frequently worry that their disabled children's sexual activity will result in the birth of kids for whom they would be unable to care. The next frontier for people with DS, however, is marriage. On *Life Goes On*, Chris Burke's character married a woman with DS and they lived in an apartment over his parents' garage. Arden Moulton described being with Chris Burke and having strangers ask for his autograph. "It was a mind-boggling experience," she said. "He was a star first, and a person with a disability second."

Tom and Karen Robards were hard-charging Wall Street types who met at Harvard Business School. Six years into their marriage, in the mid-1980s, they decided to start a family. Karen had an easy pregnancy, and they were totally unprepared for Down syndrome. Tom was crushed, but Karen said, "We're going to love David just like any other baby. When people don't know what to say, we're going to tell them to congratulate us."

The Robardses went to a pediatrician on the Upper West Side who told them there was nothing they could do. So they found a doctor who specialized in genetic defects. She told them to provide every possible form of infant stimulation. Through Early Intervention they saw physical therapists and speech therapists, who worked on feeding and chewing. They joined a support group. When Karen and some friends from that group decided to write a pamphlet about education options after EI, they encountered the staggering bureaucracy of the public schools and were also rebuffed by private schools that claimed to take children with special needs—as long as those needs weren't too special.

So Karen and the parents' group raised $40,000 to start the Cooke Foundation, now called the Cooke Center, one of the largest organizations in New York City focused on educational inclusion for disabled children. It was open to children of all socioeconomic backgrounds. It was not affiliated with any religion, but Karen persuaded the Archdiocese of New York to supply a space. That space turned out to be two large public lavatories; these were renovated into two classrooms by a member of the support group.

They hired two special-education teachers. The idea from the beginning was that their children should spend time with typically developing students, so they enrolled them in public schools for some subjects and taught others at Cooke. David continued to attend both Cooke and public school, becoming the first disabled child in New York City to be included in a regular classroom. "You have to have a place in both worlds," Karen said. "When they're younger, our kids can be more fully included in classrooms because everybody's just learning colors and social skills. As you go on, the gap grows wider, and our kids really need to be focusing on life skills. How do you join a gym? How do you take money out of the ATM? Things that come naturally for other kids require effort from our kids. So we work on building those skills so that they can be included not only in education but also in life."

When David finished high school, public special-needs education stopped. "There are very few postsecondary programs," Karen said. They finally located a school in Pennsylvania that David could attend, and at twenty-one he lived away for the first time. It was not easy for David or for his parents. When I met the Robardses, David had just begun to take Effexor after being deeply shaken by a romance gone awry. He liked a girl with Down syndrome at his school. She had encouraged David, but already had a boyfriend, who was a friend of David's. When David was closed out by both of them, he became paralyzed with anxiety.

David was twenty-three and he had done fund-raising for the International Down Syndrome Society. He had completed internships at News Corporation and at *Sports Illustrated*. He was living semi-independently in a supervised setting.

He has many friends and "a Rolodex that he works every day," according to Tom. Karen said, "David is a master of the cell phone and he loves to keep in contact, but he's also a lover of structure. So you would probably be Tuesday nights. Every Tuesday night he'll call you. We're Sundays and Wednesdays. I think the rigidity helps stabilize him."

We drifted to the question of a cure. "If you talk to people very involved in the Down syndrome community," Tom said, "you'll find a range of perspectives on whether looking for a cure for Down syndrome is a legitimate objective. There are people who won't even talk about that, because to talk about a cure is to diminish the value of the people who are alive with Down syndrome. Some would even say that if they could wave a magic wand and make their child normal, they wouldn't do it." I asked Tom what he would do if he had the magic wand. "If I could have David who he is but not have Down syndrome?" he asked. "I would do it in a minute. I would do it because I think, for David, it's hard being in the world with Down syndrome, and I'd like to give him a happier, easier life. So for David, I'd do it. But the diversity of human beings makes the world a better place, and if everyone with Down syndrome were cured, it would be a real loss."

Karen shook her head. "I'm with Tom. If I could cure David, I would, for David. But I think that we've grown so much as a result of having to deal with this. We've had so much purpose. I'd never have believed twenty-three years ago when he was born that I could come to such a point, but I have. For David, I'd cure it in an instant; but for us, I wouldn't exchange these experiences for anything. They've made us who we are, and who we are is so much better than who we would have been otherwise."

Like deafness and dwarfism, Down syndrome may be an identity or a catastrophe or both; it may be something to cherish or something to eradicate; it may be rich and rewarding both for those whom it affects directly and for those who care for them; it may be a barren and exhausting enterprise; it may be a blend of all these.

Autism

UNLIKE THE OTHER CONDITIONS DISCUSSED IN this book, autism is, mysteriously, on the rise. In 1960, one in twenty-five hundred births resulted in the condition. Today that number is one in sixty-six. Some experts argue that we are simply diagnosing autism more frequently, but improved diagnosis can hardly be the full explanation.

We don't know why autism is on the rise; indeed, we don't even know what autism is. It is a *syndrome* rather than an *illness* because it is a collection of behaviors rather than a known biological entity. Autism includes a highly variable group of symptoms and characteristics, and we have little understanding of where it is located in the brain, why it occurs, or what triggers it. It is a condition of such complexity that we will likely understand it only when we understand the brain much more fully.

Autism is deemed a *pervasive disorder* because it affects almost every aspect of behavior, as well as sensory experiences, motor functioning, balance, the physical sense of where your own body is, and inner consciousness. The primary symptoms include a lack of or delay in speech; poor nonverbal communication; repetitive movement; minimal eye contact; little interest in friendships; lack of spontaneous or imaginative play; a lack of empathy, insight, and sociability; diminished capacity for emotional reciprocity; highly focused interests; and a fascination with objects such as spinning wheels and sparkling things. Autistic children and adults often think in an extremely concrete manner. People with autism may be exquisitely sensitive to sensory overload from crowded spaces, touch, lights, and noise.

While most autistic children show early signs of the syndrome, about a third appear to develop normally and then regress, often between sixteen and twenty months. Because any of these symptoms may occur in any degree, autism is defined as a spectrum that includes varying severity of varying symptoms. The symptoms are, in fact, so variable that some clinicians refer to *the autisms*.

There is no treatment for autism, but one can educate an autistic child, administer medications, or make dietary or lifestyle changes that may relieve a child's depression, anxiety, and physical and sensory problems. No one has figured out what makes one treatment more effective than others for a particular person. Many children are unresponsive to any form of treatment, but the only way to figure that out is to treat them for a long time and then give up.

The cliché about autism is that the syndrome blocks the ability to love, but this is not quite fair. To adore a child who does not mirror your affection in expected ways exacts a greater price than other love. Yet most autistic children do develop at least partial attachments to others, at least eventually.

Betsy Burns and Jeff Hansen had planned to have just one child, but when their daughter Cece was almost two, Betsy decided she wanted another and became pregnant almost immediately.

Cece had been a good baby, happy to play by herself, though even as an infant she didn't sleep much; the new arrival, Molly, was more demanding—but also more engaged. Over time, Jeff and Betsy worried that Cece was not talking. Their doctor assured Betsy that she was just an anxious first-time mother. Betsy joined a mothers group when Cece was three and listened to the other women talk about their children. "I went cold. Something was terribly wrong," she said. Betsy requested an early-intervention assessment from the local department of health. The evaluator said, "I don't want you to be frightened when I use the word *autism*."

Betsy took Cece to a public nursery school for early intervention. Cece received speech therapy, occupational therapy, physical therapy, and music therapy. Even so, she seemed to be growing more disconnected. She injured herself and was sleepless.

Cece has spoken four times in her life. When Cece was three, Betsy gave her a cookie; she pushed it back at her, saying, "You eat it, Mommy." Jeff and Betsy waited for their world to change, but Cece said nothing more for a year. Then one day Betsy stood up to turn off the TV, and Cece said, "I want my TV." At school three years later, she turned on the lights and said, "Who left the lights on?" Then one day a puppeteer visited Cece's class; when he asked, "Hey, kids! What color is the curtain?" Cece responded, "It's purple." To have a child totally incapable of language is distressing, but to have a child who has spoken four times is almost worse. Could the right treatment make it possible for Cece to speak all the time?

"I believe that she has a wild intelligence somewhere. I worry that her soul is trapped," Betsy said. Cece's most recent therapist thinks she has no intellectual disability at all. When I first met Cece, she was ten, and her favorite thing was to hold a lot of crayons and go across a piece of table and a piece of paper so she could feel the change in sensation where the paper ended and the table began. For a brief time, she had suddenly started drawing faces. Then she stopped. "Something was coming through," Betsy said. "Just like something comes through when she says words."

Jeff and Betsy had to arrange their house around Cece's behavior. The shelves were six feet high so that she couldn't reach them; the refrigerator was padlocked because Cece would do strange things with food. Cece was frequently hospitalized because she had stopped sleeping or because she was hurling herself around. Betsy fell into a catastrophic depression, for which she was hospitalized. Toward the end of Betsy's stay in the hospital, Jeff found Cece trying to strangle Molly. The social workers arranged a place for Cece to spend three months. "They didn't tell me it was going to be permanent, 'cause they knew I would die," Betsy said. "On January first, 2000, she left our house forever." She was seven.

Three years after Cece's placement, Betsy said, "I'm allowing myself to see that I hate visiting. I feel really guilty if I don't see her on one of the prescribed days. A woman in my mothers group said, 'Because you're afraid if you don't go one day, you'll never go.'"

Occasionally Cece will show a break in her autism. "One day I was leaving and said, 'Give me a kiss!' and she rubbed her face up against mine," Betsy said. "For her, sounds and sensations might be like a radio set between dials. I mean how the world *gets in* on you, with its buzzes and demands and hangnails and phone calls and gasoline smells and underwear and plans and choices. Cece loves to put on shoes that grip her feet the right way. Sometimes, in the spring, she would put on her boots just to feel them. She loves playing with the hair of African people. And she loves french fries, that whole crunchy, salty sensation. Who doesn't? She loves salsa and things that wake up her mouth. It's very fun for her to snuggle under things. She loves motion, going for a ride and looking out the window. She used to like the soft skin on people's elbows, and she'd follow behind them and hold on to that. If I think about her sensory issues, all I have to do is pull them back a little, and they're mine. I love crunching leaves when I walk. The same is true when I walk on very thin ice, and it crackles. There are certain things that I'm afraid if I get too close to them, I'll touch them for too long."

Much of Betsy's favorite time with Cece takes place swimming. This involves going to a public swimming pool, where Cece is not capable of modifying her behavior. Betsy and Cece went to the pool at a recreation center one day just after I met them. Many families were there. The minute she arrived, Cece pulled off the bottom half of her swimsuit, defecated in the water, played with her feces, then ran around naked so that no one could catch her. One of the mothers screamed, "Contamination! Contamination!" Then all of the others began to yank their children out of the water. Lifeguards blew whistles and screamed, and Cece stood amid the chaos, laughing uproariously.

I went with Jeff, Betsy, and Molly to visit Cece at the group home on her tenth birthday. We had brought a cake in with us, but for safety reasons, there were no candles. Betsy took the presents everyone had brought out of a shopping bag. Cece climbed into the shopping bag and stayed there. The only other thing she liked were the ribbons, which she kept twining and untwining. "This party, which so disrupts routine, is probably distressing to Cece," Jeff said. "I don't know who we're doing this for." Practically speaking, their purpose was to show the workers that Cece's parents loved her, and that the staff should take care of her.

Cece periodically escalates into violence: throwing things at group-home staff, hurling herself on the ground, biting herself. Doctors have attempted to medicate away this misery; in the nine years I have known her, Cece has taken a wide range of anti-depressant and anti-anxiety drugs. Every time I saw her, the meds were being adjusted again.

In the meanwhile, the family has also had to deal with Jeff's bipolar illness. Betsy has had to warn group-home staff that they can't assume that Jeff will be entirely sane at any given time. "I don't want to demean or embarrass him. I love him. But those are calls I have to make, for Cece and not for Jeff. He thinks that if Cece had not been diagnosed with autism, the bipolar might never have been brought on. That's naive, but I think it about my depression, too. Loving Cece has done this to us." In the three years that followed Cece's placement, Jeff was hospitalized twice for mixed manic episodes; and Betsy was hospitalized three times for depression. "Maybe some people out there with a different brain constitution could have handled all this," Jeff said. "But the two of us ended up in the psychiatric ward."

At the group home, Cece and a severely autistic boy named Emmett became friends. Betsy walked into Cece's room one day and found her with Emmett, his pants and diaper off—"exploring, shall we say"—as Cece ran back and forth by the windows. The caretaker was not supposed to leave them alone, but opportunity knocked when she was called to a crisis elsewhere. "Cece and Emmett are never going to think romance, but they might think closeness and pleasure," Betsy said. "They have such hard lives, and maybe they could find a little happiness that way." The staff at the group home, however, is unlikely to tolerate such a thing, and the risk of pregnancy is alarming to all parties.

"People keep saying, 'I don't know how you do it!'" Betsy said. "It's not like I can wake up and say, 'I don't think I'll deal with it anymore.'" I replied that some people do just decide not to deal with it anymore and leave it up to the state. "Hearing that," Betsy said, "it's as if somebody took a rake and dragged it through my guts." Later, Betsy said to me, "On good days I perceive God's light about her, and on bad days I beg for God's understanding. That's the thing about autism: It just is. Cece is the Zen lesson. Why does Cece have autism? Because Cece has autism. And what is it like to be Cece? Being Cece. Because no one else is, and we'll never know what it's like. It is what it is. It's not anything else. And maybe you'll never change it, and maybe you should stop trying."

The word *autism* was used by the Swiss psychiatrist Eugen Bleuler in 1912 to describe a state in which "thought is divorced both from logic and from reality." In 1943, Leo Kanner, an

Austrian psychiatrist who had emigrated to the United States, identified autism as a distinct disorder. He chose *autistic* because it underscored the extreme aloneness of the children he had studied. Every autistic person has a unique pattern of weaknesses and strengths, and a person can be extremely competent in one area, but quite incompetent in others. At the same time, the most impaired end of the spectrum is so different from the least impaired that it is sometimes hard to accept that the conditions are related at all.

The idea that mothers with perverse desires produced deformed or troubled children had long been abandoned in relation to dwarfs and others with physical deformities, but it persisted for those with psychiatric disorders. Kanner believed that autism was instigated by "genuine lack of maternal warmth." His theory that unaffectionate parents made their children autistic led to the tragically misguided concept of the "refrigerator mother." Of course, this has since been proven to be untrue. "We mothers would have liked an apology," said Eustacia Cutler, mother of the prominent autistic intellectual Temple Grandin.

The Austrian pediatrician Hans Asperger published a case study in 1944 of four children similar to those monitored by Kanner. Asperger believed that his patients, whom he called "little professors," were capable of great improvement. He also recognized their strengths, which included creativity, a highly developed taste in art, and insight beyond their years.

Children with Asperger syndrome—which is no longer an official diagnosis but is still a colloquial descriptor for a certain subset of people with autism—are highly verbal early in their childhood, though they often use language in idiosyncratic ways. They generally have normal cognitive development and are interested in, though somewhat incompetent at, human interaction. They often lack basic social skills, and must learn patterns of interaction that are intuitive to many other people. They tend to be more aware of their condition than are people with classic autism, and this leads some to become depressed. Since the American Psychiatric Association has moved to eliminate the diagnosis, people with Asperger's are grouped among the many with *autism spectrum disorder*. The shift acknowledges that it is almost impossible to draw clear dividing lines among these diagnoses.

While many autistic people may appear disengaged, individuals with Asperger syndrome may be hyperengaged; they may stand too close and talk incessantly about obscure subjects. A psychiatrist I met described a patient who is a math genius, IQ one hundred forty, fully verbal, but socially disabled. When the pretty woman at the counter at McDonald's asked what he'd like today, he said, "I'd like to touch your crotch, please." He was completely befuddled when the police were called; he had answered her question and said "please."

Many people on the autism spectrum first learn to smile and to cry as works of theater. John Elder Robison, author of the autobiography *Look Me in the Eye*, describes hours spent memorizing human expressions so he could interpret or produce them. "As I've gotten older, I have taught myself to act 'normal.' I can do it well enough to fool the average person for a whole evening, maybe longer."

The Autism Society of America estimates that one and a half

million Americans are on the spectrum; the CDC says 560,000 people under twenty-one have autism; the US Department of Education says that autism is growing at a rate of 10 to 17 percent per year, and that numbers in the United States could reach four million in the next decade. Recent work suggests that more than 1 percent of the world population may be on the spectrum. Part of the upsurge has to do with the broadening of categories: People who might once have been classified as schizotypal or mentally retarded are now on the spectrum, as are some who would once have been thought odd but not given a diagnosis.

When I was in my twenties, I befriended an autistic man. He had not spoken until he was seven, and he laughed at things that weren't funny and ignored social niceties. He was rational, methodical, and a lightning-fast mental calculator who earned a fortune in fast stock trades. He had a photographic memory and had assembled a wonderful art collection. On one occasion, when I mentioned that I was going to Los Angeles, he volunteered detailed directions for every place I was going; he explained that he had become fascinated by the city and had spent four months driving around it for ten hours a day. We fell out after he refused to own up to something hurtful he had done. I had assumed his failure to comply with social norms was an affectation; only later did I understand that our friendship had been undermined by a neurological condition that was not subject to being fixed.

Nancy Corgi, mother of two autistic children, has been utterly responsible in her handling of her offspring, but she has kept her own cool at a considerable price. "Having advocated and fought for these kids now for nineteen years," she said, "my entire personality has changed. I'm quick to pick a fight; I'm argumentative. You don't cross me. I have to do what I have to do, and I'm going to get what I want. I never was like this at all."

Nancy's mother noticed some oddness in Nancy's eighteen-month-old daughter, Fiona, and one day at the hairdresser's she got into a conversation with a woman who had an autistic son. She called Nancy and said, "I made an appointment with this pediatric neurologist, and it would be really nice if you just took Fiona in." Nancy, eighteen weeks pregnant with her second child, decided to humor her mother. The doctor took one look at Fiona and said she had pervasive developmental disorder (PDD). Nancy was shocked. "It wasn't something that was going to be done by next week, fixed," she recalled. Fiona has classic autistic traits, is completely disengaged from other human beings, and showed no signs of developing speech on her own. She hates to be touched and wouldn't keep her clothes on. "All my food is locked up in the basement or it would be thrown on the walls," Nancy said. "Also, she could set the house on fire." At thirty-two months, Fiona started going to early intervention at the University of Massachusetts. "About three o'clock, I would start to physically shake, knowing she would be back at three thirty-ish," Nancy said. "I didn't want her coming home."

The summer after Nancy's second child, Luke, turned two, Nancy and her sister were sitting on the beach at Cape Cod, and Nancy's sister said, "You have another problem." Nancy was astounded. "My son seemed totally normal, after dealing with my daughter," she recalled. Unlike her sister, however, she had no experience of normal children. "All of a sudden my whole life was all about testing and testing and testing," Nancy said. Her husband, Marcus, is an accountant. "He copes with the IRS every day. He's used to stubborn, ridiculous bureaucracy. He has the patience and know-how to deal with insurance companies, claims, the school system's financial stuff. That was his part—my part being that I got the kids to deal with. How many years did we drive up and down the Mass Pike for evaluations at Boston Children's? My kids are seventeen and nineteen, and I'm still doing it."

Though both children are diagnosed on the spectrum, their respective autisms manifest differently. When Fiona was eight, she jumped out a second-floor window because she wanted to make mashed potatoes and knew that if she found the front-door key in the garage, she could get to the potatoes and cook them. With coaching, Fiona eventually developed language, but her syntax and affect are odd. Luke was a sweet-natured child, but adolescence hit him hard. "He is basically anxiety-ridden and really not too swift," Nancy said. "He only talks about what interests him: videos, movies, and animals. Zero common sense. If a four-year-old calls him a bad word, he might knock him out. He's angry. Two minutes later he'll be cuddly. Really crummy." Fiona was mainstreamed at school with an aide from first through eighth grade. Luke's deficits of intelligence and his disruptive behavior disqualified him from mainstreaming.

Nancy tends to express rage, but also feels despair, and when her children were young, that despair was closer to the surface. Marcus worked long days—longer, in Nancy's view, than was necessary. Her mother, who lived a few streets away, asked

Nancy how it was going, but seldom saw her. Her mother-in-law disengaged completely. "Nobody ever rolled up their sleeves to help," Nancy said. "Nobody liked my kids. They weren't likable, but if somebody had acted like they were, maybe that would have helped."

Nancy decided to enroll Fiona in a residential school at fourteen; Nancy and Marcus fought tooth and nail to get her in. "My husband broke down and cried and said, 'I just don't know what more we can do to show you what she needs.' That was one of two times I ever saw him cry." They enrolled Luke at fifteen.

Luke loves pretty girls, but his inept attentions usually meet with rejection. Nancy has to keep explaining away these painful experiences for him. He is also uncontrolled and frighteningly strong. When Nancy and Marcus went to a wedding and left the kids with a sitter who had cared for them before, Luke picked up the sitter's two-year-old son and hurled him across the room. The Corgis belong to a beach club on Cape Cod, where Nancy has been going since childhood. The year after I met them, Nancy was told that Luke had made lewd gestures to a girl by the pool and was no longer welcome—though it was in fact merely an inept attempt to strike up a conversation. Nancy drafted a letter explaining that Luke's self-control was undermined by his brain's biology. It made no difference, and Luke was not allowed back. "We're used to living in the leper colony, aren't we?" Nancy said.

In spite of her persistent outrage, Nancy can speak of her children with tenderness. "My kids are very affectionate and cuddly and sweet," she said. "Fiona wasn't so much when she was little. But now we'll sit on the couch and I will sort of pet her and hold her. I used to tuck her into bed and give her a kiss and tell her I loved her. I would say, 'Say, "I love you."' She would repeat with me, 'I love you.' Eventually she knew what it meant and would say it to me on her own. Once, I fell asleep on the couch. She got a blanket and tucked me in and gave me a kiss. Fiona is functioning way beyond what we ever expected. People say, 'You can pat yourself on the back,' and we do." But Nancy worried constantly that someone would take advantage of Fiona and was trying to get both children sterilized. "The best we can hope is that we never have grandchildren," Nancy said sadly. "My husband will sometimes say, 'Would you marry me again?' I say, 'Yeah, but not with the kids.' Had we known what we know now, we wouldn't have done it. Do I love my kids? Yes. Will I do everything for them? Yes. I have them and I do this and I love them. I wouldn't do it again. I think anybody who tells you they would is lying."

Some people with autism appear to have no language at all. Some have trouble with control over the muscles involved in producing speech and may be able to type on keyboards. The relationship between language and intellectual disability is confusing; no one really knows what may be hidden behind speechlessness.

One mother said of her adolescent son, "If he were deaf and needed to sign, I'd learn Sign. But there's no way for me to learn his language because he doesn't know it himself." In 2008, a Canadian girl with autism named Carly Fleischmann, who had never used language, began typing at age thirteen. Her parents didn't even know that she could read or understand their speech. "We were stunned," her father said. "We realized inside was an articulate, intelligent, emotive person whom we had never met. Even professionals labeled her as moderately to severely cognitively impaired." Among the first things she wrote was, "If I could tell people one thing about autism, it would be that I don't want to be this way but I am. So don't be mad. Be understanding." Later she wrote, "It is hard to be autistic because no one understands me. People assume I am dumb because I can't talk or I act differently. I think people get scared with things that look or seem different than them." When a man wrote to Carly to ask what his autistic child would want him to know, Carly wrote back, "I think he would want you to know that he knows more than you think he does." Asked by her parents about her unexpected emergence, she said, "I think behavior therapy helped me. I believe that it allows me to sort my thoughts. Unfortunately it can't make me normal. Believing helped. Then a miracle happened, you saw me type. Then you helped me forget that I'm autistic."

Bob and Sue Lehr did not intend to adopt a disabled child. However, in 1973, when Bob was working as a guest professor in Utah, the couple learned of a mixed-race child whom no one in the area wanted. They decided to make him part of their family, which already included one Caucasian biological son and one adopted mixed-race daughter. Utah required couples to wait a year from petitioning to finalizing adoption, but the Lehrs' attorney said they could bypass that system. Sue said to me, "We should have put together the clues."

After the family returned home to upstate New York, it became clear that something was wrong with Ben. The Lehrs requested his medical records. After a few months without a response, the Lehrs had an attorney write to the agency; the agency offered to bring Ben back to Utah. "Excuse me?" Sue said. "I couldn't imagine just saying, 'Well, gee, my son is damaged; I'm going to send him back,' like he was a sweater." Their pediatrician put Ben through a battery of tests. He finally recommended that Sue and Ben just take their son home and love him. Bob was an experimental psychologist and continued to work in that field, but Ben's care was to become his primary concern. Sue, who had been a gym teacher, returned to Syracuse University to earn a PhD in special ed.

The local school didn't want Ben and made his life miserable, and the Lehrs sued the district. Sue told authorities, "You can't keep him out of your building because he is brown. Tell me where it says you can keep him out because he has autism." The work at school was modified for him, but he had to do it, though he had little language and couldn't initiate speech. Some people who cannot produce oral words can communicate in writing, and some who don't have the muscle control for handwriting type instead, and some who don't have even the control for typing use other methods. Ben learned *facilitated communication*, or FC, a system in which someone helped him to use a keyboard by giving his arms physical support as he typed.

As he grew up, Ben would often smash his head on the floor, use knives to cut himself, put his head through windows. "His behaviors were a way of communicating," Sue said. "Not the best way, but other kids communicate using drugs or driving snowmobiles drunk." When Ben was a teenager, Bob and Sue took him to RadioShack, his favorite store. He panicked on the escalator, and at the bottom he sat down cross-legged and began smashing himself in the head with his hands and screaming as a crowd gathered. Sue always carried an FC keyboard, and when she took it out, Ben typed, "Hit me." "And I thought, 'Oh, yeah, in the middle of the mall with a security guard, and you're black and I'm white,'" Sue recalled. "And then he typed out, 'Like a record player.'" Sue suddenly flashed on a stuck needle; she struck him on the edge of the shoulder with the heel of her hand and said, "Tilt." Ben stood up and they walked calmly on across the mall.

In high school, Ben began having horrendous behavior problems. "I didn't like his aide, Willie, an obese, slovenly guy who always wore sweatpants," Sue said. "But I thought maybe I was just being judgmental. Then Willie was arrested for raping his own three-year-old daughter. Meanwhile, Ben was typing out that Willie had been hurting him and gave enough details to his speech therapist that she had the principal call the cops. Willie would say, 'Ben's having a hard time, so we'll go up to the weight room and lift weights.' And that's where Willie was raping him, while this other guy would watch. So we brought Ben home for a while and nurtured him, to make sure he didn't think it was his fault." When he returned to school, Ben developed meaningful relationships with his classmates, assisted by a particularly well-attuned aide. In his senior year, he used FC to write a column for the school newspaper. He invited a nondisabled girl to the prom, and she accepted (somewhat to the chagrin of her boyfriend); at the prom, he was elected to the king's court. At graduation, when he walked down to get his diploma, the whole audience stood up. Both Sue and Bob began to cry, as she described it. "Thousands of people at this graduation. And they all stood up and applauded for Ben."

I was struck by the Lehrs' early decision to help Ben but not to "fix" him. "His sister said to me, 'Do you ever wonder what it would be like if Ben were normal?'" Sue said. "And I said, 'Well, I think he's normal for himself.' Have I wished that he didn't have all of his behavior problems? Absolutely. Have I wished that he had better language? Absolutely." Much of what he types is Delphic. For a while he kept typing, "And you can cry." No one ever understood what he meant. Another day he typed, "I want to stop those, jerky feelings, jerky hurting. I get upset, then look stupid." Bob described going to conferences and being surrounded by parents desperate for a cure—"It's going to be all better next year, crap like that. We were avant-garde in saying, 'No. It's going to be better right now. Let's make it as good as possible for him.'"

After high school, Bob and Sue gave Ben the down payment for a house eight miles from their own. His Social Security check covered his mortgage and most of his utility bills. He earned money by making wooden tables to sell at craft fairs. Someone was with him constantly, either a trained aide or a lodger who shared the house in exchange for caretaking. Because water is Ben's passion, the Lehrs found him places to swim and bought him a hot tub. A decade later, Sue's mother died, and the Lehrs took their inheritance and went on a three-month family camping trip to Europe. "Each person in the family got to pick one thing they wanted to do," Sue said. "Ben picked swimming in every body of water he could find. So he's been in the Mediterranean, he's been in the Aegean, he's been in pools and lakes and streams. We have a picture of him in Athens, sitting on the top of a stone wall, the highest point in Athens. He's got his little drumsticks and he's tapping on the stones and he's got a look of sheer joy on his face."

When they returned from Europe, Bob was diagnosed with Alzheimer's, which had advanced considerably by the time I interviewed him for this book. For two years, Bob didn't want anyone but Sue to know, but Ben would type out, "Daddy's sick." Observing that Sue was upset, he'd type, "Mommy is broken." Finally, Bob sat down and explained that Ben was right, Daddy is sick, but he wasn't going to die right away. In the face of this diagnosis, the Lehrs woke up anew to the profound effect Ben had had on them. "I absolutely handled the news differently than I would have if we hadn't had Ben," Bob said. Sue said, "I think I'd learned a lot from Ben about reading people, trying to understand what they're thinking or feeling that they can't articulate. About treating someone as a human being even when his thoughts and feelings are mixed up. How do we make you feel safe, loved, okay? I learned the way it works by having Ben. And so I had it ready when Bob needed it."

Autism is associated with underconnectivity between the right and left sides of the brain. At the same time, there's an overabundance of local connections. The pruning that helps the average brain avoid overload does not appear to occur in autism. The brain consists of gray matter, where thought is generated, and white matter, which conveys that thought from one area to another. In autism, inflammation has been observed in areas of the brain that produce white matter, creating terrible noise. It's like what you might get if every time you picked up your telephone, you heard not only the voice of the person you were calling, but also a hundred other voices all on the line at the same time. The fact that you and the other person were both speaking clearly would get lost in the cacophony.

Too often the presence of autism confuses parents and doctors, so that other ailments may go untreated. Approximately one-third of autistic people have at least one psychiatric diagnosis in addition to autism, compared to 10 percent of the general population. One in five suffers from clinical depression, and about 18 percent from anxiety. They frequently don't get treatment for these complicating factors.

Is autism itself also on the rise? Inconceivable time and energy have been poured into this question, and no consensus has emerged. In children who seem to develop normally and then regress, the regression often occurs at around the same age that children are immunized. As a result, many parents have attributed their children's autism to vaccines. In 1998, British gastroenterologist Andrew Wakefield published a paper in a leading British medical journal suggesting a link between the MMR (measles-mumps-rubella) vaccine and gastrointestinal problems in autistic children. Wakefield and his colleagues described only twelve cases. The media seized upon the story, and many parents stopped vaccinating their children.

Numerous studies have consistently failed to demonstrate a link between vaccines and autism. Wakefield's study has since been discredited for many reasons, but many parents persist in the belief that vaccines caused autism in their children.

It seems that *autism* is a blanket term. Autistic behavior may prove to be a symptom of a variety of causes. No single gene or consistent set of genes causes the syndrome, although many autism-related genes that have been identified are functionally connected to one another, forming a network in the brain. It is not yet clear whether autism-related genes always or sometimes require environmental triggers to become active, nor, if so, what the triggers may be. Most such genes increase the risk of autism, some by only a small amount; none clearly determines autism consistently.

It is likely that genetics does not tell the whole story when it comes to autism, but the question as to what environmental factors are at play and how they intersect with genes will take decades to resolve.

American law guarantees education for the disabled. It does not guarantee medical care. Education is a government responsibility; medical care is a personal responsibility, controlled in large part by insurance companies. For that reason, some advocates have preferred to keep treatment for autism in the arena of education rather than of medicine. So far, the educational interventions appear to work better than the medical ones.

Despite broad agreement that early treatment is most effective, there is no consensus about what that early treatment should be. Applied behavior analysis (ABA) is based on pinpointing a child's negative or obsessive behavior and developing positive substitutes. Other successful autism treatments involve attempting to address the extreme sensitivities of autistic children. Service dogs that resemble Seeing Eye dogs are often invaluable in helping to stave off panic attacks, providing physical orientation, and building an emotional bridge between autistic people and the social world. Some parents modify their children's diets. Antidepressants have been used to control anxiety. As many as a fifth to a third of autistic people develop epilepsy, and they are helped by antiseizure medications. ADHD drugs are sometimes prescribed to calm people with autism, as are various sedatives and antipsychotics.

The results achieved with all of these treatments are inconsistent, and the effort and cost of initiating them is extreme. Even if an autistic person develops and sustains speech, functional skills, and a degree of social awareness, he or she will not become nonautistic.

The list of treatments of doubtful worth is longer than the list of treatments that help. Visionaries tout a range of bizarre procedures, and considerable time and money have been poured into minimally tested methods. Most do not pose a physical danger to children, though some do carry risks, are disorienting, and cost a lot.

While the deficits of autism are famous, the general public is less aware that people with autism may also have major abilities that the rest of us lack. The Cambridge autism researcher Simon Baron-Cohen postulates that women are empathizers, hardwired to understand others, while men are systemizers, hardwired to organize factual and mechanical information. Autism, in this view, is an overexpression of cognitive masculinity—short on empathy and long on systems.

Austistic people are indeed often systemizers; many have uncanny technical abilities. Some are savants who do not function independently in many areas of life but have extraordinary abilities in one domain—sometimes a relatively trivial one, such as the ability to immediately list the dates of Easter for every year until the end of time; and sometimes a useful one, such as the competence to create meticulously accurate drawings, or to hold in mind a complex design, or to produce a perfect map of Rome after flying over the city once.

John Elder Robison writes, "Being a savant is a mixed blessing, because that laser-like focus often comes at a cost: very limited abilities in nonsavant areas." When he improved his social abilities, his savant thinking weakened. I have heard Temple Grandin say the same thing. When you take away what's perceived as wrong, you may also take away the person's gift.

I first met Temple Grandin when she was sixty, and famous for her ability to talk about her autism to nonautistic people. Grandin is a cattle handler and livestock-facilities designer who revolutionized her field; her equipment is now used in the majority of American slaughterhouses. Grandin claims that she experiences fear as her primary emotion and has an overdeveloped startle reflex of the kind that protects animals from predators. "I think in pictures," she said. "I realized that should be able to help me figure out about animals, because I think more the way an animal does."

Diagnosed as a child in the early 1950s, Temple showed the full range of autistic symptoms, and her mother, Eustacia Cutler, was labeled a refrigerator mother. Eustacia invented her own behaviorist system to help Temple, and she and the nanny she hired kept Temple constantly interacting. Temple was given art lessons and showed a talent for perspective drawing. Her mother did all she could to encourage this skill. "You want to be appreciated for doing something other people want," Temple recalled. "When the kid is really little, you've got to get somebody to just spend thirty-eight hours a week working with that kid, keeping them engaged. I don't think the method matters that much." She expresses considerable gratitude for the attentions she received. "They put kids like me in institutions then. I had fifteen years of nonstop panic attacks, which was hard on everyone. If I hadn't found anti-depressants in my early thirties, I would have been ripped apart by stress-related health problems, like colitis. I was very lucky to get some really good mentors when I was in college."

As a teenager, Temple said to her mother, "I can't love." Eustacia wrote, "Adolescence is hard enough for any child, but autistic adolescence is something devised by the devil." But Temple's boarding school had a stable full of abused horses, and Temple found her joy in caring for them.

Temple receives thousands of letters from parents and readily offers advice. Her successes do not mean that her life has been free of disappointments. "Despite her extraordinary accomplishments, she knows that some part of the dream that I call 'life' lies a little beyond her," Eustacia wrote. Temple advocates both behavioral and medical treatments, and anything to stimulate literacy. "Your kid is throwing a fit in Walmart because he feels like he's inside the speaker at a rock concert. He's seeing like a kaleidoscope; hearing's fading in and out, and full of static." Temple believes firmly that the higher-functioning you can make someone, the happier he is likely to be. She attributes her own success to her autism; "Genius is an abnormality too," she explained to me. Temple has made what the world calls illness the cornerstone of her brilliance.

Into all of this comes the neurodiversity movement, which celebrates some aspects of autism as a horizontal identity. While opposing a cure for autism is a bit like opposing inter-galactic travel, one of the battle cries of the movement is, "Don't cure autism now." Like the rest of identity politics, this is an attitude forged and burnished in opposition to prejudice, treading a fine line between revealing a fundamental truth and attempting to create that truth. Conservatives complain that asking the larger society to accept autistic people's atypical social logic undermines the very principles that make it a soci-ety. Members of the neurodiversity movement take exception to the idea that autistic behavior lacks social logic and maintain that it is a different and equally valid social logic. They fight for their own definition of civil justice.

Jim Sinclair, an autistic adult and the cofounder of Autism Network International, wrote, "Autism isn't something a per-son has, or a 'shell' that a person is trapped inside. There's no normal child hidden behind the autism. Autism is a way of being. It is pervasive; it colors every experience, every sen-sation, perception, thought, emotion, and encounter, every aspect of existence. It is not possible to separate the autism from the person—and if it were possible, the person you'd have left would not be the same person you started with."

Many neurodiversity activists question whether exist-ing treatments are for the benefit of autistic people or for the comfort of their parents. How much torment should a child go through to be more like a typical child? They also fear that in the unlikely event of a genetic test, selective abortion would result in "genocide." The politically correct terminology in most of the world of disability is to identify the person ahead of the condition: you speak of a *person with deafness* rather than a *deaf person*, or a *person with dwarfism* rather than a *dwarf*. Some autism advocates take issue with the idea that they are a self with something added, preferring *autistic person* to *person with autism*. Others favor *autistic* as a noun, as in "Autistics should receive social accommodation." Sinclair has compared *person with autism* to describing a man as a *person with maleness* or a Catholic as a *person with Catholicism*.

Ari Ne'eman, who has Asperger syndrome and became a prominent self-advocate while still in college, uses the colloquial *Aspie* to describe himself. He said, "Society has developed a tendency to examine things from the point of view of a bell curve. How far away am I from normal? What can I do to fit in better? But what is on top of the bell curve? Mediocrity. That is the fate of American society if we insist upon pathologizing difference." Retrospective diagnosis, albeit shaky science, suggests that Mozart, Einstein, Hans Christian Andersen, Thomas Jefferson, Isaac Newton, and a great many other visionaries would now be diagnosed on the spectrum. Describe a world without those particular geniuses, and everyone would be impoverished.

In a video called *In My Language*, the neurodiversity activist Amanda Baggs describes her perspective. Baggs has repetitive behaviors and uses almost no speech. "The way I think and respond to things looks and feels so different from standard concepts that some people do not consider it thought at all," she says. "It is only when I type something in your language that you refer to me as having communication. People like me are officially described as mysterious and puzzling, rather than anyone admitting that it is themselves who are confused. Only when the many shapes of personhood are recognized will justice and human rights be possible."

Kathleen Seidel, mother of an autistic child and founder of neurodiversity.com, said, "The word *incurable* is quite devastating-sounding, but you can also look at it as being that autism is durable. Looking at this jewel through different facets does not trivialize the challenges of people who have tremendous obstacles. I'm trying to look at the whole picture, including the beautiful part of it. Autism is as much a part of our humanity as the capacity to dream. God manifests all possibilities, and this is one of the possibilities in our world. It's a part of the human condition—or conditions, as the case may be."

Bill Davis grew up in the Bronx, found his way into street gangs, and then graduated into organized crime. One day in 1979, a twenty-year-old would-be model walked into the nightclub he was managing. "She took a carnation out of a vase, put it in my lapel, and said, 'You're with me.' We've been together ever since," he recounted. After ten years Bill and Jae moved to Lancaster, Pennsylvania, where their daughter, Jessie, was born. Five years later their son, Christopher, followed. Jae stayed home with the children; Bill tended bar. At two, Chris stopped talking. By two and a half, he was rocking back and forth in a corner. Jae, who had never learned to drive, announced one morning that she was driving Chris to Philadelphia to visit the Seashore House, a children's hospital. She didn't get a satisfactory answer there, so two days later she said, "I'm going to Kennedy Krieger in Baltimore, and if that doesn't work, we're heading down to Haddonfield, New Jersey, to the Bancroft School." Bill said, "You can't drive around without a license." The next week she passed the road test.

Chris didn't sleep. He flapped his hands. He injured himself. He smeared himself with feces and flung it at his parents. He bit himself. He gouged at his eyes. He stared at the ceiling fan for hours on end. Jae had intuited that Chris would need infinite patience. She and Bill broke everything into small tasks. Chris had difficulty understanding cause and effect. He liked the motion of the car and screamed every time it stopped for a red light. Jae made red and green cards, and whenever the car approached a red light, she would show him the red one, and when it was time to go, she would show him the green. Once he understood the correlation, the screaming stopped. Jae gathered that he could absorb visual information, and she came up with a system of flash cards and symbols. "I was always watching what he saw," Jae said. She had become interested in the work of Vincent Carbone, a behavior analyst, so she drove to Penn State and cornered him in his office. When he said, "Lady, I've got to go," she said, "You don't understand. I'm not letting you out of your office until you agree to help me." After resisting for an hour, he told her she could join his next course. She stayed for a week and over the next few years developed several useful variations on his methodology. Carbone became so interested in these modifications that he sent a team up to Lancaster to observe her work with Chris.

Jae recruited interns at Franklin and Marshall College and Rutgers University to help implement her techniques, tutoring and directing them in their work at the house. She set up cameras in Chris's room and filmed the students so that she could correct their errors. She brought them to conferences and educational programs. By the time Chris was grown, Jae had trained more than forty interns; as other families in the area became aware of her work, she placed interns with them as well.

Jae refused to believe that if Chris wasn't speaking at five, he would never do so. By the time he was seven, Chris had begun to produce words; at ten, he could speak in short sentences. Chris learned to match pictures of the American presidents to their names, and Jae made numerical games so that Chris could learn math and how to count money. When I first saw Chris's room, it was overflowing with learning materials: the beads and marbles he was using to learn to count were falling out of shoe bags; a cabinet held some five hundred homemade flash cards; musical instruments were everywhere; shelves upon shelves held bowls of everything from coins to plastic Sesame Street monsters. In addition, perhaps four hundred videotapes were piled around the room, crammed into shelves, wedged underneath and next to things.

When a new intern started, Jae would say, "Here's two hundred dollars you can win. You're going to come into the next room, where we've hidden something. And you'll try and guess what it is and where it is." The person would come into a darkened room, and all the other interns would be screaming and clicking and making nonsensical remarks. The new intern would get more and more frustrated and would finally say, "I don't understand what you're doing! What do you want?" And Jae would say, "Come on, find it, and I'll give you two hundred dollars!" When the person finally walked out, Jae would explain, "That's what life is like for autistic children."

Bill took over negotiating with the state to pay for treatment. "The local schools people had been confronted by emotional parents who'd say, 'My son needs forty hours of therapy,' and they'd say, 'Sorry—you lose,'" Bill recalled. "I would say, 'Now, in *Ethridge vs. Collins . . .*' They hated me. But I grew up in the heartland of Irish gangs in New York. I certainly wasn't afraid of a schoolteacher in Lancaster." If it could be established that what Bill and Jae were doing at home was more appropriate for Chris than what the school district was offering, the district had to underwrite the program. Bill came in with an annual budget: what materials cost; what workshops cost; what the interns cost. Meanwhile, the development of therapies had become a family project. Chris's sister, Jessie, got involved too.

Still, the Davises, who had no health insurance, had a lot to pay for on their own. Chris had gymnastics, speech classes, hospital assessments, and consultations with a variety of doctors who did not take Medicaid. "I was working four bartending jobs, bringing home sometimes twenty-five hundred dollars a week," Bill said. "But, I swear to god, we couldn't pay our rent. When things got really bad, I'd hold a bar fund-raiser: I'd solicit a baseball from the Phillies; I went to the Flyers and got hockey sticks. I'd sell it all at the bar and raise six thousand dollars at a clip."

Like many autistic people, Chris has intestinal issues. Going to the bathroom can be painful for him, and he tends to hold on for as long as possible. "So his movements build up, and then movements explode behind movements," Bill said. "He'll say, 'Bath,' and he'll hug me. I clean him and disinfect the room. My god, this is filthy. It's stacked with old movies, and he's stepping on them, and he just peed over there. It's horrible. But it's what works." The place felt at once squalid and love-imbued.

When Chris was nine, the Davises decided that it was time for him to enter the school system. The school district agreed to let Jae train his teachers. The one who would be in charge of his education came to their home the summer before Chris was to matriculate. "She was open and very willing to learn and had kindness to her. I knew I could work with her," Jae said. That autumn, Chris attended school in a classroom with two other boys, the teacher Jae had trained, and four assistant teachers.

Soon after Chris started school, Jae began to say she was tired. She finally went to a doctor and found that, at age forty-five, she had a malignant cervical tumor the size of a grapefruit that had metastasized to her lungs and spine; one of her kidneys had shut down; she had suffered a minor heart attack; and she had lost enough blood through internal bleeding to need an emergency five-hour transfusion.

When I met Jae, she had been given a few months to live. A nurse came to the house to administer the chemotherapy Jae hoped would eke out a little more time. Even without hair, and somewhat emaciated, she was beautiful, and she had a gentleness that contrasted with Bill's machismo. She had insisted that I visit despite her condition. "I'm so lucky," she said to me, "that Chris started school. He's ready to do things on his own. Bill will make sure he gets what he needs. I always saw what he saw, but Bill feels what he feels. I've done what I came to do." A closed-circuit television system she'd set up to monitor Chris's teachers was still in place, so she could watch what happened in his room upstairs without rising. "It's just been such a strange experience for me, everything going on at once, my dying, Chris going to school," Jae said. "I worry more about my daughter and husband than about Chris. Honestly, he's just a happy kid. But it's hard to get him to conceptualize emotions, so I'm struggling to help him understand that I won't be around."

Chris had become aggressive, mostly toward Bill, whom he kept biting and punching and head-butting. But he had brought a lot of his videos downstairs, and he started curling up with them and his mother in her hospital bed. I arrived to find Jae drugged and melancholy; Chris was demanding and noisy and kept hitting himself and other things. "Don't hit Daddy," Bill would say, smoothing Chris's irate brow with one hand and holding Jae's hand with the other. Then Chris suddenly said to Jae in his thick voice, "I love you," and lay his head down on her chest.

Ten days after I met her, on a quiet October afternoon, Jae died. She bequeathed her teaching materials to the universities where she had found help. Shortly before Jae's death, the city of Lancaster gave her the Red Rose Award for her work. A few days later, the Intermediate Unit that had fought the Davises on their educational priorities announced the Jae Davis scholarships to pay for ten families a year to attend the National Conference on Autism. Franklin and Marshall College announced the Jae Davis Internship Program; Penn State announced the Jae Davis Parent Scholarship; the Organization for Autism

Research set up the Jae Davis Memorial Award.

Bill soldiered through his grief. "Our marriage changed completely the day Chris was diagnosed," he said. "We very rarely had sex; we very rarely had a close or romantic moment. If we went out to dinner, which was once a year, we would talk about Chris. Things just replaced other things. If Chris never works or marries, who cares? Let Chris be Chris. Chris taught us everything. He taught us how to deal with him; how he learned; how to let him live his life. We drove to a spot the other night that his mother and he used to go to, and he just started to cry. And I know it was because of that. My son is not a puzzle. I know exactly what he is."

I fell out of touch with Bill for a little while. "Jae pushed Chris so hard, and when she died, he said, 'No school,'" Bill said when we met again. "I thought, 'Well, if what he really wants is to watch television all day, should we keep pushing him to do all these other things?'" Bill was charged for truancy. Pushed over the edge by Jae's medical bills, the family became homeless and lived for a while on park benches. Eighteen months after Jae died, Chris was maturing. The smearing of feces had stopped. Chris had begun to understand that the world had other rules than his, and that he must bend to them. It was almost as though the coddling attention of his mother was needed to bring him out into communication, while his father's harder demands were needed to help him see its purpose—as if his mother gave him language and his father made him use it.

I had always been skeptical of Bill's assertions about Chris's verbal abilities; he had demonstrated only occasional comprehension of a few dozen words and spoke mostly in nouns and

memorized short phrases. During my last visit, I was astonished to find him typing complicated entries into a computer;
while I sat there, he logged on to eBay and searched for videos.
Chris actually knew many words, but did not show an inclination to use them to connect with other people. His capacity for
emotion had grown too. When I walked in, he began flapping
his hands and making high-pitched sounds; I thought that could
just be alarm, but when I sat down on the sofa, he curled up
next to me.

Temple Grandin once described herself as "an anthropolo-
gist on Mars," a description that the neurologist Oliver Sacks
appropriated as the title for one of his books. But Chris was
like a Martian in a room full of anthropologists. "In case he feels
everything," Bill said, "I talk to him about it all and I love him
totally and completely. Just in case."

There are two opposite fictions about autism. The first comes
from the literature of miracles. In its most extreme form, it
describes beautiful boys and girls emerging from their afflic-
tion as if it were a passing winter frost, and, after wild parental
heroics, dancing off into springtime fields of violets, fully verbal, glowing with the fresh ecstasy of unselfconscious charm.
Such stories of false hope eviscerate families who are struggling
with the diagnosis. The other plotline is that the child does not
get better, but the parents grow enough to celebrate him rather
than seek to improve him and are fully content with that shift.
This whitewashes difficulties that many families endure. While
the inner lives of many people who have autism remain somewhat inscrutable, the outer lives of people whose children have

autism are mostly hard. Social prejudice aggravates the difficulty, but it is naive to propose that it's all social prejudice; having a child who does not express love in generally accepted ways is devastating, and having a child who is awake all night, who requires constant supervision, and who screams but cannot communicate why—these experiences are confusing, overwhelming, exhausting, and unrewarding. It is important not to get carried away by either the impulse only to treat or the impulse only to accept. Families need a combination of the two, specific to their own child.

The world of disability has seen a great deal of *filicide*, the murder of children by their parents. Those who kill their autistic children usually claim that they wanted to spare those children suffering. Anyone who questions the autism rights movement has only to look at these stories to see how urgent a cause it is to argue for the value of autistic lives.

The list of murdered autistic children is a long one. In 2001, Gabriel Britt, age six, was suffocated by his father, who dumped his body in a lake and then received a four-year sentence for pleading guilty to a lesser crime. Also in 2001, Jadwiga Miskiewicz strangled her thirteen-year-old son, Johnny Churchi, and was sentenced to time in a psychiatric hospital. In 2003, Angelica Auriemma, age twenty, was drowned by her mother, Ioanna, who served three years. Also that year, Terrance Cottrell died of asphyxiation when his mother and other churchgoers submitted him to an exorcism. A neighbor described the mother as explaining how "they held him down for almost two hours. He couldn't hardly breathe. Then she said the devil started to speak through Junior, though he can't really speak, saying, 'Kill me, take me.' She said the church told her it was the only way to heal him." She was not prosecuted; the minister who had led the exorcism was sentenced to two and a half years in prison and fined $1,200. In 2003, Daniela Dawes strangled her ten-year-old son, Jason, and was given five years of probation. In 2005, Patrick Markcrow, age thirty-six, was suffocated by his mother, who received a two-year suspended sentence; that same year, Jan Naylor shot her twenty-seven-year-old autistic daughter, Sarah, then set the house on fire, killing herself as well, and the *Cincinnati Enquirer* wrote that they both "died of hopelessness." In 2006, Christopher DeGroot was burned to death when his parents locked him in the house and set it on fire. Each of them was sentenced to six months in jail. In 2006, Jose Stable slit the throat of his son, Ulysses. He called the police and said, "I just couldn't take it anymore." Jose Stable served a three-and-a-half-year sentence. In 2007, Diane Marsh killed her son, Brandon Williams, age five; the autopsy said he had died of multiple skull fractures and an overdose of Tylenol PM tablets; his legs were covered in burn scars because his mother used to discipline him by dipping him into scalding water. She was sentenced to ten years. In 2008, Jacob Grabe was shot by his father, who pleaded not guilty by reason of insanity.

In most cases, the courts treat filicide as an understandable result of the strain of raising an autistic child. Sentences are light. Almost half of parents who kill a disabled child do no jail time at all. The media portrays the parents as desperate victims of their child's disability and of a social service system that failed to provide support. This reinforces the idea that children with autism are burdens to their parents and to society.

Parents of autistic children are often sleep-deprived. They are frequently impoverished by the cost of care. They are overwhelmed by the unrelenting needs of children who in many cases require constant supervision. They may be divorced and isolated. They may spend endless hours fighting their insurance and health providers and the local education authority that determines what services their child will get. They may forfeit their jobs because they miss so many days to deal with crises; they tend to have have poor relationships with their neighbors because their children destroy property or are violent. Stress leads people to extreme acts; extreme stress leads people beyond our most profound social taboo: the slaughter of one's own child. Most of these parents act out of emotion so overpowering that to identify it as either love or hate is to reduce it. They themselves do not know what they are feeling; they know only how much they feel it.

More than half of the children murdered in the United States are killed by their parents, and about half of those parents claim to have acted altruistically. This is unacceptable. Societal acceptance of that label has been shown to have a toxic effect. Criminologists consistently report that the use of the word *altruism* by bioethicists increases not only the number of filicides but also the frequency of abuse, disinhibiting parents who are already inclined toward violence. Courtroom leniency sends a message to the society at large, to other parents, and to people with autism that autistic lives are less valuable than other lives. This line of reasoning comes perilously close to eugenics.

Schizophrenia

DOWN SYNDROME IS PRESENT BEFORE BIRTH and can undermine bonding between parent and child. Autism sets in or is detected in the toddler years, and so changes the child who has already bonded with parents. The shock of schizophrenia is that it reveals itself in late adolescence or early adulthood, and parents must accept that the child they have known and loved may be irrevocably lost, even as that child looks much the same as ever.

Initially, parents almost universally believe that schizophrenia is an added layer masking their beloved child, who must somehow be liberated from it. The more likely reality is that schizophrenia, rather than obscuring the person, to some degree actually eliminates that person. Yet traces persist—a sense of humor, a dislike of broccoli, a love of autumn sunlight, a preference for rollerball pens. The person with schizophrenia may retain his most basic aspects of character, including kindness.

The betrayal of schizophrenia is its irrational juxtaposition of things that vanish and things that don't. Schizophrenia can take away the ability to connect to or love or trust another person, the full use of rational intelligence, the capacity to hold a job or go to school, the basic faculty of physical self-care, and large areas of self-awareness. Most famously, the schizophrenic disappears into an alternative world of voices that he perceives to be external; these internally generated relationships become far more real and important than any interaction with the actual outside world. The voices are usually cruel and often encourage bizarre and inappropriate behavior. The person who hears them is almost always panicked and frequently paranoid. Sometimes, the hallucinations can be seen and smelled as well as heard and make the world a hell of inescapable terror. The fading away of the real world immerses schizophrenics in loneliness beyond all reckoning.

For people with schizophrenia, the membrane between imagination and reality is so porous that having an idea and having an experience are not particularly different. Because psychosis is distressing, schizophrenics often have symptoms of depression in the early stages of the illness. This is the time of greatest suicide risk. In later stages, emotional capacity altogether is reduced, and people may seem vacant and emotionless.

Schizophrenia is broadly categorized as having positive symptoms—the presence of psychotic hallucinations—and negative and cognitive symptoms—a disorganized mind, absence of motivation, blunted emotion, loss of language, withdrawal, compromised memory, and general decrease in the ability to function. One expert described it as "autism plus delusions."

Emily Dickinson described a descent into psychosis with terrifying clarity:

I felt a Cleaving in my Mind—
As if my Brain had split—
I tried to match it—Seam by Seam—
But could not make it fit.

The thought behind, I strove to join
Unto the thought before—
But Sequence ravelled out of Sound
Like Balls—upon a Floor.

Though most people experience schizophrenia as a sudden cleaving, it appears in fact to be a developmental disorder that is inscribed in the brain even before birth. Unlike autism, it becomes more disabling over time. There is a rare syndrome of schizophrenia in preadolescence and childhood. The usual course for the condition, however, is that it unfolds through five predictable stages. It is has no symptoms until puberty in the *premorbid phase*, though recent research points to delays in walking and talking, more isolated play, poor school performance, social anxiety, and poor short-term memory of words or conversations. This is followed by a *prodromal phase*, which lasts for four years on average, in which positive symptoms begin gradually to appear. The teenagers or young adults in this phase experience changes in their way of thinking, perception, sense of control over themselves, and ability to contain their movements; have strange thoughts flash across their mind; struggle to understand whether illogical beliefs are true; and become suspicious in situations that don't warrant it. Some people gradually slip into psychosis, but most appear to have a dramatic break. This marks entry into the *psychotic phase*, with the onset of hallucinations or bizarre delusions. This usually occurs between ages fifteen and thirty and lasts for about two years. No one has yet been able to discover what triggers psychosis.

After somebody becomes ill, further changes occur in the *progressive phase*, which leads to deterioration, except when controlled with medication. As the patient has repeated psychotic episodes, the condition worsens, finding its level after five years or so and settling into the *chronic and residual phase*. By this time, there has been an irrecoverable loss of brain tissue. Positive symptoms tend to fade somewhat, while negative ones become more pronounced. Patients remain disabled, and persistently symptomatic. While more than 80 percent of patients respond well to antipsychotic drugs during a first episode, only half of those treated at this stage show a comparable response.

Interviewing schizophrenics, I was struck by the way those deep in the disease seemed not to feel self-pity. People in the early stages were horrified and sad, but those who had been sick a long time were not. Illness had cut these schizophrenics off from the lives they would have led so entirely that they were hardly conscious of them. I was consistently moved by their stoic grace in relation to their illness.

When Madeline Grammont's brother William began to act erratically, their father refused to acknowledge what was going on. William had earned a perfect score on his math SATs, but by the end of his junior year at Harvard, he had to leave. William went up to his family's country place in New Hampshire. "He was subsisting on raw garlic and had knives sitting everywhere," Madeline said. "He was sleeping on the floor. My father found a small house for him in the woods, away from the summer community, so no one would see him. In fact, my father saw him only three times in thirty years."

Once a week, William walked down to the town general store, usually clothed in just a towel, talking to himself; local teenagers would taunt him. His father maintained that he was just a touch eccentric, but his sister worried, and as their domineering father grew feeble in old age, she went up to see William. "Mice and rat turds everywhere, mayonnaise jars opened and rotting," she said. "Broken dishes everywhere. His bedroom was truly disgusting. He looked at me curiously, but he had lost his language. He made little squeaking sounds, and that was it."

Madeline sought legal guardianship, obtained a diagnosis of schizophrenia, and brought William to a residential care center. There he began using rudimentary speech again. "I brought him flowers once—some lilies—and he leaned over and smelled them," she said. "I brought them every single time thereafter and I still do. I take him out every two or three weeks. He can't initiate conversation and he talks very little, but he seems increasingly able to understand. He basically saw his first treatment at age fifty-two. That kind of denial, the way my father was—it ate him alive, and now he's just a hollow wreck. A whole life slipped away, that didn't have to."

No particular form or course of schizophrenia has been linked to a particular set of genetic markers. The disease clearly runs in families; the most reliable predictor of developing the condition is having a first-degree relative who has it. But most who develop schizophrenia don't have such a relative. One possible explanation for this is that most carriers and transmitters of schizophrenia genes are not schizophrenic. So a person can have genes that make him or her susceptible to schizophrenia, not get the disease, and then pass them on to his or her children. Nobody knows what protects some gene carriers from the condition. Genetics most likely mix with environment to cause a shift in biochemistry, which then has a degenerative effect on brain structures.

Every family member of a person with schizophrenia whom I met was scared by these genetic quirks. The history of schizophrenia is the history of blame. Mothers have borne the brunt of such blame. Modern psychology has proven that this is absurd, but blame and shame remain highly operative. More recently, an epidemic of self-help books have argued that mental health is simply a matter of positive thinking. For those who are unwell, the suggestion that flawed discipline and weak character are the source of their psychosis is torture.

Genetic vulnerability to schizophrenia can be triggered by traumas in the womb, in labor, or in delivery. Maternal infections and stressful events during pregnancy have been correlated with schizophrenia. Famine in Holland during World War II led to a dramatic increase in the incidence of the disease twenty years later.

Postnatal events such as a head trauma in early childhood likewise increase the risk of developing schizophrenia. Lifetime stress plays a role, too; the risk is particularly high among immigrants who go from underdeveloped settings to cities.

The most consistent environmental factor associated with a worsening of psychotic symptoms is the abuse of recreational drugs, including alcohol, methamphetamines, hallucinogens, cocaine, and marijuana, particularly in the teen years. A seminal study done in the 1980s showed that those who had used marijuana more than fifty times were six times more likely to develop schizophrenia, though cause and effect are unclear; it may be that people who are pre-schizophrenic are particularly drawn to marijuana.

George Marcolo had a lot of friends in high school in New Jersey. He had been a pothead in his teens, and in his senior year he took LSD. A few weeks later he decided to try it again, but instead of taking one tab, he took four. "After that, things sort of felt weird," he recalled. "I think the acid sped up the progress of the disease, which I guess was already in me." In college, George was a brilliant physicist. He remembered, "November first, 1991, when I was at Boston College, I woke up and I felt like I was on acid. I had not taken anything or done anything. That didn't go away for eight years." George went to a doctor on campus, who said that it would pass. At the time, George accepted that; now he is outraged. "If I heard somebody say, 'I feel like I'm on drugs, but I'm not on drugs,' I'd be like, 'We'd better get you checked out.'"

He was reluctant to tell his parents or friends what was going on. "I was afraid they'd think I was insane. I substituted alcohol and pot for medicine. Everything was amplified. Food tasted really bad. If I had taken meds back then, I could have avoided eight years of madness." Despite his symptoms, he kept up a 3.7 average in physics. "But it is progressive," George said. "The voices became more and more prominent." He took a job with a dot-com start-up on Wall Street. After a few months, he stopped going to work, and nothing his parents could say or do would get him to go back. George's parents had divorced when he was in high school, and he was living with his mother, Bridget. She explained to me, "Young men get out of college and somebody has to kick-start them because they don't realize that they are supposed to make a life. I thought he was in an extreme form of that. I was concerned, sometimes exasperated. But I didn't see the real problem."

The Marcolos insisted that George see a therapist, and after about four months he shared that he had been hearing voices. It took some months for the Marcolos to find their way to David Nathan, a Princeton psychiatrist who has worked with people with thought disorders; he instantly recognized the severity of George's illness and put him on medication. Though it has helped to mute the voices somewhat, George has not had a job since that postcollege stint on Wall Street.

George used to hide pills in the side of his mouth and spit them out when his parents weren't looking. During a relapse, he crashed his car three times. He finally became medication-compliant after a decade. His voices are persistent, but somewhat banal. "Sometimes they say critical things, but I can ignore that," he said. "Some voices are jerks, you know? You end up having the same conversations sometimes, with a new voice that doesn't know what you told the old voices. At first I thought the voices were people around me. Then I realized that they didn't even do what they said they were going to do. So now, I hear them, I talk to them, but I don't believe they're going to do anything. While I'm talking to you, I can ignore them. The medication has never made them go away, but it makes it easier for me to deal with them. There's some I like to talk to and some that I can't stand. Even though I hate the whole thing, there are some voices I would definitely miss if they went away."

George, thirty-five when we met, was on the antipsychotic medication clozapine and had regular blood tests to guard against the drug's negative physical side effects. He was living with his father. "I'm better than I used to be," he said. "I still get a little paranoid when I'm in public, but I can function. My parents have been very vigilant on my medicines, and they pay good attention to my behavior. I don't do too much. I basically talk to the voices all day long. If Dad's home and I'm going to talk to them, I go in another room. I don't like it when people see me talking to myself, even my father."

George sees Dr. Nathan every week, and his father usually goes along and sits through the session. George likes the arrangement, which saves him the trouble of explaining everything twice, to his father and to his doctor. "There's not much I can do other than take the meds, see the doctor," George said. "Just hope that the bad events keep to a minimum. My situation is obviously stressful for both of my parents, and I know it's not my fault, but I feel bad about it."

His father said, "I don't care what it's done to me. But I sit in my room and cry because of what he's missing. What life ought to be about, could be about, and isn't about for him." His mother said, "He's such a wonderful person—decent, kind, gentle. He deserves so much better. At the beginning, I thought, he'll never have a normal life. You just think, what is a normal life? Who has a normal life? What are any of us doing here? I am so proud of my three sons for what they've accomplished. My oldest son, he's so talented and determined. My youngest son, he's so good at what he does. But George is so decent. Look at all he does with this going on in his head. I might be proudest of him."

For centuries, treatments for schizophrenia were ineffectual, barbaric, or both. In the nineteenth century, they included pulling teeth; in the middle years of the twentieth, they included lobotomy—surgery that severed part of a person's brain from the rest and altered much of his or her personality.

The development of antipsychotic medications, beginning with Thorazine in 1950, has been a miraculous breakthrough in treating schizophrenia's positive symptoms. Unfortunately, these medications have only minor effects on the negative symptoms. As Helen Mayberg, chair of neuroimaging at Emory University, said, "It's as though you've got a house that's burning down; you come in with the fire trucks and pump the place full of water; you put out the conflagration. It's still charred, smoke-damaged, flooded, structurally unstable, and pretty much uninhabitable, even if flames are no longer licking the walls."

Medications can't reverse the damage done by the disease, and they present their own problems. Thorazine flattens personalities much as lobotomy did, and while newer medications are somewhat better, the number of people with schizophrenia who go off their medications indicates how detested they are by the patients who must take them.

Successful antipsychotic drugs alone are not usually sufficient to treat the disease. Talk therapies can play an important secondary role. What you do with your brain changes it, and if you can get someone with schizophrenia well enough to think rationally for some time, the positive effects are significant. The theory is that much as someone who loses speech in a stroke can relearn talking through speech therapy, someone with psychosis may be able to train his way partially out of it.

Since the disease is associated with a progressive loss of gray matter in the brain, it makes sense that if you identify patients efficiently, treat them, and keep them well, you can sometimes prevent them from becoming irreversibly impaired. As with autism, early detection and intervention may be key, even if early means age eighteen years rather than age eighteen months.

Given the inadequacy of cures, the increasing focus is on treating people even earlier—on prevention at the prodromal (pre-psychotic) stage. It's easier to prevent the damage from occurring than to restore people after it's happened. Experts have devised a menu of symptoms that indicate the prodromal stage: suspiciousness; unusual, magical, or bizarre thinking; extreme changes in behavior patterns; decreased functioning; inability to go to school or function at a job. Confusingly, many of these are also symptoms of ordinary adolescence. It's difficult to figure out who is at the brink of schizophrenia, and therefore nearly impossible to figure out who should be treated, especially with strong medications. Antipsychotic drugs have too many undesirable effects to be used on people who may just be grumpy, and we cannot now tell the difference. While anti-psychotics are therefore not recommended until psychosis sets in, however, aggressive response to anxiety and depression is in order. Many of these symptoms are serious even if they are not about to escalate into schizophrenia.

Even with early identification, it can be a challenge to sustain treatment over a life span. Most people who receive treatment do not initially accept that it is a lifetime obligation. One doctor told me of a patient he treated early in his career: "He was twenty-one years old, Ivy League school, top of his class, popular, athlete, seemed to be destined for greatness. He developed psychotic symptoms, and I diagnosed schizophrenia and gave him medication. He had almost complete remission. Then he wanted to go back to school, and he didn't like the medication, so he stopped taking it. He became sick again, came back, we treated him, he improved, went back to school, and relapsed again. We treated him, and he made progress. Repeated again. The next time, he didn't get better. He never recovered."

Emerging beside the early-intervention movement is the recovery movement, which proposes biological treatment to address positive symptoms, and psychosocial methods to improve or lessen negative and cognitive symptoms. The focus is on improving the quality of life even for those whose clinical condition is poor, emphasizing that impaired people still have capacities that should be maximized. Case management makes certain that even patients who suffer continued psychotic symptoms have somebody to handle their health insurance, take them to doctors' appointments, and ensure that they have a place to live. Patients are helped in finding a workplace where their deficits are tolerated and supported; some are given rehabilitation training to develop job skills. Social skills training teaches them how to interact with others in more acceptable ways. Patients do computer-based brain exercises that enhance memory, decision-making, and attention. Any way that people can be knitted into the social fabric is precious.

Jeffrey Lieberman, head of psychiatry at Columbia University, has evinced considerable frustration around how little use is made of the tools we do have. "The problem is that people become mental patients in their chronic wasteland, stuck away someplace in their rooms, smoking cigarettes, doing nothing, going to see a doctor for a prescription once a month," he said. "We now have medical and social means to help people. But because of inadequate resources, low awareness, and stigma, most people aren't helped." Only a small percentage of people with schizophrenia are unresponsive to medical treatment and need permanent hospitalization, he explained. The rest could be managed with acute-care hospitals and adequate community services. "We have people in the hospital whose families don't want to or can't take them back, and they can't live independently, and we can't find them a supervised residence. You discharge them to a homeless shelter."

In the United States, 150,000 people with schizophrenia are homeless; one in five people with schizophrenia is homeless in any given year. Such people are soon off their meds and back at the hospital for acute care. This serves neither their medical advantage nor the state's economic interest.

Less than half of schizophrenics in the United States receive outpatient services; a little more than half receive prescription medication; and half of those who go untreated blame financial and insurance issues. Treating schizophrenia in the United States costs more than $80 billion a year, expenses that could be controlled with programs of active outreach to patients—most of whom could avoid both descents into raving hell and the ensuing expensive hospitalizations and incarcerations, largely funded by taxpayers. As things work now, it falls to families to organize support groups, construct community centers, create websites, and write memoirs full of advice.

Half to two-thirds of people with schizophrenia live with their families or have parents as primary caretakers, but according to a recent survey, only about 3 percent of those families deem it an appropriate arrangement. Family members frequently give up or compromise careers to do this work, resulting in economic hardship, and they face the stress of what people in the field call "unrelenting contact" with an ailing relative. While family involvement improves the lives of schizophrenics, it does not transform them into who they might have been without the illness, and a family's caretaking costs, both financial and emotional, must be weighed against the benefits that can be achieved.

The World Health Organization recently undertook a vast study to see where the best outcomes were for people with schizophrenia. The best short-term results were in Nigeria and India—where medical treatment is often extremely basic. The reason appears to be the family support structures that are built into those societies. Whether the kinship structures of developing societies are preferable to Western ones for people in perfect health is debatable, but the division of labor within extended families clearly allows for a higher quality of care for people with mental illnesses. Attention is an invaluable treatment for schizophrenics. In the West, conversely, families often disenfranchise schizophrenics. They are marginalized within their own families or institutionalized entirely. Such care as they receive is often doled out in prisons or homeless shelters.

Some people with schizophrenia lack insight into their condition and have to be strong-handled, but others are the primary experts on their own condition, and some have offered their families suggestions on how to interact with them. Esso Leete, founder of the Denver Social Support Group, has schizophrenia and pleads, "Criticize only constructively. Do not write off all conflict as symptomatic of illness. Find a role for us in the family other than being the 'sick' member." One support group website proposes, "Approach delusions in a spirit of shared inquiry. Don't push if the person starts to get upset."

While the positive symptoms of schizophrenia are most disturbing and striking to outsiders, the negative symptoms are frequently more burdensome for families coping with a son's or daughter's hostility, absence of personal hygiene, and listlessness. It is hard to remember that these are not flaws of character. The father of one schizophrenic said, "My loving, bright, amusing son was now not just very ill, but had also turned distant, cold, bitter, insultingly rude. It would have been easy to dislike him intensely." Twenty-five years later, the father was still struggling with this problem: "How do you keep on loving a son who can be an unpleasant stranger?"

Malcolm Tate, a man with severe paranoid schizophrenia, made murderous threats against his family for sixteen years while they tried persistently to find him treatment. He was repeatedly hospitalized, repeatedly released too soon, and would not take medication on his own. Finally, in December 1998, his mother and his sister drove him from their home in South Carolina, and his sister shot him to death by the road, then wept. "I was scared that one day Malcolm was going to lose his mind and harm me and my daughter, and I just didn't know what else to do," she said at her trial. She was sentenced to life in prison.

Rosemary Baglio's family is riddled with schizophrenia. Her uncle came home from World War II a little "touched." He lived with Rosemary's family in Malden, a working-class, Irish suburb of Boston, and as a girl, Rosemary loved to go up to his room. On good days, he would put rolls in the player piano and show the kids Irish step-dancing. On bad days, he would argue with his hallucinations. When Rosemary was in her late twenties, her brother Johnny became psychotic at age seventeen. Rosemary told her mother that something was wrong, but her mother refused to hear it. When Johnny started smashing things, Rosemary was the one who took him to Massachusetts General Hospital. "My mother wouldn't let anyone visit him, other than the family," Rosemary recalled. "We were never to tell anybody he was mental. So Johnny just completely lost contact with everybody."

Rosemary eventually had nine children. Her third, Joe, was the first boy in her family. "He had beautiful auburn hair and soft brown eyes and dimples, and he was just sweet," she said. "Everybody loved Joe." In high school, Joe began to have troubles. His parents thought he was getting into drugs. His grades dropped. He stayed up all night. "Finally when he was seventeen, I told him, 'Daddy and I are taking you to be examined. We have to find out what is going on.' He was terrified." That very day, he had his first real breakdown. "The kitchen had a long pantry with a window at the end of it, and the cabinets were all glass," Rosemary said. "I came home and it was all smashed, and there was blood all over the kitchen ceiling."

Rosemary found him checked into the hospital, with a severed artery in his arm. When she got there, Joey said, "I'm sorry, Ma, I'm sorry." When she wept, he reasoned, "It's better I'm here than any of my sisters." He stayed for a month.

Rosemary was determined not to repeat her mother's imposed isolation of Johnny. "I was very sad, but he was sick and that was it. I was up-front about exactly what was going on." Joey finished high school and found a job in a photography store. Then one day Rosemary got a call that he was running in traffic and screaming incoherently. When he emerged from that hospitalization, Rosemary decided to find him a halfway house, but within a year he was psychotic again. The Tri-City Authority, responsible for mental health services in Malden, insisted that he was not sick enough to be hospitalized because he knew his own name and address. He was living on a barren, rocky slope above Malden; Rosemary wouldn't let him come home because she was afraid he would harm his siblings. "Can you sacrifice the other eight for the one that's sick? He was so gentle underneath that if he ever did hurt somebody, how would he live with that afterwards? I had to protect him, too."

To keep contact, she promised to pay for Joe's cigarettes; she gave him enough money for only one pack at a time, so he had to come by her house every day. "I'd make sure he had something to eat and give him his money, and off he'd go," she said. "Thanksgiving was coming, and it was really cold," Rosemary told me. "I said to the court clerk, 'You have to get me in to see the judge today.'" Meanwhile, Rosemary told Joe that he'd have to pick up his cigarette allowance at the courthouse. She pulled him in front of the judge. "There were no soles on his sneakers. He was dirty from lying on the ground all night. I said to the judge, 'Could you serve Thanksgiving to anybody, knowing your son is living like this?' The judge committed him."

After his condition stabilized, he was released to his father's octogenarian parents in Somerville, five miles away. To maintain good mental health, Joe needed to have daily injections of Prolixin, an antipsychotic, in Malden. "He went the first day by bus from Somerville to Malden," Rosemary said. "He waited, he waited, nobody there. Got on the bus, went back to Somerville. For three days he went, but the person was out sick, and nobody told us. Joey never got his shots. The fourth day he started hallucinating. He went in the backyard at his father's, crawling on the ground like an animal. My father-in-law comes out on the back porch. He says, 'Joey, you come in and Grandpa will help you.'" Joey attacked his grandfather so savagely that he had to have brain surgery; if he'd died, Joey would have been charged with murder. Joey was committed to one year at Bridgewater State Hospital for the mentally ill.

"Oh, he was sick," Rosemary said. "Then they realized his days on insurance had run out. The very next day he was miraculously cured, and he was going to come home. I said, 'If any harm comes to anybody because of what you're doing today,

I'm taking you to court and I'm going to sue you for every penny this place is worth.'" Joey was transferred to another hospital, and he eventually got well enough to leave. By this time, he was in his mid-twenties. Rosemary was open to having Joe at home again, but if she took him in, he would lose services given only to those with no place to go. She finally installed him in a halfway house with his uncle Johnny. In his later years, he devoted himself to taking pictures of the other residents, images striking both for the desolation they portray and for the kindness with which they portray it. He also drew, a skill he'd had since childhood. His primary psychiatrist still has a picture Joey drew hanging in her office, an ink sketch of himself. "You have to really look closely," she said when I saw it, "but there's another man in Joe's ear. That's the voices whispering to him."

On April 5, 2007, Johnny choked on a piece of meat and died. Two days later, Joey was diagnosed with lung cancer. "As soon as he was diagnosed, we moved him right home, consequences be damned," Rosemary said, weeping. "Every day he had chemo. They found it in his brain, started another kind of chemo. Then it was back in the lung. And he never complained. Joey said to me, 'Ma, it looks like I'm not going to make it.' He says, 'Ma, if I'm fighting, let me fight. But if I'm slipping away, please let me slip away.' That's what happened. He just slipped away right with me sitting there." Johnny and Joe are buried side by side.

Six months before Johnny choked, Rosemary had put her parents' house, where she grew up, into an irrevocable trust. "I did it in case the halfway house didn't keep going, so that if those two were alive and we weren't, they would never be on the street," she said. "It's set up now so that if any of my grandchildren develop this, which is likely, they cannot become homeless. We're just waiting to see who's next."

Schizophrenic self-advocacy is different from Deaf rights or LPA politics or neurodiversity because members of those movements are presumed to have an accurate understanding of themselves. They are often accused of not appreciating mainstream reality; dwarfs cannot really know what it's like to be tall, and people with autism may not conceive of the pleasures of social intelligence. Their comprehension of their own circumstances, however, is usually sound. The defining quality of schizophrenia is that it entails delusion, which complicates its claims on identity. Can people with schizophrenia achieve self-acceptance, or are they in a web of denial that is a symptom of their illness? Schizophrenics' lives are complicated by *anosognosia*: having as a symptom of your illness the belief that you don't have an illness.

The Mad Pride movement believes that self-determination is a basic human right, and that it should be extended to people with schizophrenia and other mental illnesses. By bringing together people afflicted with psychosis, it builds a feeling of horizontal identity among people who may have little other community. Members seek to minimize reliance on psychotropic medications and take control of their own healing; Judi Chamberlin, one of the first activists, said, "If it isn't voluntary, it isn't treatment." Gabrielle Glaser wrote in the *New York Times*, "Just as gay-rights activists reclaimed the word queer as a badge of honor rather than a slur, these advocates proudly call themselves mad; they say their conditions do not preclude them from productive lives."

Mad Pride proponents advocate a wide range of health-promoting practices. David W. Oaks, who heads MindFreedom International and who has a diagnosis of schizophrenia, treats his condition with exercise, peer counseling, diet, and treks in the wilderness; he has refused medication and exhorts others to defy the psychiatric establishment. Of the period when he was forcibly medicated as a young man, he said, "They took a wrecking ball to the cathedral of my mind." Of his work since then, he said, "The human spirit is eccentric and unique and unconquerable and bizarre and unstoppable and wonderful. So this is really about reclaiming what it is to be human in the face of so-called normality." Sally Zinman of the California Network of Mental Health Clients said, "David is like the Malcolm X of the psychiatric survivor movement. He's out there speaking the truth in all its rawness and purity."

It is preposterous, even sentimental, to deny the biological nature of mental illness. But it would be unfortunate to dismiss David W. Oaks and Sally Zinman as merely crazy. These activists believe they are throwing off a yoke of oppression. They both have a serious illness and have suffered tyrannical subjugation; the question is whether they can address the subjugation without making false claims about the nature of mental health.

Although most Mad Pride advocates criticize medical professionals for promoting drugs as a primary treatment for mental illness, many rely on these drugs to function and support the right of others to choose for themselves whether to take antipsychotics. They insist that more can be done to ease side effects for those who must take such medications. Other activists speak of being "pro-choice" about drugs. Pharmacological treatments for schizophrenia carry risk of neurological impairment, metabolic dysfunction, long-term toxicity, diabetes, blood disorders, and rapid weight gain. Many people who initially experience their mental illness as a devastating loss may make private decisions about how much treatment is worth how much of these side effects.

A great deal can be said in favor of accepting yourself with whatever conditions you carry, but the obstacles to doing so are particularly formidable for schizophrenics. Some whom I met had found meaning in the condition, but none seemed particularly exultant about it. Despite moving statements made by advocates, Mad Pride does not have anything like the reach of the autism rights movement. I suspect that is partly because the agony can be so relentless in schizophrenia, but even more because of the illness's late onset. People with autism cannot imagine themselves or be imagined without it; it is intrinsic to their character. People with schizophrenia can imagine themselves without it because most didn't have it for the first two decades of their lives. If they posit "wellness," they are conceptualizing not an inaccessible fiction, but a familiar past. Mad Pride is positive for those who subscribe to it, and it has robust philosophical implications, but most people who descend into psychosis experience that psychosis, until negative symptoms and antipsychotics numb them, as a torment.

Alison Jost, of Yale's Interdisciplinary Center for Bioethics, wrote that it seems easy to compare Mad Pride with disability rights. "But in fact," she went on, "no matter how destigmatized our society becomes, mental illnesses will always cause suffering."

Walter Forrest's son Peter lapsed into schizophrenia his junior year in high school, arguing with his siblings so aggressively that he had to be physically restrained. "It was like the top of his head blew off," Walter said. "He'd always been Mr. Popularity, and then he had some minor social adjustment problems, and now we were wrestling him to the ground." A few weeks later in the car, Peter said, "Dad, don't hold the steering wheel that way, or I'm getting out." Walter was perplexed. "Peter had an offbeat sense of humor, so I was groping," he said. "A few days later, Peter found his way to the shrink's office at his school and melted down into total helplessness."

Peter rapidly developed acute illness. His father noted a greater loss every day. One night Peter ambushed his father and tried to push him through a window. Eventually, Peter attacked Walter with a kitchen knife, and Walter had to call the police. Peter was put in a secure ward for six months. Like most parents, Walter struggled with the gradual realization that his son's problems were not temporary. Walter explained, "The therapist who helped the most said, 'You've had the star quarterback. He's run over by a truck, breaks every limb in his body. Your hope now is not that he'll be a star quarterback, but that he'll walk again.'"

Peter is now in a residential facility, and he comes to see his father four times a year. "I take him to dinner, and he has a sleepover and goes back," Walter said. "Is there any positive in the relationship? Does it have its pleasurable moments? No. I would love him to do a minimum-wage job, bag groceries or something, and feel that he's done something to give himself worth. But the better he gets, it's almost the worse he gets, the sadder it is—because the 'might have been' just breaks your heart. Frankly, it would have been better if he'd died. Better for him, better for everybody. That sounds like the most terrible thing in the world to say. But his life is very, very hard for him, and it's hard on everyone else. Why didn't the truck just crush him completely if it was going to do this kind of damage?"

Walter looked for a long minute out the window. "And now I'm going to cry. You know, it is a death. Joy is one of the few gifts we can give to our fellow human beings, especially our children, and I haven't been able to give any to Peter."

People with schizophrenia are avoided, mocked, and misunderstood. Little progress has been made to reduce the stigmatizing use of terms such as *crazy*, *lunatic*, and *nutty*. Though the Americans with Disabilities Act is supposed to shield the mentally ill, few protections are available to them. The number of both outpatient programs and in-hospital facilities is woefully inadequate, yet circumstances under which people with schizophrenia can live independently are also scarce. An American study from 1990 showed that 40 percent of landlords immediately rejected applicants with a known psychiatric disorder. People who are open about their schizophrenia are essentially unemployable, even if they have been asymptomatic for years. Only about 10 to 15 percent of them sustain full-time employment, but the structures of work can prove enormously beneficial; one leading researcher has noted, "No treatment I have seen is as effective as a job." Homeowners fight hard to keep treatment and residential facilities out of their neighborhoods. James Beck of the NIMH put it bluntly: "Many people can't tolerate working with chronic schizophrenics. Doctors and nurses don't like to treat patients who don't recover."

Although they are erratic in their behavior, most people with schizophrenia are not dangerous to strangers. Schizophrenics are five to eighteen times as likely to commit homicide as are members of the general population, usually in connection with substance abuse; even including substance users, however, only 0.3 percent will commit homicide. A 1998 study found rates of violence in psychiatric patients who are not substance abusers consistent with those in the general population, and such violence is five times more likely to be directed at family members. Almost one in four families living with schizophrenic relatives experiences physical harm or the threat of it. Nonetheless, because schizophrenic violence may respond to hallucinations and be directed at random strangers, it has the same dark-hand-of-fate feeling as plane crashes, which frighten us so much more than fatal car accidents even though they are considerably rarer.

The facility containing the largest number of schizophrenics in the United States is the Los Angeles County Jail. At least three times as many mentally ill people are in jail as are in hospitals. In fact, nearly 300,000 people with mental illnesses are in jail in the United States, most convicted of crimes they would not have committed if they had been treated; another 550,000 are on probation. Few are in for violent crimes; most are there for the many small violations of the law that are inevitable for people who can't understand social reality. They are dealt with not by doctors, but by police officers—and then prison guards and other criminals.

Prisons are expensive to run, and American prisons are close to the breaking point. Treating schizophrenia more effectively could substantially reduce the cost of keeping people locked up for crimes they didn't understand and didn't intend. Psychiatric care is increasingly deemed a luxury, a thing reserved for people who have privilege. For budgetary reasons, we have reduced and reduced psychiatric care—closing hospitals, diminishing community supports, restricting access to doctors. If one weighs the savings achieved by this against the added burdens to the penal system, the penny-wise, pound-foolish nature of such budgeting becomes ludicrously obvious. While accommodating people with physical disabilities must be undertaken out of moral conviction, adequately treating people with severe psychiatric illness is a win-win situation; if moral conviction fails, economic self-interest should prevail.

"When other little girls were trying on their mothers' high heels, I was wrapping myself with Ace bandages, 'cause I thought it looked cool," Susan Weinreich recalled. Susan had a compulsion to bite her lips, and they were usually scabbed or openly bleeding. Ashamed, she would say to her mother, Bobbe Evans, "Why can't I stop?" Bobbe would just say, "You'll grow out of it." But schizophrenia did not manifest fully until Susan entered the Rhode Island School of Design (RISD) in 1973.

"I knew there was something wrong all along," Susan said, "but it wasn't until my freshman year that it became obvious to other people." During Susan's freshman year, her father left her mother. "That jostled everything enough so that symptoms started to bubble to the surface," Susan said. Unable to do her classwork, she began seeing a Freudian psychoanalyst, whose treatment involved returning to childhood states. Unfortunately, slipping back into a childlike state was one of Susan's symptoms, and she needed to move away from it, not deeper into it. "I was horribly dependent on him," she said. "I basically stayed in during the day and came out only at night, when I walked the streets and studied the moon. I saw deformed bodies, bloody faces, devils, bodies hanging from trees. The real people I saw all appeared distorted. They were missing arms, legs. I remember being very threatened by stains in the asphalt, and plastic bags caught in the bushes in January."

In her sophomore year, Susan entered RISD's glass-blowing department. "I had an intense need to be around fire," she said. In the first semester of her junior year, the school asked that she withdraw. "I just was imploding, burning myself with cigarettes and putting my fists through windows. In my better moments, I would go to the Brown medical library, looking, looking, looking for what was wrong with me." Susan had three separate hospitalizations that year. The doctors would explain that she needed to be on medication for the rest of her life, but wouldn't tell her why; she, in turn, refused to give the hospital the contact information for her parents. "Even though I had no understanding of what was happening, I had a very strong, strong desire to protect my family. I believed that I had baby breasts and adult breasts, and that the baby breasts were going to drop off, and the adult breasts would take their place. But I believed that if my mother came to my apartment and stayed overnight, these little men and women were going to come out of my breasts. The men were carrying scythes, and the women were carrying burlap bags. They would hurt her. I was afraid my mother would see them, which meant she would know about the devil in me. I couldn't tolerate that."

When she took in her brother's cat while he was traveling the summer following her sophomore year, the animal hid under an old, green vinyl reclining chair. "I thought the chair was infested with fleas, and then the fleas became sperm. I took out a bucket of paint and painted the whole chair white and took out a kitchen knife and started stabbing it." She didn't bathe for months on end and didn't brush her teeth for ten years. "I was like an animal, my hair knotted and greasy. I would cut myself and paint on the walls with my blood."

Bobbe had never heard the word *schizophrenia* until Susan's analyst called in 1979 to find out what kind of insurance Susan had, because he had finally decided that she needed to be hospitalized, perhaps for life. "That snapped my mother into something," Susan said, "and she came up to Rhode Island, threw me in the car, and tore me away from this guy." Bobbe took Susan to a doctor who said she should be hospitalized at once. Susan had developed facial hair, possibly in response to medication, and decided to let it grow. "When I saw this daughter, who I wanted to be this cute little thing, with hair on her face, it was just horrible," Bobbe said. Susan said, "I had all kinds of delusions about what that meant. It was down to my jawbone, and it was very thick, coarse, sexual hair." Bobbe decided to take Susan directly to Four Winds Hospital in Katonah, the best mental facility within easy driving distance. Susan was interviewed by Sam Klagsbrun, who ran the hospital. "He told me what was wrong with me. He gave me my diagnosis." Susan was admitted to Four Winds.

Susan's father had by now disappeared from her life completely; soon, Bobbe remarried. "I wanted my life to go on," Bobbe said. "To my friends, I just said, 'Susan is having a problem, and the divorce kind of triggered it.' I really wanted her out of my life, and I felt relief because somebody was taking her off my hands. I'm not proud of saying that, but it's how I remember feeling. I wish I had known someone like present-day Susan when she was so sick, because it would have given me such hope. But there was nobody."

Susan was at Four Winds for four months, then out, then back for another six, and eventually at a halfway house where she stayed for nine months in 1980 before moving back home, age twenty-four. "I would come home from work," Bobbe said, "and she would be lurking somewhere, not answering when I called her. Sam Klagsbrun said, 'You have to tell her to leave.' I said, 'But how can I?' He said, 'Just tell her that you would do anything in the world for her if she were making progress, but that this isn't helping her.' So I told her she had to leave. That was probably the hardest thing I ever had to do in my life." Bobbe wept as she told me about it. "She left, after writing a note that she was going to kill herself. Then she called Sam and went back to Four Winds."

Susan's accounts of Four Winds are rhapsodic: "It was a psychiatric utopia. There were ducks running around, and a chicken coop. I would spend my days in the pine forest. If an insurance company heard that today, they'd freak. Sam's treatment was incredible. I was an infant. He cuddled me; he hugged me. He picked me up out of a pothole in the pouring rain." Klagsbrun had started a hospice program—for nonpsychiatric patients with terminal physical illness—in the lodge where the psychotic patients lived. "You take someone like myself, who was clearly psychotic and not living in reality, and you face them with the biggest reality, which is death," Susan said. "Even in my confusion, I understood it on some level, and it shocked reality back into me. Here I am, actively self-destructive, and yet these people wanted to live so desperately. It made me ask the big question, which is, do you want to live or die? I realized I wanted to move toward life."

Susan's emotional life began to revive. "I remember the first time I felt love, after all that. I don't even remember who it was—probably Sam. I just started feeling what it felt like to love someone. I don't remember it being ecstatic; I just remember it feeling like when I would go fishing as a young girl, and a sunfish would catch the hook. Just that tug on the other end of the line. After all those years of being so isolated within myself and so disconnected, the medication sucked out some of the symptoms, and as the psychosis receded, it left room for my heart to grow. There were other psychotic episodes that followed, and I wasn't experiencing love too much during those. But during each remission, my experience of empathy and connectedness just expanded." Susan had continued to make art, and Klagsbrun adapted a little outbuilding for her to use as a studio. "My work has a dark side," she said, "but it's about creativity, and creativity is about giving life."

When Susan graduated from her most intensive treatment phase, she accepted a job at the hospital, which came with benefits, and her insurance paid for electrolysis to remove her facial hair. She was twenty-six years old. "Preparing for the larger world was still a tall order," she said. "I didn't know who the president was. My ego was like Swiss cheese. I was still having a lot of catastrophic visions. I didn't know the first thing about taking care of myself physically." She began seeing a therapist, Xenia Rose, and stayed with her for twenty years. "She had me write up a schedule. It had 'get up' and 'brush teeth' because I had no idea what a day was supposed to look like." Rose agreed to see Bobbe as well. "That was enormously helpful to me," Bobbe said, "because I had to just cry and say what I thought. But Susan's illness was not me; it was her. When I started to let go, she started to emerge."

By the time she was in her late thirties, Susan was reasonably stable. The medication Zyprexa had "revolutionized" her life. She slept thirteen hours a night, but was coherent. Eventually, she switched to Abilify, which was less sedating. "I grow like lightning," Susan said. "What you see here today is a completely different soul than I was five years ago: developmentally, physically, visually, verbally. I've worked very hard, on every level, at eradicating every remnant of the illness. Intermittently, I have little things trigger here and there, but they only last a day or two. Sensory overstimulation, a bit of paranoia, misperceptions and distortions in my thinking and visual world. Some people get stressed and their back goes out. I get stressed and my mind goes out. But then it comes back."

Of all the things that required catching up, perhaps the most challenging was romance. At the time I met Susan, she was nearly fifty and had not yet had a full sexual experience. "I'd like to experience love. But do I know what love is? So far, my mother's it." Susan laughed. "My poor mother. She signed me up for three different dating services, simultaneously. It was grueling. But I looked at it as a way to grow developmentally. The schizophrenia has given me the ability to find something inside of me, parts of myself that I might not have been able to reach otherwise."

Susan has also attempted to reconnect with her long-absent father. One day she told me she had just spoken to him on the phone for the first time in decades. "I told him that I loved him," she said. "It felt right to say that, despite his abandonment of me. I had written him a letter because he was turning eighty, and I thought I would free him from some guilt. I wanted him to know that he gave me the one tool I needed to climb out, which is my art, because he nurtured my creativity. He called after a week. We had a very superficial conversation about clamming or whatever he does down there, and then he became a little weepy, and he blurted out, 'I'll never forgive myself for walking out on all of you.' It took all I had to hold me back from jumping in my car and driving down there. But I decided not to call again. We have too much in common."

Bobbe eventually came to accept, understand, and finally be proud of her daughter. She works in the travel industry and gives all her earnings to Susan. In turn, Susan has donated most of the proceeds of her sales of her rich, strange, beautiful art to Four Winds. She has taken up public speaking. Bobbe heard Susan address a mental health dinner at Grand Central Station. "I couldn't believe it. There were like three hundred people there—and this is Susan. I mean, how did this happen?" Bobbe said. Susan's relationship with Bobbe is almost completely resolved. "She's definitely a stronger person than I've ever been," Bobbe said. "What saved her? It was her art; it was

Dr. Klagsbrun; it was the support from her brothers and me. But most of all, it was Susan. There was something in Susan that always wanted to come to the surface. I deserve a medal. I really do. But Susan deserves lots of medals. I feel really bad that she had to go through what she went through. But I also recognize that if she hadn't, she wouldn't be who she is today. And who she is today is the most wonderful, charming, beautiful woman. She used to say, 'It's the cards you have dealt to you, Mom.' I think what I've finally come to terms with is that if you learn to live with things that aren't pleasant, then, suddenly, sometimes, they are."

Families rise to the occasion of various difficulties, struggle to love across those divides, and find in almost any challenge a message of hope and an occasion for growth or wisdom. Nonetheless, schizophrenia may be in a class by itself for unrewarding trauma. The rich culture of Deafness, the LPA-centered empowerment of dwarfism, the extreme sweetness of many Down syndrome children, the self-actualization of the autism rights brigade—none of this is really present in the world of schizophrenia, Mad Pride notwithstanding. We may hesitate to cure some illnesses because they are also rich identities, but schizophrenia cries out almost unconditionally for treatment. The remarkable parents and children I met during this research would be better off if schizophrenia didn't exist. Though I liked some of them and felt they had shown remarkable courage in building lives around their complaint, the complaint itself left little room for hope; to me, their suffering seemed unending, and singularly fruitless.

Disability

DISABILITY DESCRIBES THE OLDER PERSON WHOSE bad ankles make walking long distances a trial, and the returning veteran who has lost limbs. The word is also used for people who would once have been classed as mentally retarded, and for anyone whose senses or physical abilities are severely compromised. *Multiple disability* refers to people who are impaired in more than one way. *Severe disability* indicates a considerable impairment. *Multiple severe disabilities* (MSD) refers to people with an overwhelming number of challenges.

Some people with MSD are incapable of controlled movement, verbal thought, or self-awareness. Shaped more or less like other people, they may not learn their own name or demonstrate basic emotions such as fear or happiness. They may not feed themselves. Yet they are human, and often, they are loved. Parents find beauty or hope in the existence, rather than the achievements, of such children. Most parenthood entails some struggle to change, educate, and improve one's offspring. People with multiple severe disabilities may not change or improve. Parents must love not what might or should or will be, but simply what is.

About twenty thousand people with MSD are born in the United States each year. Many who would not have lived beyond infancy are now surviving much longer because of new medical treatments that can keep them alive. People actively debate whether extending the lives of these children should always be given priority regardless of their perceived pain and regardless of the difficulties for those who will be responsible for them. Thirty years ago, parents were advised to abandon severely disabled children, often to let them die. This was because people thought that the lives of such children had no value. In the last twenty years or so, they have been told to keep and love them. That is in part because those lives are now seen to have value. Like many other identity groups explored in this book, people with MSD have made radical social progress.

Most states offer supplemental income for family members who have to give up work to take care of an MSD child, as well as respite (a weekend off for the family, when someone from outside comes to take care of the sick child), health care, and in-home services (help with feeding, bathing, and so on). People with MSD who can absorb some education have access to schools. These services are not provided out of mere kindness; higher-functioning people are less expensive across their life span. For every dollar spent on vocational rehabilitation (the process of teaching people to function better) for people with disabilities, the Social Security Administration, an agency of the United States federal government that provides benefits to citizens unable to work, saves seven dollars.

David and Sara Hadden married in their early twenties and prepared for a high-powered life in New York. David worked at one of the city's finest law firms, and Sara soon became pregnant with their first son, Jamie. Three days after he was born in August 1980, an intern entered her hospital room and said, "Your son just turned blue, and we don't know what's going on." The doctors couldn't find anything wrong and sent the family home with a monitor that would sound an alarm if Jamie's breathing stopped. It never sounded, and David and Sara thought he was fine. When he was about three months old, their pediatrician said Jamie's head size was not following the normal growth curve.

A few weeks later, a neurologist told them, "You've got king-sized problems. If you're thinking of having more kids, put it on hold. This child is blind, and probably is going to be severely retarded, and may not live long." David and Sara walked out of the office in silence.

The next morning, Sara said to David, "I don't know why I'm saying this, but I feel very strongly that we need to have Jamie baptized." They hadn't gone to church in many years, but they looked in the Yellow Pages and found one around the corner. "I didn't understand it then," Sara said to me, "but I think I was acknowledging that Jamie had a soul."

All Sara had accepted at that point was that Jamie was blind; she thought that his delays were tied to his lack of vision, and she resisted knowing that his brain wasn't growing. A month after visiting the neurologist, she and David took Jamie for an EEG. The EEG technician was digging into Jamie's skull as she applied the electrodes. "That's when we became advocates," David explained. "That's when we said, 'No, goddammit! You're not going to do that with our child.' That was a first; I had always been a well-behaved person who followed the rules. Jamie has made me a far better lawyer. He has forced me to develop advocacy skills that have sprung from passion as opposed to intellectual arguments."

At two, Jamie could push himself up into a sitting position, but at three he lost that ability; he was able to roll over until he was eleven, but can no longer do so. He has never developed speech or fed himself. He could urinate at first, but the relevant neurological processes soon failed, and he had to be permanently catheterized. "When we learned that Jamie was retarded, I was afraid," Sara said. "I had this Helen Keller vision that if I found the right key, if I could just do the signs in his hand long enough, he would learn to talk. All of his teachers were urging me, saying, 'Yes, yes, yes, that's what you need to do, the more the better; maximize his potential!' It was wonderful support in one way, and an amazing guilt trip in another way."

Jamie's doctors were fairly confident that his condition was not hereditary, and when Jamie was four, the Haddens decided to have another child. Their daughter, Liza, was born in perfect health. Four years later, they had Sam. When Sam was six weeks old, Sara was putting him to bed, and suddenly he started twitching, and Sara immediately knew it was a seizure.

Diagnosis remained elusive, even though it was soon clear that the two boys shared a syndrome. The constellation of symptoms experienced by Jamie and Sam seems to be unique, so no one has been able to predict how the boys would best be treated, how much they might deteriorate, or how long they might live.

Sam was even more fragile than Jamie. He kept breaking

his legs because he had brittle bones; he ultimately had total-spinal-fusion surgery. Fed through a tube from a much earlier age than Jamie, Sam vomited all the time. At two, he spent six weeks in the hospital for continuous seizures. When he was admitted, his cognitive abilities were greater than Jamie's, but after that six-week period, he lost them. David and Sara both became snowed under. A few months after Sam's diagnosis, Sara hit rock bottom. "I sat on the kitchen floor trying to convince myself to take both boys with me to the garage and turn on the car and let all of us go on the carbon monoxide," she said.

Yet there was joy, too. "If we had known that the condition might be repeated, we would not have risked it," Sara said. "Having said that, if I were told, 'We can just wipe out that experience,' I wouldn't. Sam got the full benefit of being Jamie's younger brother. I had a lot less trepidation taking care of him; I knew how to do it. Sam was easier to love. Jamie's a fighter; Jamie will stand up for his rights. Sam would just curl into you." David concurred, "It absolutely blows my mind, the impact that a blind, retarded, nonverbal, nonambulatory person has had on people. He has a way of opening and touching people that we can't come near. That's part of our survival story—our marveling at how he has moved so many people."

When Jamie was almost nine, Sara tried to lift him out of the bathtub and herniated a disc. All three of the children had chicken pox. The boys were in diapers and difficult to change. David said, "We had Sam, rushing off to the hospital with seizures; we had our four-year-old; and then we had Jamie, with his unpredictability. It was more than we could do." They secured an emergency placement for Jamie in June 1989, in a facility for adults about forty minutes away from their house in northern Connecticut. David and Sara became members of a class-action suit against the State of Connecticut, aimed at replacing large institutions with community care. "Jamie embarrassed the Department of Mental Retardation with the notion that the best they could offer an eight-year-old child was a sixty-bed institution with adults," David said with pride. An article about the fight ran in the *Hartford Courant* Sunday magazine, with Jamie on the cover, and in 1991, the Hartford Association for Retarded Citizens (HARC) set up a group home. The Haddens decided Sam should live there as well. They visited daily. With Liza in first grade and both boys out of the house, Sara decided that since her best means of communication with her sons had always been touch, she would go to massage school; she worked as a massage therapist for fifteen years.

Two years after Sam moved into the group home, he was having a routine bath when the staff member in charge of his care went to get some medication for him, which she was not supposed to do. While bathing, he would sit in a chair that fit in the tub, with a safety belt across his hips. Perhaps the belt had been forgotten, or perhaps the Velcro gave way. She was gone less than three minutes, and when she returned, Sam was underwater. David received the call at his office and immediately called Sara, who was driving Liza to boarding school. The three of them converged in the emergency room. "The doctor came in," David said. "We could tell by the look on his face. Sara and I were off in our own numb shock, and Liza was just furious, knowing that somebody screwed up." Sara said, "We'd talked about wanting the children to die, and then panicked if it seemed to be happening. It was best for Sam. I miss him terribly, and for me it is a tragic loss—but he had been fighting a hard fight a long time, and I have no doubt that he has gone to a better place."

The Haddens went to the home that night to see Jamie. The caretaker who had left Sam in the bathtub was there. "She was on the couch, in shock and just sobbing," Sara said. "I gave her a hug, and I said, 'Marvika, it could have been any of us.' She shouldn't have left him alone in the bathtub, but it's so hard to be vigilant every minute. We fuck up. All the time. If he had been at home, I can't say that I wouldn't have left him in the bathtub to go get a towel. It's incredibly difficult to hire and retain qualified people to do this very difficult direct-care work, and the pay is terrible. If we start charging people with crimes for making mistakes, how is that going to help? I didn't want to do anything that would discourage other people from entering this relatively thankless field."

The caretaker was charged with reckless manslaughter. "We said to the prosecutor, 'Our wish is that you don't pursue this,'" David recalled. "'This woman is going to lose her job. She'll never get another job like this. This problem has essentially corrected itself.' We both wanted the compassion and healing to set in as quickly as possible." Marvika was eventually sentenced to five years, suspended, and one of the terms of her probation was that she never again work caring for disabled children.

The videotape of Sam's funeral memorializes an outpouring of extraordinary love—much of it for David, Sara, Liza, and Jamie, as well as for Sam. "I'd imagined Sam would die,"

David said. "I thought that there would be a sense of relief. And there was. But there's also this acute sense of loss, the feeling that if I could turn back that clock and save him, I would give my right arm to do it. I didn't expect to feel that way." Four years later, when they finally interred Sam's ashes, Sara said, "Let me bury here the rage I feel to have been twice robbed: once of the child I wanted, and once of the son I loved."

When I visited Jamie for the first time, when he was in his early twenties, he seemed, at first glance, inert. I noticed how pretty his room was: framed pictures and posters adorned the walls, a nicely patterned duvet lay on the bed and attractive clothes hung in the closet. I thought that selecting pleasing visuals for a blind person was somewhat eccentric, but Sara said, "It's a gesture of respect, and it sends a message to the people who work with him that we take care of him and expect them to do so too." Jamie, who is tall and large-boned, has to be lifted from and returned to his bed with a pulley. The effort needed to keep him comfortable is tremendous, but although he seems capable of discomfort, he at first struck me as incapable of pleasure. Yet to be in the room with Sara and David and their son is to witness a shimmering humanity. "Sam's death had a mellowing effect on Jamie," Sara said to me. "But maybe the change was in us."

On later visits, I found that Jamie sometimes opens his eyes and seems to stare at you; he cries, smiles, and occasionally breaks into a sort of laugh. I learned to place my hand on his shoulder, since touch is his primary means of communication. Liza took two weeks off work to read him *The Chronicles of Narnia*, just in case he could understand it. I saw that he might be soothed by his sister's voice and presence, and that it was good for her to acknowledge his essential self. "It's raw, just being a person without trying to impress or achieve or accomplish anything," David said. "It's pure being. In a totally unconscious way, he is what human is. I find thinking about that helpful in building enough energy to counteract the demands of it."

When the group home staff unionized and went on strike, Sara said, "I strongly support their hopes and wishes, but I feel sad at how easily they can leave. I want them to love Jamie, to find it as hard to walk out on him as I would. It's a job and they do it pretty well and they are fond of him, but they don't love him. That makes it difficult for me to trust them, especially with the specter of what happened to Sam." A few years later, when Jamie had been moved to a home slightly farther away, Sara wrote to me, "Our visits to Middletown are like going out on a whale watch. Often we make the trip to find Jamie snoozing and have to settle for reports of 'You should have been here an hour ago; he was having a great time!' Or worse, sometimes we are back on the pitching seas of concern as we watch him experience discomfort and try to sort out its cause. We hope for those wonderful moments, like one we had two weeks ago, when we are there for his 'surfacing' and can feel his pleasure in being alive."

Alan O. Ross writes in *The Exceptional Child in the Family* that parents' expectations "invariably include that the child will be able to surpass, or at least attain, the parents' level of sociocultural accomplishment." He continues, "When the child does not conform to this image, the parents often need help in adapting their behavior to the reality—they must learn to cope with the dissonance between their image of 'a child' and the reality of 'their child.'"What rewards do parents expect in return for the sacrifices they make for their children? The answer changes not only from family to family, but also over time.

Among other mammals, parents are primed to form attachments to their newborns by their hormones and the act of birth, but in order for their behavior to continue, they must have babies that are responding appropriately. Nurturing has to be reinforced and maintained. Of course human beings are not lower animals and our experience of parenting is far more subtle and complex. But even human parents mostly want to see their love rewarded with smiles or snuggles or other signs of adoration. What happens to parents of an MSD child, who can often express only appetite or pain?

Despite not getting the typical, seductive responses, parents get attached to their children with MSD time and again. Like all love, theirs is partly an act of projection. One thinks that one loves one's children because they are genuinely beguiling and one's parents because they have given care, but many children whose parents have neglected them go on loving such parents, and many mothers and fathers of disagreeable children are enchanted by them. As one sociologist observed, we not only take care of our children because we love them, but also love them because we take care of them.

While some people with severe disabilities may experience acute health crises or frightening seizures, much of their care has a rhythm, and human nature adapts to anything with a rhythm. An extreme but stable stress is easier to handle than a less extreme but erratic one. This is one reason why parents of people with Down syndrome have an easier time than parents of schizophrenics or of people with autism: with Down syndrome, you know with whom you are dealing from day to day, and the demands on you change relatively little; with schizophrenia, you never know what weirdness is about to strike; with autism, you never know whether you are at the brink of a severe meltdown moment.

Once the course of care is clear, most people can accept it. Since knowledge is power, even very serious illnesses that you understand can be easier to deal with than less severe ones about which you know nothing. Identity is a function of certitude.

When Max Singer was born, one of his eyes was fixed to the left, and the other had an enlarged pupil. A leading pediatric neurologist in New York examined Max, then turned to Peter Singer and said, "You should take your pretty wife home and make yourself another baby, because you're never going to get anything out of this one. I don't know if he'll ever be able to walk or talk or recognize you or function or even think." The neurologist said that Max had Dandy-Walker syndrome, a congenital brain malformation involving the cerebellum and the fluid-filled spaces around it.

Susanna Singer described the day she got the diagnosis as one of the worst of her life. "I'm not sure that we benefited from knowing instantly that there was something wrong," she said. "That slowed down my attachment to him." The Singers next took Max to a neurological ophthalmologist to figure out what was happening with his eyes. The doctor determined that Max could see. Everything else was open to question. "The first doctor told us he would be a vegetable," Susanna said. "The next one said he could be slightly delayed. We had these diagnoses but no predictions about what they meant and were told that we wouldn't know what was going on until autopsy. It's very hard to live without clear expectations."

Susanna chose not to discuss Max's problems publicly when he was little. "I was keeping him hidden. I regret that secrecy. It was lonely for both of us." When Max was three months old, the Singers hired a Trinidadian nanny named Veronica, who stayed with them for the next twenty years. "She was like a third parent, and maybe more than that," Susanna said. "If he had had to choose between us and her, he would have chosen her. She was with him all the time. She never ran out of patience."

The Singers tried for another baby, but Susanna kept miscarrying. They decided to adopt; while Susanna and Peter were sitting at their chosen adoption agency, they got a call from Veronica, saying that Max had come home from school with a fever. Susanna left the meeting so she could take him to the doctor. "Max isn't often sick; aside from his disabilities, he's actually very healthy. But the agency told us that, really, Max took too much work, and we couldn't give what was needed to another child. They rejected us. Maybe it would have been difficult for another child to have Max as a brother—but I think both would have benefited a lot."

Max can walk if someone has an arm around him and is holding him up. "Unless he decides he doesn't want to," Susanna said, "in which case he will stop and cross his legs, and it is virtually impossible to move him. If he wants to go to a movie or get to a television, he can practically run." Max can use a bathroom, and he has good movement in his left arm and right leg. "He can do a lot more than he does," Susanna explained. "He'll wait you out." Max understands language, but is incapable of producing speech. This comes with its own frustrations; to understand and be unable to respond is maddening. Max can nod or shake his head. Max also lacks the motor control he would need for Sign, though he can sign "more," "finished," "music," and "I'm sorry." He does not like speaking devices, but when he's forced to use a talking machine, something that translates typing or other symbols into sound, he can make fairly complicated sentences. He can read short words; he can write his full name.

"Max gets a real kick out of almost everything," Susanna said. "He's full of curiosity. There's nothing that makes him scared, except very big dogs. He's well-adjusted and feels very loved. Because he goes to a special school, he's never been ostracized or teased. Also, Max doesn't have any physical deformities that make people shy away. That's helped him a lot. I, frankly, was never all that good-looking. But I think he really is. He's extremely affectionate. He doesn't have the muscle control to kiss, but he hugs hard and often. It used to happen all the time that we would sit around with Veronica, and Max would put his arm around her. If we were laughing, he'd look at her, to make sure she was laughing too. He's very sweet that way."

Max went off to a special summer camp for the first time when he was nine, and Susanna phoned the camp every day to check on him. Finally, one of the other campers took the call and offered some friendly advice: "Mrs. Singer, Max is having the time of his life. My parents always go away when I'm at camp; maybe you should consider doing that." Later, Max attended a camp run by the Hebrew Academy for Special Children. The Singers are secular Jews, but summer camps for special-needs children are often run by religious organizations. "I don't like religion, but I've learned it's not about me," Susanna said. "Every year Max goes to that camp, he comes back more mature, and he learns incredible amounts."

Max is comparatively well socialized and psychologically independent. When he got on the bus to go to the Special Olympics for the first time, he pushed Susanna away. "I was proud of that," she said. "From the beginning, I wanted this child to feel like he was the greatest thing in the world. I succeeded in that. Sometimes I wish I hadn't because he can be so arrogant, but I did." She smiled. "It is not a joyful thing, by any means, to have a special-needs child. But Max himself has given us a lot of joy. I had to change my ideas when he was born, about what it means to be successful, for him and for me; his happiness is his success for him, and mine for me. I wish that he would work a little harder at school. I wish he were willing to accomplish more, rather than be satisfied with hanging out. But maybe he would have been that kind of kid anyway. His basic disposition is like mine. Maybe that's why I like it. Buoyant and even. Basically happy, and willing to adjust."

Max loves Jim Carrey movies, has a sense of humor, and is a classical-music enthusiast. "My father's a huge opera buff, and I was named Susanna after *The Marriage of Figaro*," Susanna said. "Somebody gave me a CD of Cecilia Bartoli, and I put it on, and Max was entranced." Susanna has taken Max to see Cecilia Bartoli, one of the world's most famous opera singers, at the Metropolitan Opera and at Carnegie Hall. They went to see her give an interview at Hunter College. He has gone to her record signings. "He's a groupie," Susanna said. "Cecilia Bartoli, who has a dog named Figaro, has, I have to say, been very nice to Max over the years." She's signed albums to him; she's even signed a photograph for him. Susanna herself had an old, mean dog who died when Max was twelve. "Nobody particularly liked him except for me, and Max, who loved him like a brother," she said. "Max was going off to camp, and I said, 'Max, I really want a new dog. Is that okay?' He kept saying, 'No, no, no, no.' Finally I said, 'Max, suppose we name it after Cecilia Bartoli? He said, 'Yes.' We got the dog, but it was a boy, so the name is Bartoli, and we call him Bart."

When I first met the Singers, Max was twenty. "Adolescence is not easy with children like this," Susanna said. "This little angel that I once had, I don't have anymore, at least not so much of the time. He loves girls, especially pretty girls, but he's not necessarily appropriate with them. He has friends in a way, but I wouldn't say that they're really bonded together. I know he knows the difference between people like us and himself; he's dependent on everybody."

Things had taken a sharp turn for the worse earlier that year, and Peter and Susanna couldn't understand why. Max's behavior became so bad that they took him to a neurologist, who put Max on medication that seemed only to make things worse. Eventually, they learned that Veronica had been telling Max that she was leaving after the summer. She hadn't yet mentioned this to Susanna or Peter. Max had no way to explain what was wrong. "That's one of the hardest things about having a child who can think, and react, and love, and have the feelings we have, but not be able to tell us. I can't even imagine not being able to express such incredible fear and sadness. Once we talked it through, he accepted it; by the time he got back from camp, we had a new person and he's very fond of her. He's adjusted better than I thought, and better than we have; I cried and cried."

Veronica's departure was occasioned by her being tired after twenty years, by Max's being so large that he was becoming physically difficult to move, by her wish to return to Trinidad, and by her horror at the thought that Max would someday be moved to a group home. "Every time we talked about it, she cried," Susanna said. "I kept saying, 'You know this is the best thing for him.' She knew that. I felt like Max should be out of the house around the time he would have been going to college. I find it sad to see kids in their forties living with aging parents. I'd like to be around while he's transitioning, to help him, so when something happens to Peter and me, he isn't suddenly thrown into chaos."

It can be hard to find a place that will deal with someone who is as physically disabled as Max, but where staff are prepared to talk to him even though he can't speak and to cope with the depth of his understanding. His parents eventually found a place that seemed right, but it was still under construction when I met them, and they were waiting. Susanna is matter-of-fact about the group home. "It's not going to feel like a big void when he goes. It doesn't when he's in camp. Peter and I get along better when Max is away. We don't have help on weekends, and if Peter plays golf all day one day, that means I have to be with Max all day. Peter has the same problem if I need to do something. I don't believe that we'll have an empty-nest problem. I think that would have been very different with a normal child, so I get sad about not being sad."

I have heard mothers of healthy children express a fantasy of the child who would be forever tender and vulnerable and dependent, who would not go through the rebellion of adolescence or the detachment of adulthood. Be careful what you wish for. Disabled children are forever the responsibility of their parents; 85 percent of people with intellectual disabilities live with or under the supervision of their parents, an arrangement that often persists until the parents become disabled or die. This has its up and down sides. It can cause the parents terrible anxiety as they age; it can also give them a permanent worthy focus. For the parent the initial stress is often overwhelming. However, one research group found that nearly two-thirds of aging parents felt their continuing role as caregivers gave them a sense of purpose, while more than half felt less lonely with their child still at home.

Some parents who begin with gusto become overwhelmed by children who require special attention and, in midlife or later, begin to despair. Others who had originally wanted to give up their children for adoption fall gradually in love with them. The life expectancy for people with disabilities is increasing; in the 1930s, the average age at death for institutionalized mentally retarded males was about fifteen and for females about twenty-two; by 1980, the figure for males was fifty-eight and for females it was up to sixty, though people without mobility die younger.

Siblings of severely disabled children have been studied extensively, but with inconclusive results. One study mentions that persons with disabled siblings "felt that living with a disabled brother or sister helped them be more responsible, be more tolerant," better able to see "the good in others, develop a better sense of humor, and be more flexible." However, these siblings also reported "embarrassment, guilt, isolation, and concern about the future of their disabled sibling." Another study of siblings of disabled children found that while they were in general more unhappy, they did not suffer from more diagnosable psychiatric problems than their peers. Often, the more obvious or severe the handicap, the easier it is for the nondisabled sibling, because the disabled child doesn't look as if he or she should be acting like any other child. Children who seem normal when people first see them and then turn out not to be require more explaining. The most profound impairments seem to be associated with the best sibling adjustment. Having a clear diagnosis also makes a big difference for siblings, allowing them to use a simple, logical explanation with friends; those with a sibling with no clear diagnosis have to struggle more.

The reason most commonly given for institutionalizing children in the heyday of institutionalization was that keeping a disabled child at home was unfair to healthy siblings, because the disabled child would take too much of the parents' energy and focus and embarrass the nondisabled child. Now, it has been observed that siblings of people given up are often terrified that if they became unwell, they, too, might be abandoned. So the interests of the nondisabled sibling are now more often held to require keeping the disabled sibling at home. This may be better for the disabled child as well, but it's striking how the conversation continues to prioritize the interest of the nondisabled sibling over that of the disabled one.

The field of profound disabilities does not often have breaking scandals, but the Ashley treatment rocked that world. Ashley X, whose last name has never been revealed, was born in 1997, an apparently healthy baby. When she seemed irritable at about three months, her parents thought it was colic. It turned out to be a brain injury of unknown origin. Ashley will never talk, walk, or feed herself, and she cannot turn over. She can sleep, wake, and breathe—and she can smile.

In a bid to defend his own and his family's privacy, her father has refused to meet face-to-face with anyone from the media; he refers to himself as AD (Ashley's Dad). He explained to me over the phone that he and Ashley's mother (AM) had initially resisted giving Ashley a feeding tube because they had a visceral negative response to the idea of surgery. "She cannot chew, and she was always struggling with the bottle," he said. "We would spend six to eight hours a day to get enough nutrition into her." Finally, they had a tube inserted. Despite compromised brain function, Ashley is not unresponsive. "Ashley enjoys our company and voices," her parents said in a written statement. "When we sweet talk to her, she often radiates with a big smile. She enjoys rich music, walks outdoors, a swim on a warm day, the swing, etc." Ashley's parents started to call her their "pillow angel" because she was generally lying on a pillow and never gave them deliberate trouble; they have proposed the term be used for other people with MSD.

As Ashley grew from infancy to childhood, her care became more challenging. Hourly, her parents change her position and prop her back on her pillow. "We make sure she is well covered and pull her shirt down to cover her tummy; we wipe her drool, etc.," AD explained to me. "Also there are diaper changes, tube feedings, dressing, bathing, teeth cleaning, stretching, entertainment." All of this became harder as Ashley grew larger. "You start having difficulty including her in activities," AD said to me. "You want to be able to carry her, but your body aches. The notion formed gradually that her added size and weight were her worst enemy, and the idea to do something about it was an epiphany." When Ashley was six, AM was talking to her own mother, who reminded her of a neighbor who had had hormone treatments to prevent her becoming extremely tall; this procedure was not uncommon in the 1950s, when girls over five feet ten inches were considered unattractive.

Upon hearing of their concern over Ashley's height, their family pediatrician suggested that AD and AM visit Dr. Daniel Gunther, an endocrinologist at Seattle Children's Hospital. At their appointment several weeks later, Gunther acknowledged that Ashley's growth could be attenuated by administering estrogen, which would close her growth plates. Since Ashley will cry for an hour when she sneezes because she is so upset by slight discomfort, AD thought she would have a hard time with menstruation and the cramping it can cause. He proposed a hysterectomy. He thought breasts would get in her way when she was turned on her pillow or strapped in a wheelchair and asked that his daughter's breast buds, the small, almond-shaped glands that enlarge into breasts at puberty, be removed. All this would result in a person who was easier to move—which, in turn, he argued, would mean better circulation, digestion, and muscle condition for her, and fewer sores and infections. Giving Ashley a permanent child's figure would leave her with what her father called "a body that more closely matched her stage of mental development."

AM and AD had to persuade the hospital ethics committee that this was a viable set of procedures. Eventually, the committee decided it was the right thing to do. In 2004, Seattle Children's Hospital doctors performed a hysterectomy and a bilateral mastectomy on Ashley, who was then six and a half. While Ashley's abdomen was opened for the hysterectomy, they also removed her appendix, anticipating that she would not be able to communicate the symptoms of appendicitis should she ever develop it. Ashley's adult height is four feet five inches, her weight is sixty-three pounds, and she will never menstruate, grow breasts, or have the breast cancer that runs in her family. "It has been successful in every expected way," her parents wrote.

AD encouraged Ashley's doctors to publish the protocol, which appeared in October of that year in the *Archives of Pediatrics & Adolescent Medicine*. A firestorm ensued. Arthur Caplan, of the University of Pennsylvania Center for Bioethics, characterized it as "a pharmacological solution for a social failure—the fact that American society does not do what it should to help severely disabled children and their families."

He suggested that with better support services, Ashley's parents wouldn't have been driven to their radical act. Feminist and disability activists protested at the American Medical Association's headquarters, asking them to issue an official condemnation. One blogger wrote, "If 'Ashley' were a 'normal' child and the parents decided to have her surgically mutilated, the parents would be thrown in prison where they rightly belong. The 'doctors' involved in this case should have their licenses revoked." FRIDA (Feminist Response in Disability Activism) wrote that they were "not surprised that the initial recipient of the 'Ashley Treatment' was a little girl, given that girls, and girls with disabilities in particular, are perceived as easier subjects for mutilation and desexualization." The *Toronto Star* complained about "designer cripples."

Parents of other disabled children joined the fray. Julia Epstein, communications director for the Disability Rights Education and Defense Fund and the mother of a disabled child, called the term *pillow angel* "terminally infantilizing." Another wrote, "My son is eleven, doesn't walk, doesn't talk, etc., etc. He's not going to get easier to carry. And still, I don't understand removing healthy tissue and functioning organs." Yet another parent wrote, "Caring for a five feet something, 110-plus pound adult with physical disabilities is no walk in the park. I've got the trashed lumbar discs to prove that. But I am truly just sick to my stomach to imagine that it's acceptable medical practice to surgically stunt a child's growth. Using their logic, why not just perform quadruple amputations? I mean, really, she's not going to use her arms and legs." These comments about growth attenuation echo in some way attitudes toward limb-lengthening for people with dwarfism.

The backlash shocked the hospital administrators, as it did AD and AM. The debate has gone on ever since, with many commentators opining that the whole question is beyond the scope of medical ethics. In late 2010, the Seattle Growth Attenuation and Ethics Working Group issued new guidelines based on an uneasy compromise: "Growth attenuation can be an ethically acceptable decision because the benefits and risks are similar to those associated with other decisions that parents make for their profoundly disabled children and about which reasonable people disagree. But clinicians and institutions should not provide growth attenuation simply because parents request it. It is important to have safeguards in place, such as eligibility criteria, a thorough decision-making process, and the involvement of ethics consultants or committees."

Writing in the *Hastings Center Report*, one member of the Working Group complained of the assault on the Ashley treatment, saying, "This remarkable intrusion into private medical decisions lacks any plausible claim of harm to third parties other than emotional distress on becoming aware that one's moral or political views are not shared by everyone. By this criterion, parents seeking cochlear implants for a deaf child, surgical correction of club feet or scoliosis, or a do-not-resuscitate order for a terminally ill child should be reminded that their decisions may be offensive to others." But in the same issue, another author argued, "If growth attenuation should not be done on children without these impairments, then it should not be done on any children. To do otherwise amounts to discrimination."

The moral questions enmeshed in cases such as Ashley's

have become steadily more complex in the last fifty years. It's a problem to cure someone's identity by making it go away, and it's a problem to neglect medical or social trouble that could be treated. AD set up a webpage to tell his side of the story; it has since had nearly three million hits, and at the time we spoke, AD told me he spent about ten hours a week blogging. Describing the protesters as a loud minority, he said that about 95 percent of the e-mail he and AM received was supportive. An MSNBC survey with more than seven thousand respondents showed 59 percent in support of the treatment. "More than 1,100 caregivers and family members with direct experience with pillow angels took the time to e-mail us with their support," Ashley's parents wrote. "If parents of children like Ashley believe that this treatment will improve their children's quality of life, then they should be diligent and tenacious in providing it for them." In the wake of the controversy, however, the procedure is unavailable.

One of Ashley's doctors said, "The argument that a beneficial treatment should not be used because it might be misused is itself a slippery slope. If we did not use available therapies because they could be misused, we would be practicing very little medicine." Writing in the *New York Times,* the Princeton ethicist Peter Singer said, "What matters in Ashley's life is that she should not suffer, and that she should be able to enjoy whatever she is capable of enjoying. Beyond that, she is precious not so much for what she is, but because her parents and siblings love her and care about her. Lofty talk about human dignity should not stand in the way of children like her getting the treatment that is best both for them and their families."

My conversations with AD made it clear to me that he loved Ashley, and that he believed fervently in the Ashley treatment. While writing this book, I met family after family who didn't know what to do as their children grew up and became too big to handle. Disability activists often referred to Ashley's loss of dignity, but having seen a number of similarly disabled people lifted up in pulleys with chains to be removed from bed, put in metal standers to preserve muscle tone, conveyed on rope systems into showers, I cannot see much dignity there. Arthur Caplan and others referred to the need for better social supports for families of people with disabilities, but AD and AM undertook the treatment not because they didn't have resources to get ropes and pulleys and even nurses, but because they felt a different intimacy in carrying their child themselves. Most human beings—children or adults, physically impaired or able-bodied—prefer human touch to mechanical support. Whether that intimacy warrants surgical intervention is open to discussion, but to discount the intimacy and say all that is needed is more access to assistive devices is to miss the point.

Some activists said that the procedure was not for Ashley's benefit but to make her parents' lives less stressful. These things cannot be separated. If the lives of Ashley's parents are made easier, then they will be able to devote more calm and positive attention to her, and her life will be better. If she is in less pain, her parents' lives will be improved. They are yin and yang, those lives, and far more important than the choice to undertake a procedure is that AD and AM have not separated from Ashley, nor indicated any wish to do so. Ashley likes rides in the car, and the sound of voices; she likes to be lifted and held; and this treatment appears to mean that she can have many years of these experiences instead of going to a group home. Parental care, which so often outclasses other forms of care, will also probably increase her longevity.

Activists are outraged at the things Ashley has lost: being tall, being sexually mature. These attainments are all part of the natural life cycle, but they are not exalted simply because they happen to most people. It's a subtle moral calculus to weigh out what is lost and what is gained by growth attenuation and hysterectomy. No one has said that the Ashley treatment is appropriate for people with significant cognition.

The calculus is very much complicated, however, by stories such as Anne McDonald's. She, too, was a pillow angel, permanently unable to walk, talk, feed, or care for herself; she remained small because she was malnourished in the Australian hospital where she was placed in the 1960s. "Like Ashley, I have experienced growth attenuation. I may be the only person on Earth who can say, 'Been there. Done that. Didn't like it. Preferred to grow,'" she wrote in a column for the *Seattle Post-Intelligencer*. "My life changed when I was offered a means of communication. At the age of sixteen, I was taught to spell by pointing to letters on an alphabet board. Two years later, I used spelling to instruct the lawyers who fought the habeas corpus action that enabled me to leave the institution in which I'd lived for fourteen years." Anne McDonald eventually graduated from a university with majors in philosophy of science and fine arts. She traveled around the world. "Ashley's condemned to be a Peter Pan and never grow, but it's not too late for her to learn to communicate," McDonald continued. "It's profoundly unethical to leave her on that pillow without making every effort to give her a voice of her own."

McDonald's story and writing point to the mysteriousness of people who cannot express themselves. Nonetheless, her growth attenuation was caused by horrible neglect in the institution where her parents had abandoned her, while Ashley's was brought about by parents who love her, to keep her with them. McDonald's intelligence had no chance to emerge; Ashley's has been given every encouragement. "I hope she does not understand what has happened to her; but I'm afraid she probably does," McDonald wrote. AD is mistaken in suggesting that Ashley is definitively incapable of mental development; the plasticity of even the most basic parts of the brain means that most people develop with the simple passage of time.

Higher-functioning disabled people of necessity speak for lower-functioning disabled people, and the insights of higher-functioning disabled people are precious; their situation is, after all, closer to that of low-functioning disabled people than is that of the general population. A higher-functioning person who used to be lower-functioning—such as Anne McDonald— has particular authority. Nonetheless, claims to common cause are often muddied by projection. McDonald seems to be retelling her own history rather than responding to Ashley's. Ashley is essentially unknowable both to her parents and to the vocal advocates who believe they have spoken on her behalf. Disability rights advocates complain of a world that refuses to accommodate their reality, but AD makes a similar complaint: that a tyrannical group of empowered people prevents accommodation of an individual and her specific needs.

"A collective agenda/ideology is being shoved down the

throat of all individuals with disabilities, whether it serves them as individuals or not," AD wrote. "This is disturbing in a society that believes strongly in the well-being of children and in individual rights. We feel the benefits to Ashley on a daily basis. We care about how this might help other kids in her situation. A lot of the criticism came from people who themselves have disabilities and was based on their feeling about how inappropriate the treatment would be for them. Clearly Ashley is in a vastly different category of disability than someone who is able to blog and write e-mails and make decisions for themselves. A chasm separates the two, not a slippery slope like some fear or claim. Newtonian physics works well in most cases, but not in extreme cases. As Einstein pointed out, it fails at high speeds. Relativity explains that very well. So, this ideology of the disability community works well. We support it. In this extreme case, however, it fails miserably."

Our understanding of brain science is so advanced and yet so primitive. We still have much to learn about how areas of the brain change their function when they have to, and also about the possibility of growing new neurons. The nature of anyone's silence is always a matter of speculation. We make mistakes both in doing too much and in doing too little. Norman Kunc, who was born with cerebral palsy and is now a consultant and speaker on disability issues, has described how much of a gap there can be between the caring intention and problematic consequences of treatment for people with disabilities. He characterized his own early experiences with physiotherapy as akin to rape. "From the age of three until the age of twelve, three times a week," he said, "women who were older than I was, who were more powerful than I was, who had more authority than I had, brought me into their room, their space, their turf. They took off some of my clothes. They invaded my personal space. They gripped me and touched me, manipulating my body in ways that were painful. I didn't know I had any other choice than to go along with it. To me it's a form of sexual assault even though it was completely asexual. It's the power and domination that is part of the abuse. Obviously the therapist does not have the same intent as a rapist, but there is a difference between caring and competence. Many human service professionals assume that, because they care for people, their actions are inevitably competent. As soon as you challenge the competence of their actions, you're seen as questioning their caring for the person."

Kunc argues that doing something with love does not necessarily make it good. Even outside the world of disability, we all perpetrate and are subject to loving yet damaging acts within our families. That damage is likely to be greater and more frequent with horizontal identities because the good intentions are less informed. Because I am gay, my parents hurt me in ways they wouldn't have if I'd been like them—not because they wanted to hurt me, but because they lacked sufficient insight into what it was like to be gay. Their essentially good intentions, though, are crucial to my adult identity. I can't be sure whether AD harmed his daughter or helped her, but I believe that he acted in good faith. Parents are broken and full of error. Intention does not obliterate that error, but I think, contrary to Kunc, that it does at least mitigate it. Being hurt by those you love is awful, but it's less awful if you know they meant to help.

The word *genocide* gets thrown around a lot in identity movements. Deaf people speak of a genocide because so many deaf children receive cochlear implants; people with Down syndrome and their families speak of a genocide achieved through selective termination of pregnancies. Few people, however, would propose that people who are deaf or who have DS should be killed or left to die. Though some parents murder their autistic children, the practice is commonly held to be shocking and wrong. In cases of multiple severe disability, however, far more people feel comfortable with such a solution. This is in part because these children often live only by way of extreme medical intervention; they are a modern invention, and the idea of letting them die can be held up as "letting nature take its course."

In *Rethinking Life and Death*, Peter Singer quotes an Australian pediatrician, Frank Shann, who described two children in his care. One had had massive bleeding in his brain and therefore had no cerebral cortex; he was capable only of automatic function. In the next bed was a child who was healthy except for a damaged heart, and who would die without a heart transplant. The vegetative boy was a blood-type match, and his heart could have saved the other child, but this would have required that his organs be harvested before he was legally dead. Since this was impossible, both children died within weeks. Shann said, "If the cortex of the brain is dead, the person is dead. I suggest it should be legal to use the organs from the body of the dead person for transplantation." Singer does not agree that obliteration of the cortex is equivalent to death, but he nonetheless feels that the death of both children was a tragic waste. Disability advocates would say it is as unthinkable to kill a severely disabled child to save a nondisabled child as it would be to kill one nondisabled child to save another. Dead people clearly have fewer rights than living people, and Shann held that the first child in his scenario was exempt from the rights of the living. There may be science in this, but it feels weird to describe as dead someone who is breathing, sneezing, yawning, even producing some form of reflex smile.

Peter Singer maintains that what is in question is *personhood*. He proposes that not all persons are human beings; animals of higher awareness are also persons. He likewise opines that not all human beings are persons. In *Practical Ethics* he wrote, "Killing a disabled infant is not morally equivalent to killing a person. Very often it is not wrong at all." Elsewhere he has contended, "If we compare a severely defective human infant with a nonhuman animal, a dog or a pig, for example, we will often find the nonhuman to have superior capacities, both actual and potential, for rationality, self-consciousness, communication, and anything else that can plausibly be considered morally significant." Singer in effect reverses "I think, therefore I am" and says that those who do not think do not exist.

Most people agree that one cannot kill disabled children against their parents' will, but whether they can be kept alive against their parents' will is a tougher question. In 1991, Karla Miller, five months pregnant, went into labor and was rushed to her local hospital in Houston. Doctors told her she was having a "tragic miscarriage" and asked whether she and her husband preferred to let nature follow its course, or to have an experimental procedure that would probably leave the child alive but severely brain-damaged. The couple prayed and decided to forgo heroic measures. The hospital administration then informed them that hospital policy was to resuscitate all babies born over five hundred grams, and that if they did not want the baby saved, they should leave the hospital immediately. As Karla was hemorrhaging and in danger of bleeding to death, they chose to stay there. Though in many states Karla could have aborted a fetus at this stage of development, she did not have the right to refuse life support once the child had come out of her. When the baby arrived at 630 grams (just 1.4 pounds), medical personnel inserted a tube into the newborn's throat to give oxygen to her undeveloped lungs. She is blind and has never walked or talked.

The Millers took care of her, but they brought a wrongful-life case against the hospital, claiming that the hospital had acted against their wishes and should therefore provide a financial settlement to finance the child's permanent care. A court awarded the Millers $43 million in damages and expenses, but that decision was overturned on appeal. Official policy had kept their child from dying; official policy said it was their problem to deal with her needs for the rest of their lives.

The Miller case prompted enormous protest and a coalition of seventeen disability organizations filed an amicus (friend of the court) brief that stated, "Most adults with disabilities, including those who have had a disability since birth, choose life and have quality in their lives. Most parents of children with disabilities value and believe their children's lives have quality." The disability-focused *Inclusion Daily Express* wrote, "Many disability rights advocates believe that the Millers' suit promotes infanticide—the murder of babies—particularly of those with disabilities." Among people outside the disability rights community, opinions were less decisive. George Annas, a health-law and bioethics expert at Boston University, said, "The truth is, no one really knows what's best for kids like this, and there should be no hard-and-fast rule."

For legal purposes, the referent was a 1978 decision made in New York, in which the judge wrote, "Whether it is better never to have been born at all than to have been born with even gross deficiencies is a mystery more properly to be left to the philosophers and the theologians. Surely the law can assert no competence to resolve the issue, particularly in view of the very nearly uniform high value which the law and mankind has placed on human life, rather than its absence. The implications of any such proposition are staggering."

In Peter Singer's definition, Ashley, Jamie, Sam, and others like them are not persons. Nonetheless, the parents I met who lived with and cared for such children often described a great deal of personhood in them. It's impossible to establish in any given case in what measure such personhood is observed and in what measure imagined or projected. Singer does not argue that parents who believe in the personhood of their children have to act toward them as they would toward nonpersons, but he opens the moral framework for someone to think that these children are expendable. I am not sure that, as activists claim, this will lead us into Hitlerian proposals to eliminate a much broader range of the disabled, but neither am I sure that Singer's arguments are as rational as he makes them out to be. His fallacy is his assumption, for himself and for science, of omniscience.

The Australian disability advocate Chris Borthwick has written that for ethicists pondering such a question, "The identification of a class of people who are 'humans' but not human, if any such could be found, would be central." Borthwick says that we accept someone's state as vegetative when that person fails to persuade a doctor that he is conscious—in other words, what is in question is not consciousness, but the legible manifestation of consciousness. Borthwick views consciousness as largely unknowable. He points to a study published in *Archives of Neurology* in which nearly two-thirds of a group of eighty-four people judged to be "in a vegetative state" had "recovered awareness" within three years. "One must ask," he writes, "in the light of the evidence, why it is that reasonable, moral, and ethical writers can extract these qualities of permanence and certainty from data that is, to put the matter no more strongly, clearly capable of other interpretations." Borthwick maintains that even if some human beings are nonpersons, we cannot identify them definitively. It's hard not to think of Anne McDonald, who seemed to many professionals to be a nonperson, and who ultimately emerged into obvious personhood. The same rationale that makes us deplore the death penalty in cases where the evidence is not entirely conclusive should give us pause in these supposedly clear-cut disability cases.

Contemplating Singer and Borthwick, I was reminded of the work on Deaf culture that shows how Sign emerges unbidden when there are two people to communicate in it, but lies dormant in children isolated from others who might employ it. I recalled the outrage one man I interviewed expressed at the suggestion that his brother's schizophrenia could be defined in chemical rather than in spiritual and personal terms. I dislike both the conceited science behind Singer's position and the mawkish sentimentality of those who insist that we treat all human life equivalently, always. Of course, practical answers must be sought, but to think of those answers as better than approximate is foolishness. We assign personhood to one another, and we assign it to or withhold it from these disabled children. It is not discovered so much as it is introduced. The psychoanalyst Maggie Robbins once said, "Consciousness is not a noun; it's a verb. Trying to pin it down like a fixed object is a recipe for disaster."

The daughters of the ant queen take care of their mother and siblings; in some bird species, older fledglings help parents raise younger chicks; but overall, little reciprocity is attached to nonhuman parenting. Human parenting is an ultimately two-sided lifetime relationship rather than a one-sided temporary one. Even before the ultimate turnaround in which children in their prime care for incapacitated elderly parents, the manifestations of reciprocity may determine the parents' social status and self-regard. For the parents of MSD children, early reciprocity may be infrequent and ultimate reciprocity impossible.

But the pleasure of caring for children does not lie only in reciprocity. The French writer Annie Leclerc has spoken of "the profound taste we have for children," and the feminist psychologist Daphne de Marneffe has said that a mother's skill in responding to her child contributes "not only to her recognition of her child, but to her own sense of pleasure, effectiveness, and self-expression as well." Psychoanalysis has long proposed that mothers' early caretaking is a form of self-care.

This commonality of interest seems to have strengthened most of the parents I interviewed for this chapter, but not all parents can achieve it. Some disability activists, abortion opponents, and religious fundamentalists have argued that those who are unwilling to parent disabled children shouldn't allow themselves to become pregnant in the first place. The reality, however, is that most people embark on parenthood in optimism, and even those who soberly consider a worst-case scenario cannot adequately predict their response to such a situation until they are in it.

The British opera director Julia Hollander has written about her experience of giving up a disabled child to foster care. "Severe epileptic fits should have been killing her," Julia said. "That was nature's way of destroying this person. But, no. There was a drug that could stop the spasms. It's a very hard thing to want your child to die. To some degree, my anger is about the invention of these children. Because when I was born, they didn't survive. These Imogens are on the increase as the sophistication and tyranny of intervention escalate."

Julia continues to see Imogen from time to time. The day of our last interview, she explained, "Yesterday, I pushed Imogen along the street. It's a nightmare getting six blocks with a wheelchair. All the large cars are parked on the pavement, so you go along two cars' worth, where there's a big enough gap, and then you go onto the road, with the oncoming traffic. By the time you get six blocks, you're a serious martyr.

Every time she's around, I experiment with being the mother of the disabled child. People walking along the pavement get out of the way and smile at you, that smile that goes, 'You poor thing, I'm glad I'm not you!' I can imagine polishing my halo at the end of every day. At the very same time, I can imagine being the most furious person in the world."

Ambivalence exists in all human relationships, including parent-child. Anna Freud maintained that a mother could never satisfy her infant's needs because those are infinite, but that eventually child and mother outgrow that dependence. Children with MSD have permanent needs far beyond that infinity. In *Torn in Two*, the British psychoanalyst Rozsika Parker complains that in our open, modern society, the extent of maternal ambivalence is a dark secret. Most mothers treat their occasional wish to be rid of their children as if it were the equivalent of murder itself. Parker proposes that mothering requires two impulses—the impulse to hold on, and the impulse to push away. To be a successful mother you must nurture and love your child, but cannot smother and cling to your child.

The dark portion of maternal ambivalence toward typical children is crucial to the child's ability to grow up and separate from his or her parents. But severely disabled children who will never become independent will not benefit from their parents' negative feelings, and so their situation demands an impossible state of emotional purity. Asking the parents of severely disabled children to feel less negative emotion than the parents of healthy children is ludicrous. My experience of these parents was that they all felt both love and despair. You cannot decide whether to be ambivalent. All you can decide is what to do with your ambivalence. Most of these parents have chosen to act on one side of the ambivalence they feel. Others choose to act on the other side and give up their children. I am not persuaded that the ambivalence itself is so different from one of these families to the next. I am enough of a creature of my times to admire most the parents who kept their children and made brave sacrifices for them. I nonetheless esteem those who made the other decision for being honest with themselves, and for making what all those other families did look like a choice.

Prodigies

BEING GIFTED AND BEING DISABLED ARE surprisingly similar: isolating, mystifying, petrifying. Dazzling brilliance is an abnormality, as horizontal an identity as any in this study. Prodigiousness and genius are as little understood as autism. Like parents of children who are severely challenged, parents of exceptionally talented individuals are custodians of children beyond their comprehension.

A *prodigy* is able to function at an advanced adult level in some domain before the age of twelve. I've used the word to include anyone who develops a profound innate gift at an early age, even if he does so more gradually or less publicly than classic prodigies. *Prodigy* derives from the Latin *prodigium*, a monster that violates the natural order. These people have differences so evident as to resemble a birth defect. The designation *prodigy* usually reflects timing, while *genius* reflects the ability to add something of value to human consciousness. Many people have genius without showing early development. Others have prodigiousness without brilliance. But there is considerable overlap.

A child with incredible abilities may alter his or her family as much as a child with schizophrenia or disability would. Like a disability, prodigiousness forces parents to redesign their lives around the special needs of their child. Experts must be called in and, often, they seem to challenge the parents' absolute authority. A child's prodigiousness requires his parents to seek out a new community of people with similar experience; they must decide whether to place their child with, for example, people who share their child's interests but who don't want to make friends with a six-year-old, or with other six-year-olds who will have no idea what their child is talking about. The health and happiness of families of prodigies do not surpass those of others in this book.

Prodigiousness manifests most often in athletics, mathematics, chess, and music; I have focused on musical prodigies because my ability to understand music exceeds my comprehension of sports, math, or chess. A musical prodigy's development hinges on parental support; without it, the child would never gain access to an instrument or the training that even the most devout genius requires.

There is no clear line between supporting and pressuring a child. You can damage prodigies by nurturing their talent at the expense of personal growth, or by cultivating general development at the expense of the special skill that might have given them the deepest fulfillment. You can make them feel that your love is contingent on their dazzling success, or that you don't care about their talent. If society's expectations for most children with profound differences are too low, expectations for prodigies are often perilously high.

Just as deaf children will begin to communicate with physical gestures, musical prodigies may use musical tones to convey information from the outset. For them, music is speech.

It is said that Handel sang before he talked. The pianist Arthur Rubinstein would sing a mazurka when he wanted cake. As with spoken and signed language, there must be not only a means to express, but also people to receive, respond, and encourage, which is why parental involvement is crucial.

That music is a first language does not guarantee brilliant use of that language, however, any more than American children's fluency in English makes them all poets.

Sue and Joe Petersen always put their son Drew's personal needs before his talent, but the two often seemed to overlap. Drew didn't speak until he was three and a half, but Sue never believed he was slow. When he was eighteen months old, she was reading to him and skipped a word, whereupon Drew reached over and pointed to the missing word on the page. Drew already cared about sound deeply. "Church bells would elicit a big response," Sue said. "Birdsong would stop him in his tracks."

Sue, who had learned piano as a child, taught Drew the basics on an old upright, and he became fascinated by sheet music. When he began formal lessons at five, his teacher said he could skip the first six months' worth of material. Within the year, Drew was performing at Carnegie Hall and was flown to Italy to perform in a youth festival where the other youths were a decade older than he. Sue said, "I thought it was delightful, but I also thought we shouldn't take it too seriously. He was just a little boy."

Sue was advised to seek out a teacher named Miyoko Lotto, who warned that she didn't have time to teach Drew, but would listen to him play and then refer him to someone else. When he finished playing, Lotto said, "I have time Tuesdays at four." Her enthusiasm was not entirely welcome. Sue said, "It was so extreme, and it gave me the creeps." Sue could not take Drew into Manhattan every week, but she enrolled him with a teacher in New Jersey whom Lotto recommended. Lotto e-mailed Sue every couple of weeks to ask how things were going. Every few months, she'd invite Drew to play for her. "It felt very casual, but in retrospect, it was regimented and purposeful," Sue said.

On his way to kindergarten one day, Drew asked his mother, "Can I just stay home so I can learn something?" Sue was at a loss. "He was reading textbooks this big, and they're in class holding up a blowup M," she said. Drew said, "At first, it felt lonely. Then you accept that, yes, you're different from everyone else, but people will be your friends anyway." Drew's parents moved him to a Montessori school, then to a private school. They bought him a new piano because he had announced, at seven, that their upright lacked dynamic contrast. By junior high, he was performing frequently and had taken up competitive swimming. When Drew was fourteen, Sue found a homeschool program created by Harvard; when I met Drew, he was sixteen and halfway to a Harvard bachelor's degree.

The pull of music is inescapable for Drew. He said, "I thought at Harvard I would find some subject that I was really interested in, maybe even more than music. I haven't, and I'm not sure I really want to." Since Lotto was at the Manhattan School of Music, Drew has pursued his musical education there. "He said, 'I don't want management and publicity now; I don't want a childhood in music; I want a life in music,'" Sue recalled. At sixteen, Drew still didn't want management. "You have to be able to fight back," he explained.

I asked Drew how he could express so much through music after so little life experience, and he said, "I can only express it through music, not through words. Maybe I can only experience it through music too." A year after I met him, Drew was selected for a master class with the Chinese pianist Lang Lang, then twenty-eight, and I went to watch them interact. Lang Lang, for whom speech is easy, coached six students. He said the least to Drew, and Drew the least to him, yet Drew's playing changed to incorporate Lang Lang's insights with a fluency none of the others could muster. Sue said, "His talent is a magnifying glass on what I need to do. To be honest, I have no way to know what I'm doing right or wrong except to ask him." Drew said to her, "You're always questioning. As much as I am a nonconformist, you're a questioner." She said, "Fortunately, your answers are very convincing."

The origin of genius has been a topic of philosophical debate for at least twenty-five hundred years. Plato believed that genius was bestowed by the gods. The early Christian philosopher Longinus proposed that it was something a person does—that the genius does not receive divinity, but creates it. John Locke (who, tellingly, had no children) thought that parents could stimulate genius. This idea from the Age of Reason, the period in which *genius* took on its current meaning, gave way to a Romantic image of mysterious, incomprehensible brilliance.

The question of how high IQ correlates to genius has been in debate ever since intelligence tests were used to categorize army recruits during World War I. Eugenicist Lewis M. Terman, who developed the tests, followed a group of about fifteen hundred children with very high IQs; seventy years later, his critics claimed, they had accomplished no more than their socioeconomic status would have predicted. One child Terman had excluded as not bright enough, William Shockley, had coinvented the transistor and won the Nobel Prize in Physics. Measurements of this kind were nonetheless championed by people who believed you could purify the race by ensuring that gifted people reproduce while "inferior" people were subject to forced sterilization. Hitler was well versed in these ideas.

The history of high intelligence is no less political than the history of intellectual disability or of mental illness. If genius springs from genetics, we must bow down to inborn superiority. If genius results from labor, then brilliant people deserve the applause and wealth they reap. The communist perspective is that everyone can be a genius if he will only work at it; the fascist perspective is that born geniuses are a different species from the rest of humanity.

Many people fall short of their potential through lack of discipline, but a visit to a coal mine demonstrates that hard work on its own neither constitutes genius nor guarantees riches.

Musical prodigies are sometimes compared to child actors, but child actors portray children; no one pays to watch a six-year-old playing Hamlet. Musical performance can be learned quickly because it is rule-driven, structured, and formal;

profundity comes later. Mozart was the archetypal prodigy, but if he hadn't lived past twenty-five, we'd know nothing of him as a composer.

Most people who receive rigorous early training do not become singular musicians. Veda Kaplinsky, who teaches at the prestigious Juilliard School and is perhaps the world's most highly esteemed piano teacher for younger students, explained, "Until the child reaches eighteen or nineteen, you don't know if he'll have the emotional capacity for expression." A mature childhood can be a recipe for an immature adulthood—a principle most publicly borne out by Michael Jackson.

It is best to accomplish something before becoming famous, because if the fame comes first, it often gets in the way of the accomplishment. The best music teachers see a child with remarkable skills rather than a set of skills inconveniently attached to a child. Many parents cannot see this crucial difference. Karen Monroe, a psychiatrist who works with prodigious children, said, "When you have a child whose gift is so overshadowing, it is easy for parents to be distracted and lose track of the child himself."

Van Cliburn was among the preeminent prodigies of the twentieth century. He catapulted to fame at twenty-three, when he won the Tchaikovsky Piano Competition in Moscow at the height of the Cold War and was welcomed home with a ticker-tape parade. His mother was his piano teacher, and when she was teaching him, she would say, "You know I'm not your mother now." Of his childhood, Cliburn said, "There were other things I would like to have done besides practicing the piano, but I knew my mother was right about what I should do."

Cliburn lived with his mother all her life. But he largely abandoned his career after the death of his father, who was also his manager, because he could not bear the pressure. He suffered from depression and alcoholism, becoming the figurehead of the Van Cliburn Piano Competition, which has become as prestigious as the one that he won.

In 1945, there were five piano competitions worldwide; there are now seven hundred and fifty. Robert Levin, a professor of music at Harvard, said, "The favored repertoire is music of such technical challenges that, as recently as thirty years ago, less than 1 percent of pianists were playing it. Now, about 80 percent are. It isn't an improvement. It reflects a purely gladiatorial, physical behavior. You should not tell a young student to learn the notes and then add the expression. You might as well tell a chef, 'First you cook the food, then you add the flavor.'"

Mikhail and Natalie Paremski held comfortable positions within the Soviet system: Mikhail with the Russian Atomic Agency, Natalie with the Physics Engineering Institute. Their daughter, Natasha, born in 1987, showed a precocious interest in the piano. "I was in the kitchen, and I thought, who is playing?" Natalie recalled. "Then I saw, it's the baby, picking out nursery songs. My husband said music was a terrible life; he begged me not to give her lessons." But she thought a few lessons could do no harm. Six months later, Natasha played a Chopin mazurka in a children's concert. "She decided, 'I'm going to be a pianist,' at four years old," Natalie said. "We didn't worry about music, because she was so good in math, physics, chemistry. She could have easily done something else if she ran out of talent for this."

When the Soviet Union collapsed, people with Soviet-era privilege were figures of suspicion. In 1993, Mikhail was brutally beaten on his way home from work late one night. A corporate recruiter had been pestering Mikhail for years to work in the United States, but the Paremskis didn't want to leave Russia. After the attack, Natalie changed her mind.

Mikhail went ahead; the family followed in 1995. Natasha entered fourth grade, where everyone else was two years older than she. Within a few months, she was speaking English without an accent and coming in first on every school test. Natalie persuaded the school to let Natasha do independent study so she could perform. Natasha said that her own impulse, not her parents, drove her success. "What did they do to make me practice?" she asked. "What did they do to make me eat or sleep?"

Natasha graduated with top honors from high school at fourteen and was offered a full scholarship by Mannes College for Music in New York. She signed with management, moved East, and began full-time study there. Natasha and her mother spoke by phone constantly. Her mother worried about the deficit of soul in New York. "There is no time for vision! People are just struggling to survive, like in Moscow," Natalie said—to which her daughter replied, "Vision is how I survive." Nonetheless, Natalie said, "That was my present to her: I gave her her own life."

At Mannes, Natasha rapidly emerged as a star. I met her when she was fifteen, and I first interviewed her when she was sixteen. A year later, in 2004, I went to her Carnegie Hall debut, for which she played Rachmaninoff's Piano Concerto no. 2. She's a beautiful young woman, with cascades of hair and a sylphlike figure, and she wore a sleeveless, black velvet dress, so her arms would feel free, and a pair of insanely high heels that she said gave her better leverage on the pedals. Her playing was as virile as her clothing was feminine, and the audience gave her an ovation. Her parents were not there. "They're too supportive to come," Natasha told me just before the concert. Natalie explained, "If I am there, I am so worried about every single note that I can't even sit still. It's not helpful to Natasha."

In 2005, Natasha was invited to perform a benefit concert for the Prince of Wales with Sting. "She made friends with Madonna," her mother said. "I didn't make friends with her," Natasha protested. "She told me, 'You classical musicians are too stuck-up. You really should think about wearing hot pants.'"

"When I play, I use my brain and I breathe and everything like that. But I'm not—" Natasha was at a rare loss for words. "Thinking of yourself," her mother finished. Natasha nodded. "That's why I worry," Natalie said, "because she loses weight, she forgets to eat because she is playing the piano."

Natasha shook her head. "The rest of life is so distracting."

Like so many other aberrations, musicality can be mapped physiologically. People with absolute pitch (about one in a thousand to one in ten thousand people) can name any note just by hearing it. They have an enlarged area in the auditory cortex of the brain, which sorts out sounds. Violinists have an enlargement of the area of the brain that controls movement of the left hand. The parts of the brain that control motor coordination and language are greater in volume or metabolism among many musicians, suggesting that music is both athletic and linguistic. It is unclear, however, whether these characteristics are the basis of musical ability, or the result of repetitive practice.

Throughout much of history, prodigies were thought to be possessed; Aristotle believed that there could be no genius without madness. The great nineteenth-century violinist Paganini was accused of putting himself in the hands of the devil. Recent neuroscience demonstrates that the processes of creativity and psychosis map similarly in the brain. A continuum runs between the two conditions; there is no sharp line.

Prodigies often have a mix of abilities and challenges including dyslexia, delayed language acquisition, and asthma. These can be severe. One family told me that their son could identify more than fifty pieces of music when he was two. He would call out, "Mahler Fifth!" or "Brahms Quintet!" At five, the boy was diagnosed with borderline autism. Their pediatrician's instruction was to break the obsession by taking away music completely, which they did. The autism symptoms abated, but he lost his affinity for music. Some researchers claim that musical predisposition is a function of an autistic-type hypersensitivity to sound. Music may be the organizing defense of such children against the clatter that assaults them. A number of the musicians described in this chapter likely meet clinical criteria for autism-spectrum disorders.

The association between genius and madness makes many parents wary of prodigious children. Anyone who has worked with prodigies has seen the wreckage that can ensue when someone has intellectual, emotional, and physical ages that do not align. It is no easier to have an adultlike mind in a child's body than to have a childlike mind in a mature body. Julliard's Veda

Kaplinsky said, "Genius is an abnormality, and abnormalities do not come one at a time. Many gifted kids have ADD or OCD or Asperger's. When the parents are confronted with two sides of a kid, they're so quick to acknowledge the positive, the talented, the exceptional; they are in denial over everything else."

Even those without a sideline diagnosis need to find a way to lessen the loneliness of having their primary emotional relationship with an object. The psychiatrist Karen Monroe explained, "If you're spending five hours a day practicing, and the other kids are out playing baseball, you're not doing the same things. Even if you love it and can't imagine yourself doing anything else, that doesn't mean you don't feel lonely."

Suicide is an ever-present risk. Brandenn Bremmer had prodigious musical abilities, finished high school at ten, and told an interviewer flatly, "America is a society that demands perfection." When he was fourteen, his parents left the house to buy groceries and returned to find he had shot himself in the head, leaving no note. "He was born an adult," his mother said. "We just watched his body grow bigger."

When these suicides occur, parents tend to get blamed— and some do push their children to the breaking point. The presence of the stage mother, or the demanding father who is never satisfied, runs through the professional literature. Some parents are focused on helping their kids, and others, on helping themselves; many don't recognize a gap between these objectives. Robert Sirota, president of the Manhattan School of Music, said, "Mothers had their little boys castrated in Renaissance Italy to preserve their high, clear voices and give them a music career, and the psychological mutilation of today is equally brutal." The violinist Jascha Heifetz once described prodigiousness as being "a disease which is generally fatal," and one that he "was among the few to have the good fortune to survive."

The crudest and most straightforward form of exploitation is financial. In "The Awakening," Isaac Babel describes the subculture of prodigies in prewar Russia, where they represented a possible path out of poverty for their families. "When a boy turned four or five, his mother took the tiny, frail creature to Mr. Zagursky. Zagursky ran a factory that churned out child prodigies, a factory of Jewish dwarfs in lace collars and patent leather shoes." The prodigy pianist Ruth Slenczynska wrote in *Forbidden Childhood* of the beatings she endured from her father: "Every time I made a mistake, he leaned over and, very methodically, without a word, slapped me across the face." Her 1931 debut, when she was four, met rave reviews. One day, she overheard her father say, "I teach Ruth to play Beethoven because it brings in the dollars." She crumpled; when she gave up piano, "I was sixteen, felt fifty, and looked twelve." Her father threw her out; his parting words were, "You lousy little bitch! You'll never play two notes again without me."

Cruel parental control is hardly a recent invention. Mozart's childhood mantra was, "Next to God comes Papa." Paganini said of his father, "If he didn't think I was industrious enough, he compelled me to redouble my efforts by making me go without food."

Ken Noda's mother saw an ad for piano lessons in the *Village Voice*, and enrolled Ken when he was five. Within two years, his teacher had suggested that he audition for Juilliard's pre-college division. Ken's mother had wanted to be a dancer, but she came from a prominent political family in Tokyo, and her father had forbidden it. She hoped to give her son the artistic opportunity she had been denied. "Suddenly my mother was sitting next to me, watching me practice, making sure I did two hours, punishing me when I made mistakes," Ken recalled. "I loved music, but I started to actually loathe the piano."

As his parents' marriage disintegrated, his practice sessions became more grueling. "Violent yelling," Ken said. "It was nightmarish. You should have to pass a bar exam to qualify as a parent for talented children. I tried desperately to believe she was not the prototype of a stage mother, because she always used to tell everyone else she wasn't, but she was. She was very, very loving when I did well, and when I didn't do well, she was horrific." Meanwhile, Ken's father effectively abandoned him. "He often expressed contempt for what I was doing. It wasn't really for me; it was contempt for her. Since I didn't have time for friends, and since I needed someone to love me, I kept working so she'd love me, at least sometimes. You see, I was born with two umbilical cords: the physical one that everyone is born with, and another that was made of music."

What Ken refers to as his "first career" began when he was sixteen. After an auspicious 1979 debut concert, with Daniel Barenboim conducting, he was signed by Columbia Artists Management. Barenboim said to Ken's mother, "There's so much emotion, and so much going on inside him, but physically, he's so tense, so almost contorted when he plays, and I'm afraid he's going to hurt himself." Ken became Barenboim's pupil. Technical proficiency was hard for him, but he played with poignant insight. When Ken was eighteen, his mother left his father for an Italian painter. "That's when suddenly every-thing clicked, and I realized she herself was trapped, and that I had become her outlet."

At twenty-one he came out of the closet, publicly declaring that he was gay, which was necessary for both his mental health and his music. "Young people like romance stories and war stories and good-and-evil stories and old movies because their emotional life mostly is and should be fantasy, and they put that fantasized emotion into their playing, and it is very convincing. But as you grow older, fantasy emotion loses its freshness," he said. "For some time, I was able to draw on this fantasy life of what loss would mean, what a failed romance would mean, what death might mean, what sexual ecstasy might mean. I had an amazing capacity for imagining these feelings, and that's part of what talent is. But it dries up, in everyone. That's why so many prodigies have midlife crises in their late teens or early twenties. If our imagination is not replenished with experi-ence, the ability to reproduce these feelings in one's playing gradually diminishes."

Ken had a run of concerts with formidable conductors; management had him scheduled years in advance. When he was twenty-seven, he had a crisis that brought him to the brink of suicide. "I was suffocating. My playing began to be care-ful, a little bit anal-retentive. I never miss notes; I've always been a very clean player, but the cleanness became almost hypochondriacal. I felt unable to express anything." He walked into the office of the head of Columbia Artists Management and announced that he was quitting. His manager said, "But you have concerts booked for the next five years." Ken said, "I want to cancel my whole life." Fifteen years later, he told me, "It was the single most thrilling experience I've ever had."

Ken had saved enough money to live comfortably for some time without working. "So I just walked around New York for a year. I sat in parks; I went to museums; I went to libraries, all these things I had never been able to do. People would ask, 'Where are you playing next?' and I'd say, 'Nowhere.' That was the best year of my life, because my identity and self-worth had absolutely nothing to do with my talent."

Then James Levine, artistic director of the Metropolitan Opera, offered Ken a job as his deputy. Ken coaches the singers; while Levine is somewhat socially disconnected, Ken's sparkle and warmth draw out the performers. "The musical life I'm having now is a dream," he said. "I love the theater. I love singers. I love the Met." He performs occasionally, usually as an accompanist, taking the non-spotlit position he prefers. "I do it to prove to myself that I didn't stop because of stage fright," he said.

"With middle age, I started yearning for life—life that I'd always been reading about in books, or seeing in movies, or witnessing in other people's homes," he said. He began his first serious relationship at forty-seven. "I'd had many love affairs, and they'd all been somewhat theatrical, shooting-star kind of romances," he said. "When I finally started to live, I had this incredible fear that my ability to produce art would dissipate." Periodically, this fear would spur him to withdraw. "The first time I broke up with Wayne, he was heartbroken," he recalled about his first serious relationship. "The second time, after three weeks, he just came back to find me." Ken described, as well, a social incompetence that was the legacy of his isolation. In the middle of a Gay Pride party, he announced that he had to go practice at the Met. Wayne said, "You're my partner. You can't just leave. You can't just run back to the Met and hide in a practice room." Ken said to me, "I never played with other children, so why at forty-seven would I go out and play with my partner?" Soon thereafter, Ken donated his piano and sheet music to charity. "It's a wonderfully simple feeling to come home and not have a piano."

After a period of estrangement, Ken has a cordial relationship with his father; Ken's mother has expressed enormous regret over his childhood, and they, too, have reconciled. "I can have overwhelming feelings of love for her," he said. "I don't hate her, ever. But the connection is so powerful, and I have to fight to have another focus in life." Then he paused. "The drive and focus that I have came from the way my mother drove me. That took me very far. I will never forgive her for my first life in music, which I hated, but I will never be able to thank her enough for my second life in music, which I love."

Developing a life in music takes tremendous will. Deciding *not* to develop a life in music after a prodigious beginning also takes will. Veda Kaplinsky said, "By the time they become adults, it's very difficult for them to differentiate the profession from themselves. They can't imagine themselves doing anything else, even if they really don't want to be musicians." Some wonderful musicians simply do not want the performer's life.

On the other hand, some who love applause confuse that fervor with a passion for music. "Unfortunately," Veda Kaplinsky said, "they're going to be miserable. Because most of the time, it's you and your music, not you and your audience." The critic Justin Davidson said, "When you're fourteen, you do it because it's expected of you, you're good at it, and you're getting rewards. By the time you're seventeen or eighteen, if that's still why you're doing it, there's a good chance you're going to crash. If music is about expression, you have to be expressing yourself by that point, not somebody else."

Still more problems arise in dealing with the adults in one's life. Sometimes the adults a prodigy wants to please compete with one another. Like deaf children who learn Sign at school, many musicians share with teachers a language that their parents cannot master. The relationship between teacher and student often triangulates the parent-child bond. It can be like a messy divorce, with the teacher and the parents giving different instructions and the child caught in the middle. One teacher told me about a student so anxious about the divergence between her mother's suggestions and the teacher's that she abandoned a promising career and switched to mathematics.

While a taste for wealth and fame can propel parents of prodigies into exploitation, most are not evil or greedy; they are just not good at separating their wishes from their children's. If you dream of having a genius for a child, you will spot brilliance in your child, and if you believe that fame would have soothed all your own unhappiness, you will see a longing for celebrity in your son's or daughter's face. While many performers are self-involved, it is often the parents of prodigies who most obviously invest their own hopes, ambitions, and identities in what their children do rather than who their children are. The abuse reflects a tragic misunderstanding of where one human being ends and another begins. Absolute power corrupts absolutely, and no power is more absolute than parenthood. The children of these parents, despite being the subjects of obsessive attention, suffer from not being seen. Their sorrow is organized not so much around the rigor of practicing as around invisibility. Accomplishment requires giving up the pleasures of the present moment for triumphs in the future, and that is an impulse that must be learned. Left to their own devices, children do not become world-class instrumentalists before they turn ten.

When I spoke to Marion Price to set up our interview, I invited her to bring her violinist daughter, Solanda, for dinner, but she said, "We have a family of fussy eaters, so we'll eat before we come." The Prices arrived wearing coats, and I offered to hang them up. Marion, speaking for her husband and daughter, said, "That won't be necessary," and they sat through the interview holding their outerwear. I offered them something to drink, but Marion said, "We are so used to our schedule, and it's not time for a drink right now." In three hours, none of them had a sip of water. I had put out homemade cookies, and Solanda kept glancing at them; every time she did, Marion shot her a look. When I asked Solanda a question, her mother constantly jumped in to answer; when Solanda did reply, she did so with an anxious glance at her mother, as though worried whether she'd delivered the right response.

The Prices live around their musical talent. Sondra, ten years older than Solanda, is a pianist; Vikram, four years older than Solanda, is a cellist. When Solanda was five, her parents had all three children in a children's orchestra; they now perform as a trio. Marion is African-American; Solanda's father, Ravi, is Indian, and he writes and plays smooth jazz. "We're hearing the word *gifted*, we're hearing the word *musical*," Marion said. "We see three children who, when they practice together, it seems like one person."

Solanda started piano lessons at four. "But she fell in love with the musician Itzhak Perlman and the violin. Solanda got that violin when she was almost five," Marion said. Solanda explained, "I chose the violin because I thought it sounded like my voice." She began studying at Julliard just shy of six. But her instructor "was kind of scrambling to keep up with what Solanda really needed," Marion said. "Solanda was digesting everything on the spot. She wanted to play the Beethoven D Major Concerto, the Brahms D Major, the Mendelsohn E Minor. And music theory is just the air she breathes."

All three Price children have been homeschooled. I asked Solanda about having friends, and Marion said that Solanda's siblings were her best friends. I asked Solanda what she did for fun. "Basically, Julliard," Solanda said.

Solanda had been asked to perform at an important ceremony in the nation's capital. "I was nervous," Solanda said. "It was very, very shocking to be there, but I played my best and I didn't mess up." Marion said that both Solanda and the trio had been invited to play all around the country. In a rare interpolation, Ravi said, "We need to take it up to the next level, where it would be, as necessary, profitable." Marion was clearly embarrassed by the mention of money. There had been a few paid performances, she said, but her children mostly played for joy—"and it just so happens that their joy is something that brings joy for others," she explained. "I don't consider us to be pushy parents. Involved parents. Supportive parents. But I don't think we're pushy. I know what that looks like. I think we're just able to respond to what our children are asking for."

In general, I don't ask musicians to perform when I interview them. Marion was holding a violin case in her lap, however, so I asked Solanda if she wanted to play. Marion said, "What do you think you'll play, Solanda?" Solanda said, "I think I'll just play the Bach *Chaconne*." Marion said, "How about the Rimsky-Korsakov?" Solanda said, "No, no, no, the *Chaconne* is better." I was struck that Solanda had chosen the instrument for its resemblance to her voice; now it provided her only chance to be heard over her mother. Solanda played the *Chaconne*. When she finished, Marion said, "Now you can play the Rimsky-Korsakov." Solanda launched into *"Flight of the Bumblebee,"* the proof of every virtuoso. Marion said, "Vivaldi?" and Solanda played "Summer" from *The Four Seasons*. She played with a clear, bright tone, although not with such brilliance as to resolve the question of why a childhood had been sacrificed for this art. I had hoped Solanda would light up at her instrument, but instead she brought out the violin's searing melancholy.

Gore Vidal wrote, "Hatred of one parent or the other can make an Ivan the Terrible or a Hemingway: the protective love, however, of two devoted parents can absolutely destroy an artist."

Early trauma and deprivation become the engines of some children's creativity. One researcher reviewed a list of eminent people and found that more than half had lost a parent before age twenty-six—triple the rate of the general population. A horrific upbringing can kill talent or bring it to life. It is a matter of having a match between how the parents act and what a particular child needs.

Lang Lang, often billed as the world's most famous pianist, is the embodiment of brilliance honed in punishment. His father, Lang Guoren, wanted to be a musician but was assigned to a factory during China's Cultural Revolution. When his eighteen-month-old son showed signs of being a prodigy, Lang Guoren's longing reared up. From the age of three, Lang Lang woke up every morning at five to practice. "My passion was so huge that I wanted to eat the piano up," he said. At seven, at China's first national children's competition, he took an honorable mention and rushed onto the stage shouting that he didn't want anything less than first prize. He threw his reward, a stuffed dog toy, in the mud and trampled it, but his father picked it up and kept it on the piano at home so Lang Lang would never forget how much work he had to do.

Lang Guoren decided that he had to take Lang Lang from their home in Shenyang to Beijing to seek a place at the Attached Primary School of the Conservatory of Music, while Lang Lang's mother, Zhou Xiulan, would stay behind to earn money to support her son and husband. "I was nine, and it was really painful to leave home, and I realized that my father was quitting his job to be with me," Lang Lang said. "I felt such pressure."

Lang Guoren rented the cheapest apartment they could find, without heat or running water, and to keep the pressure on, he told his son that the rent was much higher than it actually was. Lang Lang missed his mother terribly, and he often cried. The teacher they had come to see in Beijing assessed Lang Lang harshly. "She said, 'Go home. Don't be a pianist.' Then she fired me," he recalled.

Shortly thereafter, Lang Lang stayed after school to play piano for the celebration of the founding of the People's Republic of China, and he was two hours late coming home. When he walked in, Lang Guoren beat him with a shoe, then proffered a handful of pills, and said, "You're a liar and you're lazy! You have no reason to live. You can't go back to Shenyang in shame! Dying is the only way out. Take these pills!" When Lang Lang refused, Lang Guoren pushed the boy onto the apartment's balcony and told him to jump. Lang Guoren later explained that coddling exposes everyone to disaster. But Lang Lang was furious and refused to touch the piano for months, until his father swallowed his pride and begged him.

Lang Guoren had begged another teacher to work with his son and sat through the lessons so that he could reinforce the instruction at home. "He never smiled," Lang Lang said. "He was scaring me, sometimes beating me. We were like monks. The music monks." A family friend observed that Lang Guoren never showed affection or let his son know that he was pleased. "It was only when his son was sound asleep that he would sit by him silently and gaze at him, fix his quilt, and touch his small feet," the friend wrote.

When they went back to Shenyang for the summer, Lang

Guoren treated the visit as a mere change of location. Zhou Xiulan fought with him, demanding, "What does it matter to be a 'grandmaster' or not a 'grandmaster'?" Lang Lang tried to distract them with music. Every time they fought, his playing progressed. He worked so hard that he collapsed and had to go to the hospital for intravenous fluids every day, but his practice schedule never changed. "My father is a real fascist," Lang Lang said. "A prodigy can be very lonely, locked out of the world."

He was finally accepted into the Attached Primary School and then, at eleven, he auditioned to represent China at the International Competition for Young Pianists in Germany. He was not selected. Lang Guoren told his wife that she had to raise enough money to enter Lang Lang privately, which was contrary to etiquette and potentially humiliating. Before the contest, Lang Guoren identified a Japanese pianist as his son's most serious opponent and told Lang Lang to draw out his competitor about technique. Lang Lang then attempted to integrate the same approach to his own playing. Lang Lang won, and his father sobbed for joy. When told of his father's response, Lang Lang replied that his father was incapable of tears.

In 1995, at thirteen, Lang Lang entered the second International Tchaikovsky Competition for Young Musicians. His father would eavesdrop on the other contestants practicing and urged Lang Lang to do the same if anyone was working on the same piece that he was. He adjusted his tactics accordingly, and Lang Lang won. In Lang Guoren's view, if the pianist before you played with strength, you should play with delicacy; if the he played softly, you should begin with power. This tactic would make it easier for the judges to remember you, and capture the attention of the audience. When someone later asked Lang Guoren how a thirteen-year-old could play something as heart-breaking as Chopin's Piano Concerto no. 2 for the finals, he said he'd told Lang Lang to think about his separation from his beloved mother and his beloved country. Lang Lang won.

Within months, Lang Guoren arranged an audition with Gary Graffman at the Curtis Institute of Music in Philadelphia. Lang Lang was accepted on the spot, and he and his father moved to the United States. During his first lesson, Lang Lang said, "I'd like to win every competition that exists." Graffman asked why. Lang Lang said, "To be famous." Graffman just laughed, while the other students told Lang Lang he should focus instead on being a superb musician, but he didn't understand the differ-ence. Though he has since learned tact, he has never entirely renounced this Olympic model. Graffman said to me, "With most students, you want to get them excited about the emo-tional content of the music. With Lang Lang, it was just the opposite: I had to calm him down enough so he could learn."

At seventeen, Lang Lang acquired a manager, who got him his first big break at the Ravinia Festival, outside Chicago. The critics were enraptured, and for the next two years Lang Lang sold out every concert, made numerous recordings, graced the covers of glossy magazines. "The higher the expectations, the better I play," he told me. "Carnegie Hall makes me play best of all."

The extent of Lang Lang's self-branding is indicated by his having trademarked his name; he performs as "Lang Lang™." He has signed endorsement deals with Audi, Montblanc, Sony, Adidas, Rolex, and Steinway. Anthony Tommasini of the *New*

York Times wrote that Lang Lang's solo debut at Carnegie Hall in 2003 was "incoherent, self-indulgent and slam-bang crass."

I first sat down with Lang Lang in 2005, in Chicago, when he was twenty-three. Following his performance that afternoon, a line of some four hundred people waited patiently to get this autograph on their CDs, and Lang Lang never flagged. Afterward, he invited me to talk in his room. When we arrived, Lang Guoren was watching television. He shook my hand, we exchanged pleasantries, and then, with his characteristic mix of brusqueness and intimacy, he took off his clothes and lay down for a nap. "When I turned twenty and became a huge success, I started to love my father," Lang Lang told me. "He listens very well, and he helps me do the laundry, pack. I'm a spoiled kid. After a big recital, nobody else is going to do a little massage at two o'clock in the morning while talking about the performance."

I once told Lang Lang that by American standards his father's methods would count as child abuse, and that the clear friendliness he had with his father was startling to me. "If my father had pressured me like this and I had not done well, it would have been child abuse, and I would be traumatized, maybe destroyed," Lang Lang responded. "He could have been less extreme and we probably would have made it to the same place; you don't have to sacrifice everything to be a musician. But we had the same goal. So since all the pressure helped me become a world-famous star musician, which I love being, I would say that, for me, it was in the end a wonderful way to grow up."

Several recent books hark back to the adage that practice makes perfect, setting the workload for mastery at ten thousand hours. Recent surveys in which people were ranked for talent and then followed for practice time showed that practice time mattered more than talent. The ability to develop a strenuous and boring practice routine may, in fact, be more important than a natural gift.

There is considerable truth to this idea; if this were not the case, education would be futile and experience would be a waste of time. But the inclination to practice tirelessly may itself be inborn, and nourishing that inclination may be as important as nourishing basic talent.

Is giftedness innate or accrued through labor and study? Veda Kaplinksy jokingly compared the question to what she'd once heard a psychiatrist say about sex in marriage: "If the sex is good, it's 10 percent. If it's bad, it's 90 percent." She explained, "If the talent is there, it's 10 percent of the package. If the talent is not there, it becomes 90 percent, because they can't overcome the lack of it. But just having talent is really a very minor part of what is necessary in order to make it in music."

Musicians often talked to me about whether you achieve brilliance on the violin by practicing for hours every day, or by reading Shakespeare, learning physics, and falling in love. The violinist Yehudi Menuhin said, "Maturity, in music and in life, has to be earned by living." The composer and performer Gabriel Kahane said, "There is always a Korean girl who has been locked in the basement practicing for longer than you have. You can't win that game." But more profoundly, *normal life* in these contexts is a euphemism for a richer life. Single-minded devotion to an instrument builds proficiency—but music embraces experience.

Classical music is largely a meritocracy, which makes it a fit route to social mobility for industrious people isolated by geography, nationality, or poverty. For many years, the prodigies were mostly Jews from Eastern Europe; now the field is dominated by East Asians. The general theory about the Asian dominance of classical music is that it reflects a sheer numbers game. "There are more than three hundred thousand children in China learning instruments," Gary Graffman said. "If you see a child in Chengdu who is not carrying a violin case, it means he's studying the piano." Chinese and other tonal languages reinforce hearing acuity in infants and toddlers, and the typical Chinese hands, with broad palms and generous spaces between the fingers, are especially well-suited to the piano. Discipline and competitiveness are deeply valued and reinforced in many Asian cultures.

Many Westerners, meanwhile, are leery of "tiger mother" stereotypes. The question of when to specialize receives very different answers from place to place; European students narrow their fields of study much earlier than Americans, and Asians focus earlier still. Early specialization requires sacrifices. "Upper-class American parents want their children to have arts, athletics, and community service," said Robert Blocker, dean of the Yale School of Music. "But it's very distracting for someone who really wants to be a musician. Profound achievement is usually the result of early identification and specialization."

If the gamble pays off, the sacrifices are easier to live with. When Lang Lang told me he was reconciled with his upbringing, I thought of the people who, long after the fact, were glad that their parents had encouraged them to undergo limb-lengthening—of how what looks like abuse in the present does not necessarily seem so once it's been completed successfully. On the other hand, how many children have hated practicing the piano and then, as adults, failed at music? The danger is that being pushed toward early specialization can leave children believing that they have only one way to succeed. Prodigies who don't make it will have worked insanely hard on something that can no longer sustain them, after having neglected skills needed to pursue any other kind of life.

Prodigies are not covered by the Americans with Disabilities Act; there is no federal mandate for gifted education and little support is offered to gifted students. It falls to parents to advocate for their children's needs, often in the face of a hostile or indifferent educational system. A bias against excellence accompanies our American pursuit of equality. This bias is portrayed as democratic, when it is often dishonest. One study of super-high-IQ students showed that four out of five were constantly monitoring themselves in an attempt to conform to the norms of less gifted children. It smacks of misguided efforts to make gay kids act straight.

It used to be believed that promoting prodigies academically damaged them socially—even though many were already ostracized for their abilities. The Internet has given prodigies, like other horizontal identity communities, a society where they can connect with like-minded people and underplay differences.

In the 1990s, Miraca Gross studied children who were radically accelerated, starting college between the ages of eleven and sixteen. None regretted the acceleration, and most had made good and lasting friendships with older children. By contrast, gifted children stuck with age peers experienced rage, depression, and self-criticism. Today, most gifted programs keep children in an age-based setting some of the time and a skills-based setting the rest of the time. Neither affords a perfect fit.

Two distinct kinds of people are grouped under the *prodigy* rubric: the driven, single-minded baby virtuoso, and the youth who loves music in his bones and therefore has a better shot at a sustained career. The latter kids are more broadly intelligent, curious, often articulate, and possessed of a sense of humor and perspective about themselves. They pursue some semblance of normal sociability during adolescence and end up going to college instead of conservatory. Being pragmatic, smart, poised, and healthy is in their makeup, just as their musical enthusiasm and aptitudes are.

Joshua Bell is good at everything. He is the most prominent violinist of his generation; placed fourth in a national tennis tournament when he was ten; is the all-time high scorer on several video games; is one of the fastest solvers of the Rubik's Cube; holds an appointment in the MIT media lab; and is truly funny when he appears on the talk-show circuit. He's handsome, charming, and seems riveted by whomever he's talking to, and yet he also evinces the impenetrability of someone who wants privacy in the public eye. People meeting him for the first time are amazed at how accessible he is, and people who have known him forever, at how unknowable he is.

Josh's parents were not an obvious match; when they met,

Shirley was fresh from a kibbutz, and Alan was an Episcopal priest. Alan left the ministry, earned a doctorate in psychology, and took a senior position at the Kinsey Institute for sex research in Bloomington, Indiana. "He was so nonjudgmental versus me," Shirley recalled. "I knew the answers to everything." Shirley is a strong presence with a disregard for boundaries. She wants to feed you, drink with you, play poker with you, sit up late talking. Dark, lithe, and pretty, she appears immensely powerful and touchingly vulnerable—willing to be honest with anyone else to the exact extent that she is honest with herself.

Josh was born in 1968. At two, he stretched rubber bands from knob to knob on a dresser, pulling out the drawers to vary the tensions and create different sounds when he strummed them; as an adult he joked that he had progressed "from credenza to cadenza." He started violin at four, learning new music quickly. "It goes in one ear and it just stays there," Shirley said. Music became a world they shared intimately, but his creativity was always tinged with sadness. "He would wake up in the night crying," she went on. "My other kids, I could always hug and console. But with Josh, there was nothing I could do."

Josh became a local celebrity at seven, when he played the Bach Double Concerto alongside his teacher with the Bloomington Symphony Orchestra. His playing was elegiac, but lacked technical mastery. "My mother, even though she was invested and practiced with me, was not a great disciplinarian, and neither was my father," he said. "I crammed for tests the morning of the test, and crammed for concerts the day before, and lived by the seat of my pants. I sometimes went days without touching the violin at all, sneaking out the back door of the music building when I was supposed to be practicing, playing video games all afternoon, and rushing back for my mother to pick me up." In hindsight, he believes this lack of supervision was beneficial. "Doing nothing but music is not so good for your mental health," he said, "and it's not so good for the music, either."

Shirley read about a competition sponsored by *Seventeen* magazine for high-school musicians; having skipped a year of school, Josh just barely qualified. Shirley was too fretful to accompany him there. "When I got the phone call that he won, I screamed," she recalled. Then she sighed. "I loved having children. My kids became my life. But my youngest daughter was neglected. If Josh was performing on her birthday, we'd be at Josh's concert. I was on tour with Josh when she was growing up, and didn't hear her screams inside. But gifted children have needs, too, and who's going to meet them?" The problem was not just time allocation. "I received such tremendous joy from Josh's music," Shirley said. "Every success he had gave me pleasure. The other kids could see that, and it hurt them." Josh has his own regrets about the effect his career had on his sisters, but feels that his mother's involvement was so crucial "that there was almost no way around it."

As Josh began performing extensively, his mother worried about how he could sustain his momentum with audiences. "When he's fourteen, it's less of a miracle than when he's twelve, even though he's playing much better," she said. Meanwhile, Josh's situation at school became increasingly uncomfortable. "I had that tall poppy syndrome," he said. "Some teachers were threatened by anybody doing something out of the ordinary, and they made my life miserable." He graduated high school at sixteen. "It was unthinkable for me to stay home after high school," Josh said. That meant Shirley's role had to change.

"It takes two for that kind of symbiotic relationship, and it takes two to handle the separation," she said. She was pained that Josh did not want her to manage his affairs. He moved into a condo in Bloomington that his parents had bought, and Shirley went over to do his laundry, "to stay involved," Josh recalled.

Josh made his Carnegie Hall debut at seventeen and almost immediately won the prestigious Avery Fisher Career Grant; his co-recipient that year was Ken Noda. He now headlines more than two hundred performances a year. Additionally, he has been leading the Saint Paul Chamber Orchestra. Josh was among the first classical musicians to do crossover, making a modish VH1 video of a Brahms Hungarian dance. He has bowed his fiddle with bluegrass bassist Edgar Meyer, and has collaborated with jazzmen Chick Corea and Wynton Marsalis. He was featured on singer-songwriter Josh Groban's album *Outside*. Every one of Josh's albums has made Billboard's Top 20; *Romance of the Violin* sold more than five million copies and was Classical Album of the Year. He has been nominated for several Grammys and has won one, and he owns a $4 million Stradivarius. He likes the high life and is classical music's equivalent of a rock star. But rock stars' lives don't look entirely glamorous up close. "Josh is so stressed, you can't get his attention on anything," his mother said, bemoaning that he started taking blood-pressure medication before he turned forty. I asked if the downside made her sad. "What gives me the greatest pleasure is when he calls me to ask my opinion about something, where I can still be a mother," she said. "We have a real musical connection. I have to be careful not to be too intrusive, which is my nature. I don't know him that well anymore."

When I related that conversation to Josh, he was indignant. "She knows me very well," he said. "Even now, I trust her opinion more than anyone's." Josh had moved in with his first serious girlfriend, Lisa Matricardi, when he was twenty-two; they broke up seven years later. But in 2007 they had a baby boy together, and Josh spoke about how Lisa and the baby were "basically one, which is normal with a mother and baby. When you're fifteen and your mother is still so enmeshed, it's unhealthy. When I was in my twenties, my mom was still doing my taxes." He did not consult Shirley about his decision to father a child. "Her approval or disapproval still has such power," he said, "it's best not to let her in when it comes to some of the important things."

Like most parents of kids with horizontal identities, Shirley fears that her child is lonely. "He has an issue with intimacy," she said. "He doesn't want anybody on his back. I know, because he doesn't want me on his back. He's totally free, joking, and very funny in public. It's humbling to be in his presence. I mean, what's going to come out of his mouth? I'm always waiting to hear. But deep down, he's a little bit of an enigma. I think that's why people are drawn to him, because they can't know him. Neither can I. I couldn't comfort him when he was an infant, and in some ways, that's never changed. I think that's part of the nature of his genius, and it breaks my heart."

The advent of sound recording in 1877 had sweeping social consequences, making music ever-present even for those who could neither play it nor afford to hire performers. There is nothing exclusive about hearing music today. Like Sign before the cochlear implant and painting before photography, live performance had a different urgency before the phonograph. Although the causal relationship is less direct, new science and technology is clouding the future prospects of musical prodigies as surely as it is threatening the Deaf and gay cultures and the neurodiversity perspective on the autism spectrum. The arguments about adaptation and extinction are as relevant here as they are to many so-called disabilities.

Despite the ever-increasing number of superlative musicians, audiences who know how to listen are dwindling—because of the jarringly alien qualities of much contemporary music, the surge in anti-elitism, the escalating cost of concert tickets, the elimination of childhood music-education programs, and the technology-spurred dispersal of media users into small, narrowly focused groups. This echoes the experience of other identity groups that are gaining acceptance just as medicine threatens to eliminate them. We have disembodied music in modern life. The exploitation of prodigies is part of the re-embodiment of music. If you see an eight-year-old perform, you see a miracle child, which is very different from merely hearing his playing online.

The gap between classical and popular music keeps widening, and the first approach to that problem has been for classical composers to try to move in with music that speaks to both audiences. Fearful that their language appears to be dying and eager for widespread acclaim and the financial rewards that come with it, composers and performers have entered a mainstream they might once have disdained. Lang Lang appears in popular ads. Young composer-performers such as Christian Sands strive for music of wide appeal that soft-pedals the differences between classical and pop. They are fighting to save their own identity from erasure.

Christian Sands grew up on gospel, jazz, and pop. He won first place in the church talent show when he was three after only a year of piano lessons; at four, he won a local composer's award in New Haven, Connecticut. His father, Sylvester, worked a night shift, so Chris was at home nights with his mother, Stephanie. "Music made me feel safe, so music was the way that he and I coped with having to be strong," she said. When Chris started kindergarten, the teacher told Stephanie that her son was incapable of sitting still and seemed to be on some other planet. Stephanie said, "He's not on another planet, he's just composing music in his head. He'll stop squirming if you let him play a lullaby or something for the other kids at naptime." After he went to bed at night, his parents would hear the clicking of his fingernails on the desk, as if it were a keyboard.

From the outset, Chris would improvise. When he was seven, his teacher said he should switch to a jazz teacher. "With jazz, I could make things up, and nobody would say, 'Don't do that,'" Chris recalled. "I used to think my hands had their own brains. I call them 'the little people,' because each finger just does a different thing when it wants to do it."

Chris's teacher arranged a gig for him at Sprague Hall, the

large concert venue at Yale. "It was a trio," Chris said. "The bass player is sixty-five, the drummer is maybe fifty-eight, and I'm nine, and I'm the leader. I didn't pay attention to the audience. It's almost like when you're a child and you're playing with a toy, and your parents have company; you don't care if they're in the same room with you; you're just making your train go or finishing up your tower of blocks. The piano was my toy, and I was in my own world that I created." Chris received a standing ovation, but never came out to bow again. His parents found him backstage, lying on the floor in his tuxedo and reading a book.

The invitations started to pour in. By the time he was eleven, Chris's music was airing on the radio, and he was selling homemade CDs. The next year, he played a special concert for all fifteen thousand sixth graders in the New Haven school district. He was asked to entertain at a cocktail party at Skull and Bones, a Yale secret society. One of the guests was doctor to jazz pianist and composer Dave Brubeck, and he subsequently arranged for Chris to take lessons from Brubeck. At fifteen, Chris made his first major recording. In high school, he was playing as many as four gigs a week.

Chris's modesty slyly invites a little awe. He's handsome and affable and likes to pretend that even hard work is easy. When a friend complained that Chris was never available, he replied, "You are my friend, but music is my love, and it will always come first." Stephanie said, "He has to isolate himself, even from us. That could be painful. He's always been the one steering the boat, and we're just making sure it's not sinking." All the same, his parents don't want him to forfeit the usual pleasures of youth. During the breaks of his late-night concerts, they'd sneak out the stage door to play tag and roughhouse.

In 2006, at seventeen, Chris was invited to perform at the Grammy Awards for the legendary jazz pianist Oscar Peterson. He had been warned that Peterson would be onstage in a wheelchair. Chris began to play Peterson's tune "Kelly's Blues." "Right in the middle of my second chorus, I hear some applause, and I'm thinking it's for me," Chris said, "and all of a sudden I heard a chord and I thought, 'Wait, I'm not playing that chord,' and I looked up." Peterson had pulled himself out of his wheelchair and made it over to the other piano on stage, and they began something halfway between a pianistic dialogue and a duel, which ended the show exultantly.

Chris went on to the Manhattan School of Music, where, Sylvester said, he learned the names for what he was already doing. When I visited the Sands family at home, Chris was twenty-one, and in the middle of writing an opera, half jazz, half classical, loosely based on his romance with a mezzo-soprano from Dubai. "Her story's as weird as mine," he said. "So my opera's about my doing jazz when everyone else was doing sports, and her doing opera when everyone else was doing shopping and Islam." He laughed. "Do I want to make operatic music, or do I want to do cutthroat, in-your-face jazz, or to be Afro-Cuban, or to use this new Latin style? From the dawn of time, man put sticks over here, berries over here. It's been like that forever, so everything is categorized, and that's why there's so many genres and subcategories. My music is a new beast, and it's untamed, and it's running rampant through the streets of New York."

In some ways, genius is the ultimate horizontal identity. A man with a natural aptitude for skiing who is born into poverty in Guatemala will most likely never discover it; someone whose primary talent is as a computer programmer would not have gone far in the fifteenth century. How would Leonardo have busied himself if he'd been born an Inuit? Would Galileo have advanced string theory if he'd been around in the 1990s? Ideally a genius should have not only the necessary tools and conditions to realize his gifts, but also a receptive society of peers and admirers.

Like sainthood, *genius* is a label that cannot properly be affixed until considerable time and a few miracles have ensued. We help the disabled in a quest to make a more humane and better world; we might approach brilliance in the same spirit. Pity impedes the dignity of disabled people; resentment is a parallel obstacle for people with enormous talent. The pity and resentment alike are manifestations of our fear of people who are radically different.

It has become fashionable to dismiss classical and experimental music as elitist. Classical music, which may look dull to the uninitiated, contains complexities that can make it electrifying for those who study it. With a myriad of perceived flaws, people have learned to find meaning in difficulty, and while the challenges of deafness or Down syndrome may overshadow the rigors of learning to like classical music, the quest for meaning via hard work is not dissimilar. In both cases, earned pleasures supersede passive ones.

Better services for people with disabilities and disadvantages allow them to function better and thereby pay for themselves in many ways. Educating the gifted is likewise in the public interest. If we credit scientific and cultural advances to this identity group, refusing them acknowledgment and support is costly to the population at large. We live in an anti-intellectual society in which people of extraordinary achievement are as likely be considered freaks as to be celebrated as heroes.

Rape

A CHILD CONCEIVED IN RAPE GETS as rough a start as
a child with dwarfism or Down syndrome. The pregnancy is
usually greeted as a calamity, upending family life that may
already be very troubled. The mother is uncertain whether she
will ever get over the very fact of the child's existence. Rarely
is a reliable partner on the scene to help. All new mothers are
prone to ambivalence, but the hostility and revulsion often
experienced by the mother of a rape-conceived child may be
reinforced by her family. Society is likely to judge both mother
and child unkindly.

Facing most disabilities, those who do not share a given
condition struggle to find the humanity within it, while those
who do share the condition gravitate toward one another for
support, validation, and collective identity. With children of
rape, however, the flaw is invisible to strangers, sometimes
to family and friends, and often to the child, who must cope
with its psychological shadow nonetheless. You can keep your
child's deafness or genius or autism secret only for a short time.
Others are sure to notice; the child himself will usually notice.
Children conceived in rape may go a lifetime without knowing
their own identity.

Horizontal identities usually originate in the child, then

spill over to the parents. Children conceived in rape, however, acquire their horizontal identity by way of their mother's trauma; here, the children are secondary, and they are much less likely to find others who share their identity. The mother has the stronger horizontal identity, and the child has an aloneness that follows from it. The mother of a schizophrenic may find herself in a club she never meant to join, but that association is defined by her child. The mother of a child conceived in rape has her own, separate, primary damage to negotiate. Her identity as a mother proceeds directly from her identity as a rape victim. Her child embodies the violence against her and gives permanence to what she may ache to forget. Instead of being unhinged by a startling discovery about her child, she knows what is wrong even before she learns that she's pregnant. Soon thereafter, like many other mothers of exceptional children, she must figure out whether she can love a child who is antithetical to anything she imagined or wanted.

Many people see children of rape as defective—including, often, their mothers. Unlike other factions perceived this way, this one has not come together into a thriving identity group. Even once a child knows his or her origins, he or she cannot easily locate others who share this identity. One of the few organizations founded to address this vacuum, Stigma Inc., took as its motto, "Rape survivors are the victims . . . their children are the forgotten victims."

Marina James assured me that there was a good, quiet spot to talk at her neighborhood library in Baltimore, but when we got there, it was closed. It was a raw March day, but Marina guided us to a bench in a public park, where other people could see us, but not hear us. At twenty-six, she punctuated her most shocking thoughts with the word *obviously*, and seemed to believe that her decisions were the ones anyone else of even moderate intelligence would have made.

Marina had gone to Antioch College in 2000. At a campus party when she was twenty, the student DJ slipped a disabling sedative into her drink and then violently raped her. "It's more of a physical memory than an intellectual memory," she said. "I don't have pictures in my head but I have feelings in my body."

She didn't press charges. "I know what defense attorneys do to rape victims," she said. "I drank, I did drugs, I had a good time. What justice would I get? It seemed like so much grief for nothing." When Marina learned that she was pregnant, she assumed she would have an abortion. But in her third month, she changed her mind; she had had a previous abortion, and it wasn't something she wanted to go through again. She would have the baby, she decided, then give it up for adoption. But as the months passed, she became disillusioned about adoption. She had used recreational drugs just before finding out that she was pregnant, and an adoption administrator told her not to say so on the form because it might put off prospective parents. The deceit upset her. "My child was going to be biracial and all the families were white and liked the fact that I was a well-educated white girl," she said. "The construction of her racial identity was going to be important and I didn't think any of these people could help her with it."

So Marina decided to keep the baby. "Now that I have Amula and I have been really successful at being her mom, obviously I know I made the right decision. But at the time, I didn't know that. So it was torture." She gave birth and chose the name, derived from *amulet*, because she wanted the baby to be a sign of good luck and a protection against the evil that had produced her. Afterward, Marina was paralyzed with post-traumatic stress disorder (PTSD), perhaps mixed with postpartum depression. "I felt like I was a different person, and I couldn't even remember what the old person was," she said.

Marina went on to graduate school in social work, bringing her daughter to classes, but began to have frequent nightmares and had difficulty eating as well as sleeping. Amula started day care, and saw other children dropped off and picked up by their fathers. Before she was two, she was asking, "Why don't I have a daddy?" It made Marina cry, and she didn't want to cry in front of her daughter, so she started getting counseling. "A lot of my Antioch friends are gay, and so I tell her lots of kids have two mommies or two daddies," she said. "I try to be proactive about how I frame it."

Marina is attractive, poised, and somewhat severe. She talks about her own vulnerability easily, but she does not demonstrate it. It is impossible to know to what degree she was always like this, and in what measure being raped reshaped her. Like many of the women I met who had borne children conceived through rape, Marina James sustained both revulsion at the origin of her pregnancy and profound joy in her child. "I thank God every day that I have my child. But I can't ignore the fact that it's a very painful thing, why she's here."

Marina eventually promised Amula that she would look for a daddy for her, but she shows very little interest in having a partner herself. "I don't consider myself a sexual person," she said. "I was before all this. I feel sad that Amula does not have a father—but not for me." Of course Amula does have a father, in the biological sense, and Marina knows his name. "Protecting her from him is the best thing I could do for her," Marina said. "My friends keep saying, 'You have to be able to forgive him in order to accept it and move on.' I want to punch people when they say that."

Although the rape and its aftermath tested Marina's belief, she has increasingly turned to God in a quest for greater insight. She was Christian, but her childhood friends were all Jewish, and after she returned to Baltimore, she reconnected with them and began the process of converting. "Studying Judaism has enabled me to feel emotion, which I haven't felt in years," she said. "It's enabled me to feel hope and to feel faith and it's definitely helped me to feel better. It's my way to not retreat from the world."

Marina has told her boss and several colleagues about Amula's origins. "People ask me and I don't like to lie," she said. "It makes people uncomfortable." For someone who deplores lying, it's all the more difficult to field Amula's increasingly complex and urgent questions. She says she doesn't feel ashamed, but remains concerned about how Amula would incorporate the rape into her own identity. "I just want her to know that she is always wanted, that I chose to keep her, and feel that it was the right choice. Even when I was struggling every day with being a survivor, I never thought, 'I wish I didn't have this baby.'"

She worries that her bright, charming daughter might

share personality traits with her rapist. "Half of her genes are evil," Marina said. "I can do whatever I should as her mom to make her this loving, wonderful, caring person. But in her is the DNA of a person who is really sick, and is that DNA stronger than what I can do?"

Historically, rape has been seen less as a violation of a woman than as a theft from a husband or father to whom that woman belonged. In ancient times, rape victims were described as adulterers.

Classical mythology is full of rape, often by a lustful god. Zeus took Europa and Leda; Dionysus raped Aura; Poseidon, Aethera; Apollo, Euadne. It is noteworthy that every one of these rapes produces children, and that rather than being marks of shame, they are half immortal. The rape of a vestal virgin by Mars produced Romulus and Remus, the twins who founded Rome. Romulus later organized the rape of the Sabine women to populate his new city. In the Renaissance, representations of that event often decorated marriage chests.

Yet the hostility such children's origins may inspire has also long been acknowledged. In ancient and medieval societies, women who bore children conceived in rape were permitted to let them die of exposure. Misogyny is present in writings about rape throughout history. The Roman physician Galen claimed that women could not conceive in rape—nor otherwise without an orgasm based in pleasure and consent. While Augustine promised women that "savage lust perpetuated against them will be punished," he also noted that rape keeps women humble.

A woman in the American colonies could not make a claim of rape; her husband, her father, or, if she was a servant, her employer, needed to present the case to a magistrate. The understanding was that women were prone to bring such charges to disguise illicit consensual sex. These women were considered guilty unless they could prove their innocence. In Puritan Massachusetts, a woman pregnant through rape was prosecuted for fornication.

These habits of blaming the woman began to change only with the social justice movements of the early nineteenth century. Rape of black women in the United States was not acknowledged as rape; you could not violate your own property, and children conceived through such rapes were themselves slaves. Black men accused of rape were frequently found guilty if they had not already been killed without trial; white men often made cash settlements with their white victims to avoid prosecution. In the 1800s, the courts' primary concern was protecting white men who might be falsely accused.

Rape remained underreported through the mid-twentieth century because women feared adverse consequences if they spoke out. The rise of psychoanalysis did not help. Freud's followers saw the rapist as someone suffering an uncontrolled sexual appetite who fed into women's "natural" masochism. As late as 1971, one highly regarded criminologist described how women have "a universal desire to be violently possessed and aggressively handled by men," and concluded, "The victim is always the cause of the crime."

Feminists of the 1970s began arguing that rape was an act of violence and aggression, not sexuality. Rape, they said, had little to do with erotic desire and everything to do with domination. They called for laws that would purge rape of its sexual content to moot the idea that both parties were implicated. American law had defined rape as "an act of sexual intercourse undertaken by a man with a woman, not his wife, against her will and by force." Feminists attacked this definition, broadening it to include nonconsensual sex within relationships and marriages, extending it to include involuntary sexual contact other than intercourse, removing the burden of proving that the encounter had been caused by irresistible force, and eliminating gender specificity.

The new view of rape encompassed sexual stalking by a known assailant, and coerced contact even after consenting words had been spoken. Terms such as *sexual assault* and *criminal sexual conduct* address the primacy of violence and change our understanding of rape from something the victim experiences to something the perpetrator does.

One August day in 1975, Brenda Henriques left her home in the projects in Queens to pick up her paycheck for working as an urban summer-camp counselor. She had tied the front tails of her shirt to show off her tanned belly in defiance of her mother, Lourdes. She got off the subway and was passing a parked cab when its door swung open and a man pulled her inside. "It was just so fast. I was on the floor. There was that hump in the middle of the car floor. So my butt was up on the hump and my face was down on the floor." The driver came into the back seat, and the two men raped her in sequence, then handed her jeans to her and pushed her back into the street with blood running down her legs.

Back home, she took a very long shower, and didn't say a word about what had happened. "Mom warned me about my shirt and I didn't listen, and look what happened," she said. "So I blamed myself. I felt like everybody knew. It was like I had a sign on me. 'Not a virgin anymore,' or 'Rape victim: asked for it.'" When she missed her first period, she told her best friend, and they snuck out during recess and went to Planned Parenthood for a pregnancy test. When she broke the news to her parents, her father, Vicente, said, "Are you sure that's what happened? Why didn't you go to the police?" Years later, Brenda shuddered. "Why, why, the whys came," she said. "I said, 'Mommy, I was wearing the shirt you told me not to wear.' And my mother says, 'You could be standing there naked on that corner, and no one would ever have a right to do that.' I cried with relief."

Still, they wanted to keep the pregnancy secret. Her Catholic father wanted her to go to stay with relatives in Puerto Rico and give the baby up for adoption. Her grandmother told everybody that she had been married secretly and her husband was in the military. The High School for the Performing Arts wanted her to withdraw from classes, but one of her friends circulated a petition, after which the school administration backed down, but moved her to a less visible place in the orchestra. Brenda felt she had to be her baby's champion.

Brenda gave birth the last week of her junior year. She wanted to name her daughter after her paternal grandmother, but her father said, "I don't want my mother's name on that baby." She said, "I wanted her to have a crowning name that she wouldn't be ashamed of. I went through the Bible and Rebecca means *captivating*, and that just clicked." When her father saw the baby, he had a change of heart, and wrote Brenda a card that said, "Thank you for giving me my first granddaughter."

Vicente was a car mechanic and Lourdes was a nurse; Brenda's ambition was to be a doctor, but there was no way she could reach so far with an infant at home. "So I volunteered for the ambulance corps," she said. "I would go into the training class dragging my daughter, and put her in one of those little portable playpens, and that's how I got my EMT." Brenda loved working the ambulance, and eventually became a qualified paramedic.

But she was still trying to process the rape. She became promiscuous for a few years, until she met a guy named Chip Hofstadter, who owned a fish store in Queens. They married eight months later, when Rebecca was four, because Brenda needed a way out of her parents' apartment, and Chip was willing to be a father to Rebecca. They had two more children, and all three grew up believing that Chip was their father.

Brenda and Chip separated when Rebecca was fifteen, and one of Brenda's subsequent boyfriends raped Rebecca. Brenda decided it was time to tell Rebecca about her own rape. "It wasn't good for her to live with lies anymore," she explained to me. Rebecca was furious, and grew increasingly rebellious. She became pregnant by her first boyfriend, and Brenda became a grandmother at thirty-five. Two years later, Rebecca had another child by another father. When Rebecca became pregnant with the third, by yet another man, Brenda took her for an abortion, saying, "You're ruining your life, and I can't let you do this. I'll probably burn in hell for it, but there comes a time when I have to step in." Rebecca eventually joined the air force.

When I first met Brenda, Rebecca was stationed in Iraq, and Brenda was raising Rebecca's children. "My grandchildren are my heartbeat," Brenda said. "I didn't think that I could love like that, and I didn't love like that with my own children—maybe I was too young, maybe the rape. But when I felt that love, I had to let the rape go. I've asked myself, if I ever saw my attackers in the street, would I recognize them? All I know is I have something that these people will never know. Never know that they have a beautiful daughter. Never know that they have beautiful grandchildren. They'll never know. But I do. And so we're the lucky ones, as it turns out."

Both medical professionals and law enforcement officers are now widely trained to respond to evidence of rape. Legal definitions still vary from state to state and do not always accord with those used by the FBI and other federal agencies. Definitions vary even more internationally. Because my focus is on women who bring up children conceived in rape, I did not speak to men, children, and postmenopausal women who have been raped, but no one is immune to rape's humiliating expression of a power differential.

As other social awareness movements have transformed the experience of rearing a child with a disability, so feminism has changed the experience of rearing a child conceived in rape. The idea of a "proud victim" would have seemed laughable only a few decades ago. Despite these strides, rape often remains invisible. Our warnings to our daughters caution them against getting into a car with a stranger or going home with a man they meet in a bar, but 80 percent of rapes are committed by someone the victim knows. More than half of rape victims in the United States are under eighteen, and nearly a quarter of those—an eighth of the total—are under twelve. Rape is often habitual in abusive relationships. Impoverished women who depend on men for survival feel like they have less control over their own bodies. The Centers for Disease Control have asserted that rape is "one of the most under-reported crimes," estimating that only 10 to 20 percent of sexual assaults are reported.

There is not much writing about keeping children of rape, and the books that do exist mostly address genocidal conflicts abroad or are packaged in antichoice invective. The women I interviewed were eager to tell their stories in the hope that doing so might help others. It was painfully apparent, though, that they did so at considerable cost. Many would agree to meet only in extremely public situations because they felt they could not trust me enough to be in a more secluded location. Others insisted on extremely private places because the subject was so loaded that they couldn't bear to speak of it where they might be overheard.

Melinda Stephenson knew from childhood that she wanted to go into deaf education. Her father was deaf and her mother, hearing; as a hearing child fluent in Sign, she served as her father's translator. In her native Indiana, Ball State University was the only college that gave degrees in deaf education, so that's where Melinda went. In her sophomore year, she lived off-campus and commuted via the university-run shuttle service. The shuttles were driven by students, and Melinda occasionally chatted with them, including one, Ricky, who was a childhood-education major.

One evening on her way home, Melinda noticed a car idling in front of her building. She assumed it was someone dropping off her roommate, so she left the door unlocked. When she heard it close, she turned and saw Ricky. "He shoved me on the bed and said, 'If you scream, I will kill you.' I remember looking at my clock. It was eight forty-seven." The phone was ringing, but he cut the cord. "I was banging on the wall, I was kicking him, but then he showed me a knife, and I wanted to live. He left at eleven twenty-three."

Melinda sat on her bed without moving until five thirty the next morning, when she finally asked a friend to take her to the hospital. The nurse expressed doubt that it had been a rape and did not offer emergency contraception. She did, however, summon the police, and Melinda made a report; the police asked if she wanted to press charges, and she said she couldn't. Melinda finished the fall semester with plummeting grades and dropped out halfway through the spring semester, paralyzed by anxiety. "I was petrified to leave my apartment," she recalled.

She moved back in with her parents and enrolled at a community college that had no deaf-education program. When she realized she was pregnant, it was already too late for an abortion. Melinda couldn't bear the thought of relinquishing the baby anyway. "I had to change and adapt or be stuck in fear," she explained. Anxious and deeply depressed, she was hospitalized twice—once on suicide watch.

When her son, Marcus, was born, Melinda's parents refused to treat him as their grandchild. "We have a secured area in the living room where we stay," Melinda explained. When her father is home, Marcus has to stay within five feet of her. When Melinda's sister adopted a daughter, Melinda's parents would take the little girl to the park and go to Grandparents Day at her school. But when a coworker asked Melinda's mother how her grandson was doing, she said, "What grandson? I don't have a grandson."

After college, Melinda got a job at Head Start. By then, she had developed compulsions, could not have different foods touch, began cutting herself, and couldn't go to a new place on her own, even a Starbucks. She angered easily. Melinda started seeing a therapist who was a rape survivor herself. At first, Melinda couldn't talk about what had happened. When she did, she insisted that the door be locked. Her therapist suggested that Melinda send anonymous postcards to Ricky laying out her accusations. She sent one every other day, from different towns. She mailed some to his job, others to his home.

After six months of postcards, Ricky brought charges against her for stalking, so she was fired from Head Start, where employees cannot be the subject of a criminal investigation. Ricky then announced that he was going to sue for custody, and Melinda broke down. She took Marcus to Child Protective Services (CPS) and announced she was signing him over. Her therapist met her there and convinced her to take Marcus home, but her mother offered to drive her back to CPS if she changed her mind again.

Melinda found another job in a toddler day-care center. Her mental state remained fragile, and the line between Marcus and Ricky seemed blurred for her. "What if I go to hurt him, thinking he's his dad? I'm petrified. Marcus is the spitting image of my rapist." She got a glazed look. "There's some things that he does, and I'll think, 'Oh, I'm so proud of you.' And then he'll talk to me and suddenly I can't even acknowledge him. Without him, what's going to make me get up in the morning? I guess I'm much less likely to kill myself if I've got him."

Within a year, Melinda wrote to me that she'd been dating a man for eight months and they were expecting a child. "Marcus is excited about being a big brother," she continued. "I am happy, therapy is going in a good path, and the best part, my parents can't tell us what to do anymore." Two months later, she wrote, "The guy I had been dating decided that I wasn't for him. He is now living in Michigan with his new wife. I named my daughter Eliza. Sad news is she was born dead."

Six months later, she gave up Marcus; he was placed with a foster family that was considering adopting him. "I see him as much as I want," Melinda wrote, "which is not as much as I should. He is getting everything that I could not provide. I am not allowed to spend time alone with him, and I think that is very smart. I struggle a lot with losing Eliza. For Eliza's birthday I am having a cookout with some friends. I am so excited to make her 'gunk' cake. It's a nine-by-eleven yellow cake with peanut butter icing covered in birdseed with whatever writing I decide to put on it. I will be putting this cake on her grave so the wildlife can enjoy her presence and life as all of us do every day."

So Melinda struggled on, in love with a child who was dead, and unable to love the one who was alive. Rape engenders both rage and sadness, and even as it had made Marcus the object of Melinda's displaced fury, it had made Eliza the safer receptacle of her despair.

There is a war of statistics about the correlation of rape and pregnancy, and the confusion is only made worse by the warring agendas of the pro-choice and antiabortion movements. Studies have found that between twenty-five thousand and thirty-two thousand rape-related pregnancies occur each year in the United States. In a 1996 study of rape-related pregnancy, half of the subjects terminated their pregnancies; of the rest, two-thirds kept the child, one-fourth miscarried, and the rest gave the children up for adoption. Extrapolating from those figures, at least eight thousand women in this country keep rape-conceived children every year.

Access to safe abortion allows a woman who keeps a child to feel that she is making a decision rather than having the decision forced upon her. Even opponents of reproductive choice often allow for a "rape exception." Raped women need independence in this arena: to abort or carry to term; to keep the child or give him or her up for adoption. Women who choose to raise such children, like parents of disabled children, choose the child over his or her challenging identity. They and their children may struggle with society's condemnation.

Many women keep children conceived in rape because they have no access to abortion, because of religious beliefs, or because of a controlling partner, husband, or parent. I also met women who completed their pregnancies because deep self-examination led them to that decision and women who described keeping their pregnancies as a kind of reenactment of the forced passivity they had experienced in rape. Some said their children felt like evidence—as if to abort them would be a denial of the rape. Because the option to terminate any pregnancy is strongly associated with feminism, many of these women found their only support in the antiabortion movement. Many women said they felt intense social pressure to abort.

For some women, the rape-engendered fetus represents the unwelcome conquest of her body; for others, it seems to be an extension of herself. Some women experience attachment and revulsion in rapid alternation. In other instances, an initial hatred can give way to love—sometimes when movement of the fetus is first felt, sometimes not until the child has matured into adulthood.

American abortion law from the colonial period through the mid-nineteenth century was predicated on the English common-law principle that life begins with quickening—the moment when the expectant woman feels the fetus moving inside her, usually at four to five months. In 1857, the newly formed American Medical Association (AMA) began a crusade against abortion even prior to quickening, and laws passed in 1860 and 1880 made abortion illegal at any stage unless the mother's life was at risk. In 1904 the AMA concluded that the fetus's rights trumped the mother's, even in cases of rape.

The 1930s saw a rise in illegal abortion as the Great Depression made large families harder to sustain. Many women died as a result of backroom procedures. Unsuccessful efforts were made to pass laws that would permit abortions for rape victims, girls under sixteen, mentally retarded women, and "poorly nourished" women with large families. Abortion was, however, openly discussed.

In 1939, the first US Hospital Abortion Committee was formed to determine case-by-case eligibility, and by the 1950s such committees were common. They often accepted the recommendations of psychiatrists who stated that a patient's pregnancy endangered her mental health. Rape victims who could not pay a psychiatrist had to show that they were nearly deranged in order to obtain an abortion. Some were diagnosed as immoral and were forced to agree to sterilization.

In the 1960s a dozen states passed laws that legalized abortion if the pregnancy was the result of rape. But the standard treatment in most states for unwed women who had been raped was to send them to maternity homes, where they were encouraged to surrender their children for adoption. Women who wanted to abort were considered murderous; women who wanted to keep their children, selfish.

In 1973, the Supreme Court affirmed a woman's right to an abortion in *Roe v. Wade*. In 1976, the Hyde Amendment cut off Medicaid funding for abortion except when the mother's health was at risk, and not until 1993 was a further exception made for women pregnant through rape or incest. While abortion of fetuses with disabilities is often constructed as saving the child from suffering, the rape exception is held to be about saving the mother. By the late 1980s, polls showed that while half of Americans opposed abortions for most women, only a small percentage opposed abortion for rape and incest victims. The debate continues, often on religious grounds.

Younger women and girls, who don't have a clear idea of

their own future, often decide to continue or end a rape-related pregnancy in rebellion against or compliance with the wishes of parents and other elders. Other women are in denial: one-third of pregnancies resulting from rape are not discovered until the second trimester. Any delay in detection or action reduces women's options, but many women are still recovering from being raped when they are called on to make up their minds whether to carry though their pregnancy. No matter which choice is ultimately made, pregnancy after rape can lead to depression, anxiety, insomnia, and PTSD. Rape is a permanent damage; it leaves not scars, but open wounds. As one woman I interviewed said, "You can abort the child, but not the experience."

Rapists are often repeat offenders; it is less well-known that women who have been raped before age eighteen are twice as likely as other women to be raped as adults. The two statistics have an appalling symmetry. As aggression is rewarded in the rapist, the victim's ego becomes frayed and vulnerable. Then her understanding that the world is unsafe becomes a self-fulfilling prophecy.

For years, Lisa Boynton thought her most important secret was that she had been abused by her grandfather since she was five. When Lisa was in seventh grade, she saw a census form on which her father had identified her as "stepdaughter." He had never wanted Lisa to know because he was afraid Lisa wouldn't love him anymore. Louise, Lisa's mother, said she'd become pregnant at fifteen by a boy from school. "I was angry," Lisa said. "I'm still angry. My whole family knew that he wasn't my real dad, but no one told me."

The following year, Lisa and some friends were hanging out with a friend of theirs, Donny, who was "mentally retarded." Lisa was in eighth grade; Donny was twenty; they had made out a few times, but she never expected it to go further. She went upstairs with him to see something, and he raped her. She screamed, but nobody responded. When she came downstairs, shaking, and asked her best friend why she hadn't helped her, the friend said, "Oh, I thought you were just getting it finally. It always hurts the first time."

Ironically, only after Lisa's rape—which she kept a secret—did her grandfather's abuse come to light. Her mother overheard her telling a friend about it and prodded her into confessing the whole story. Her parents notified the police. Her stepfather's father pleaded guilty and was sentenced to five years on probation. Lisa received a letter of apology from him, but it sounded "as though a lawyer wrote it," she said. "To me, it meant nothing." Lisa's stepfather cut off relations with his own father.

The relationship between Lisa and Louise, despite this support, remained strained. "My dad went above and beyond to make me feel like I was loved and part of the family," Lisa said. "It was my mother who always blamed me for things. My sister was always innocent." After the rape, Lisa became promiscuous. Like many victims of child sexual abuse, she had no sense of boundaries about physical intimacy. "I would sleep with anybody," she said. "Even though I'd been raped by Donny, I continued to have sex with him willingly up until I was in eleventh grade." She added, almost in bewilderment, "I guess I'd confused sex with love ever since my grandfather began abusing me."

Then one day, when Lisa was twenty, Louise confessed that

she herself had been raped and that she didn't know who Lisa's father was. "I couldn't tell her that I was angry that she never told me, because I could hear the sadness in her voice. And I never wanted to bring it up again. I'm going to die with a lot of unanswered questions."

All the secrets and lies have had a corrosive effect on Lisa, who, in her thirties, still doesn't feel like a part of her own family. She has spent a good bit of time looking at online forums that have made her feel less alone. She eventually got a degree in social work, and as a group-therapy leader she counsels women who've experienced similar traumas. Her personal and professional lives are devoted to recovery. "I minimize my issues and problems," she reflected. "But I'm the first to say, 'Don't minimize yours.'" She lives with a female partner and has a daughter from a previous relationship, to whom she is deeply attached. "I want my daughter's life to be completely different from mine," she said.

"Where did I come from?" is one of the first urgent questions of childhood. A response that includes terror and powerlessness can undermine a child's feeling of safety. Many rape victims who bear children have to explain why they've had babies at an inappropriate age, in the absence of a stable romantic relationship, or despite lacking financial or emotional resources to provide care for the child. The extent to which a woman feels judged may determine the scope of her concealment or denial.

Telling a secure child who isn't looking for answers the story of his or her conception can itself feel like an act of violence. Mothers who were unable to protect themselves are gratified by their ability to protect their children, and shielding them from such awful knowledge is part of that safeguarding. Withholding the information, however, can be as loaded as the telling; often, the child gleans knowledge accidentally from other people, then feels betrayed by a lifetime of secrecy. In short, there's no good time or safe way to share the news, but concealing it can spell disaster.

To learn that you are the kind of person most mothers would prefer never even to imagine can produce an angry self-doubt. Some rape-conceived people have become antiabortion activists as a way of marking the fact that they were born. Some speak grandiosely about how they evaded abortion, as if they had been wily double agents in utero. Others fail to empathize with the trauma to which they are connected.

Prejudice against rape victims and their children is as real as it is irrational. One blogger wrote, "Hmmm, so many children, born out of incest and rape. The CWS [Child Welfare System] is overwhelmed and unprepared. My suggestion? PUT THEM TO SLEEP LIKE UNWANTED PETS!" Even among people with less extreme points of view, prejudice is deeply ingrained. Liberal acquaintances who were all for Deaf politics and neurodiversity expressed unease about raising a child with "those genes." To the mother, the child is an incarnation of the rape; to the world, he or she is the rapist's heir.

When she was three, Tina Gordon called her mother "Mom" and was immediately rebuked. "Don't you ever call me that again," Donna said. "I'm not your mother." Tina's great-grandmother told her later, "It's not your fault. She was raped when she had you." Tina had no idea what her great-grandmother was talking about. "When I learned how to read, I looked it up in the dictionary and understood the violence part, but not the sex part," Tina said. "For a lot of my life, though, I felt damaged." Tina watched her older sister, Corinna, say "Mom" over and over and watched her receive at least sporadic flashes of love and attention. Ironically, however, Tina's estrangement from Donna may have afforded her a measure of protection from her mother's destructive tendencies.

Donna had had a nervous breakdown in college and was abusive to both Tina and Corinna when they were young. Donna was living in Florida when Tina was born, and a friend called Donna's mother to say that there was a new baby. "It might already be too late for the older daughter," the friend said, "but you've got to come and get these kids and maybe save this baby." So Tina's grandmother went to fetch the two girls. She found that Corinna was missing parts of her finger pads because Donna had put her hands on the stove as a punishment.

Tina and Corinna grew up in Mississippi under the far more loving care of their grandmother, who taught school by day and cleaned houses by night. Donna would visit and say that she was going to reclaim Corinna as soon as she got back on her feet. She made no such promises to Tina, who soon gave up seeking any kind of approval from her mother and focused on her grandmother and aunts. As a result, Tina saw her mother's hypocrisies with greater clarity than her sister did.

When Tina was eight and Corinna was ten, their grandmother died at fifty-eight. Donna, close to forty, was clearly unable to handle them. A great-uncle they barely knew felt they shouldn't be split up and agreed to take them both, so they moved to Connecticut. Aunt Susan and Uncle Thomas gave them material security, but ran a strict household, and the girls were unhappy. Donna would send care packages and Christmas presents to Corinna, but nothing to Tina. Uncle Thomas told Donna that if she couldn't send presents for both daughters, she shouldn't send anything. After that, there were just letters: cold and formal ones to Tina, effusive ones to Corinna promising to take her back. Two years after a fire at the house in Connecticut, Corinna was caught trying to set fire to it again, and she was sent to a juvenile facility. Another uncle took her in briefly after she was released, but she wanted to move back in with Donna. Donna would have none of it, and Corinna was devastated. At fifteen, she ended up living on the streets in Mississippi.

Tina found it painful to be in her uncle's house when Corinna was not allowed to be there and decided to go to boarding school. "I've always just had maybe a little bit of a survivor instinct," Tina said. She was admitted to a girls' school, where she was one of seven black students in a population of one hundred and sixty. Her aunt and uncle cut her off after she was disciplined for smoking pot. "I started to be known at school as 'the orphan,'" Tina recalled. Meanwhile, Corinna was hustling and doing drugs; she had developed AIDS by the time Tina started college at New York University (NYU). "Donna contacted me to disparage Corinna," Tina remembered. "I said, 'I understand why she's made the choices she's made. Other people have had a huge part to play in that.' Donna said, 'What other people?' I said, 'You and others.' That was the end of her trying to reach out to me." The sisters, however, kept in touch, and Tina visited her sister repeatedly in the last year of Corinna's life, when she was twenty-three.

"No matter what Donna said or did, Corinna would tell me that I should reach out to Donna, forgive Donna," Tina said. "Because I knew it would mean a lot to Corinna, I actually called Donna and asked her to call Corinna and say that she loved her and that she was in her prayers—just to reach out to her before she died. Donna said, 'I don't think I can do that.' Then she said, 'I know I haven't necessarily made good choices, but if I can make that up to you, tell me what I can do.' And I said, 'If you call Corinna, all is forgiven and forgotten.' She said, 'I've heard that she's prostituting, and I heard she was using drugs.' And I said, 'First of all, you don't know if that's true or not, and secondly, what does it matter? She's dying. You don't have to call and talk about her life or what she's done. It would just mean a lot to her if you would call and say that you're praying for her, thinking of her. Something. Anything.' She said, 'I don't know if I can do that.' And she didn't."

Tina enrolled in Columbia Law School, and as her accomplishments accrued, Donna began to seek her out. Donna called to ask whether she was going to be invited to see Tina graduate with honors. Tina said. "I haven't talked to you in years, and the last time I talked to you I made a request of you and you couldn't even do that. So why are you trying to be a part of my life now?"

Tina became a public defender. Having accepted injustice from birth, she found solace in defending other people. When I met her, she was seven months pregnant. I wondered whether she had fears about being a mother. "Despite all the things that happened, in a lot of ways I do feel very fortunate, very blessed," she said. "My grandmother was able to give us so much love. Even though I was only with her for eight years, she made such a huge impression." Tina was engaged to a man with a warm, supportive family, "the exact opposite of mine." Her fiancé is naturally affectionate, "and there are times when I'm suddenly, like, 'Every time you come in the room, you don't have to touch me.' He knows how I'm damaged." Tina had worked hard to build a life that can subsume the past. "I don't know what happened to Donna when I was conceived," she said, her hand on her pregnant belly, "but that curse has run its course, and it's going to stop here."

In the late eighties and early nineties, the marital exception to rape laws was gradually removed from the books in most states, despite protests from the political right, including some who claimed that the accusations of rape within marriage would be used by vengeful wives to persecute innocent husbands. In fact, marital rape most commonly comes up in court within a larger pattern of domestic violence.

Louise McOrmond-Plummer, coauthor of *Real Rape, Real Pain* and herself a rape survivor, wrote, "The woman raped by her partner was routinely blamed and told that since her rapist was her partner, it wasn't 'real' rape. Women such as myself were being told that our pain was an overreaction; the fact of being in a relationship meant that any sexual rights were void."

A recent study has identified "coerced childbearing as a weapon in the arsenal of power and control." Numerous women who have been raped within relationships speak of the rape as a means used by a man to keep her under his thumb, the classic ploy of domination by keeping a wife "barefoot and pregnant." A women in one survey said, "They own you when you have a child by him—part of the purpose in having a baby is to control you." As the mothers' children bear witness to ongoing sexual violence, they are more likely to be traumatized, and to be both victims of and perpetrators of sexual abuse themselves.

Although no one ever deserves to be raped, a woman's actions can have an enormous impact on her own safety. Yet some women repeatedly put themselves in situations of extreme vulnerability. Talking to many women who had borne children of rape, I was struck by their inability to foresee the likelihood of danger inherent in their choices. Every bad thing that befell them, even at the hands of previous aggressors, came as a surprise. They could not tell the difference between people who warranted trust and those who didn't. They lacked guiding intuition and were blind to bad character until it manifested itself.

Nearly all such women I met had not been cherished or protected as children. At the most basic level, they did not know what caring behavior felt like, so they were unable to recognize it. Some were desperate for love and attention, which made them easy targets. Most were so familiar with neglect or abuse that they accepted it when it came their way; for many, abuse was synonymous with intimacy. Some who actively strove to improve their situation kept falling back into the familiar muck.

When Emily Barrett would hug her mother, Flora, she was always pushed away. "But it took a minute for her to realize that she wanted to shoo me off," Emily told me, "and I miss those moments right before she did." Flora was a light-skinned Jamaican woman who had immigrated to New York for a better life. By the time Emily was twelve, Flora was on her fourth husband. "She was extremely charismatic, and beautiful, and she was funny," Emily said. "Other people loved her. She was a hypocrite, but it was still interesting to watch, almost like a science project." As an only child, Emily was lonely. Before she turned thirteen, she developed a crush on a good-looking nineteen-year-old, Blake. He took to giving her rides to and from school, and one day in the car he leaned over and kissed her. As the years passed, her attachment to him grew. When she was fifteen, Emily gave him her virginity, even though she knew he had a girlfriend.

Soon after, Flora moved to Virginia, taking her reluctant daughter with her. In Virginia, Emily's mother found her a job doing bookkeeping for friends who owned a restaurant; Emily called them Uncle Eric and Aunt Suzette. Uncle Eric asked Emily to help out his brother, who owned a store, and the brother raped her while he was driving her to work. "It's not like on television," Emily said. "There's no black eye, and there's no knives and guns. It's five seconds. I was just stunned." She spent the next few days in a haze, and then she finally called the police, by which time the man had fled.

In the weeks that followed, Emily had severe headaches, and her breasts began to hurt. When Flora found out Emily was pregnant, she locked the doors and unplugged the phones while she decided what to do about it. "She told the school I had appendicitis," Emily said. "Every day she would come home and just scream. And then I'd hear her in her room crying and wailing in her shower. Then Uncle Eric and Aunt Suzette were coming over saying how I'm ruining their reputation. I was sixteen and I had no business having a child. But that whole experience was just insanity." Flora finally took Emily to the clinic for an abortion. "For a long time, I would calculate in my mind and imagine how old that baby would be from when I was sixteen," Emily said. "I would see a baby and start to cry."

As abruptly as she had relocated to Virginia, Emily's mother moved them back to New York. For a few years, life returned to normal. Emily resumed her friendship with Blake. She went off to college, but dropped out to take care of her mother after Flora was diagnosed with advanced colon cancer. Flora left Emily a small inheritance. Emily got a call from Blake asking for an urgent loan, and she gave him $5000, and he vanished.

Emily located him after a few years, and asked about the loan; he said that he had some money to give her and told her to come over to collect it. "He gave me a drink with something in it," Emily said. "Next thing I know, I feel my clothes coming off. I'm seeing flashing lights and pictures. He was positioning my body, he was moving me around. I couldn't believe it. When I woke up, he was in the shower and I was shaking." Emily gathered her clothes and drove home. She was dating a policeman at the time, and when she told him what had happened, he took her to the precinct to report it. Blake was arrested, and the process of bringing charges began.

Emily sensed that she was pregnant but couldn't face it: She took seven pregnancy tests, hoping that eventually one would be negative. She broke up with the policeman; her emotional life centered on Blake, the rape, and the pregnancy. At a hearing in her case against him, when she realized that he might go to prison, she told the assistant district attorney during a recess that she couldn't see it through, because she was pregnant by Blake. The attorney asked for a continuance, and Emily left the courthouse. "Blake ran after me, and asked, 'What's going on?' And I told him, got in the car, made this crazy U-turn, and I drove."

Blake first convinced Emily not to have an abortion. "Then he said I didn't want my child to have its father in prison," she remembered. "'What are you going to tell it when it asks you where I am?' he said. I couldn't sleep, I couldn't eat. I was losing it." Eventually, she told the ADA that she would not go forward with the rape case. She asked Blake to leave her alone. "But he just kept checking in with me, I guess to make sure that I didn't change my mind. When I was five months and a week pregnant, he told me that he was with another woman, that she was five months pregnant, and that she was moving in with him." Though she had not imagined building a life with him, Emily was crushed.

Then Delia was born. "She was like a salve, like a panacea, which is a lot of responsibility for a newborn," Emily said. She began to think about the blank line on Delia's birth certificate, the one for the second parent, and she decided to add Blake's name in case Delia ever needed another close genetic relative for a medical emergency. What Emily hadn't considered was that Blake would be notified, and when she went to the courthouse to pick up the revised document, he was there. A judge granted him visitation rights. "I realized, he's going to be tied to me for the rest of my life," Emily said. "I didn't sleep for days before his first visit." So began an uneasy détente. Blake paid child support, and saw Delia erratically for two years, then drifted away again. "I was so attached to Delia that I couldn't let go at all," Emily said. "When she was small, she was like a toy, so cute, all huge cheeks. But when she was about four, she started asking me questions about her father and where she came from, and it was like someone took a hammer and cracked me open and I spilled out all over the room."

Emily became intensely agoraphobic and lost her job. "I don't remember how Delia got food," she said. "It got done. I couldn't leave the house, except to go to therapy. Then I couldn't leave the room. I wasn't sleeping for days at a time. I was fragmenting." A psychiatrist put her on anti-depressants, and she did constant talk therapy with him, and she gradually began to reemerge. "He saved me," she said. Just as she was getting it together, Blake turned up at the front door to say that he wanted to see Delia. The familiar cycle recurred. He would come occasionally to visit, then vanish, over and over. Emily decided she had to be strong for Delia and not keep her from her father, but Blake's motives always seemed unclear. "I didn't know what to do, because he was her father, and she knew it," Emily said. "If something happened to me, he could get her. So I had to make sure he wouldn't hurt her, and the only way to do that was to let him know her so he would care about her."

Emily had had a brief romance, and given birth to a son, Gideon, seven years younger than Delia. Blake told Emily that she belonged to him and that her new child was a betrayal. The sexual brutality his argument implied frightened her, and she decided to flee, so she moved the kids back to Virginia.

When I met Emily, Delia was ten, and had recently won a national academic award and matriculated in a magnet school for gifted children. "She's never asked about how she came to exist, and I know she wonders," her mother said. "She and I have had conversations about my prickliness, how I pull away. I would never, ever, ever tell her that it has anything to do with her. I always tell her it's because of me, and because my mom pulled away from me. But I don't do it with her brother." Emily had recently become engaged, and she told me that her fiancé, Jay, found this coldness toward Delia very upsetting.

"Fix me," Emily said to me as we sat on the floor of her office, late at night, doing this interview. "Why can't I hug my daughter? I love her, but when she touches me, it feels like hundreds of razor blades scraping across my skin, like I'm going to die. I understand that I just have to let her because she's a child, and so I do, but in my mind, I go someplace else, and I know that she knows it. So now she asks permission. I prepare myself. There are rules, like, she can't come up behind me. Sometimes she forgets, and I'll jump, like a cat that you put water on, because her father had this stealth ability to just appear in front of you, and you don't know where he came from. She inherited that. She looks like Blake in some ways, but not as much as she did when she was small. She reminds me of me, and I attempt to focus on that. Even if I don't always love myself, I can love myself in her. But there's always that other part that makes me struggle every single day, because while most mothers just go with their natural instincts, my instincts are horrifying. It's a constant, conscious effort to keep my instincts from taking over."

More than any other parents coping with exceptional children, women with rape-conceived children are trying to quell the darkness within themselves in order to give their progeny light. For no other exceptional families is there less support than for these. These mothers and children need an identity community, a place to find more dignity than can be achieved in the piecemeal world of online supports. The children described in the rest of this book sustain injuries; these children, through no fault of their own, *are* injuries. But the ordeal that produces them does not shrink their mothers' hearts so much as those mothers themselves often fear. Maternal love can captivate these women even as they guard against it.

Crime

UNLIKE MOST CONDITIONS DISCUSSED IN THIS book, criminality is the child's fault, something he or she has done deliberately and with choice. It is also the parents' fault, something they could have prevented with decent moral education and adequate attention. These, at least, are the popular conceptions, and so parents of criminals live in a territory of anger and guilt, struggling to forgive both their children and themselves. While parents of children with disabilities receive state funding, parents of criminals are frequently prosecuted. If you have a child who is a dwarf, you are not dwarfed yourself, and if your child is deaf, it does not impair your own hearing; but a child who is guilty of serious crime seems like an indictment of the mother's and father's moral character.

Having a child with physical or mental disabilities is usually a social experience, and you are embraced by other families facing the same challenges. Having a child who goes to prison frequently imposes isolation. Aside from those communities in which illegality is the norm, this is a misery that doesn't love company. The parents of criminals have access to few resources. No colorful guides suggest an upside to having a child who has broken the law. This deficit also has advantages; no one trivializes what you are going through; no one urges you to celebrate what you want to mourn.

Parents whose kids do well take credit for it. The equivalent belief is that parents whose kids do badly must have erred. Unfortunately, good parenting is no warranty against corrupt children. The force of blame impedes parents' ability to help—sometimes even to love—their felonious offspring.

Thousands of institutions have been designed to ease the challenges attached to many horizontal identities: schools for the deaf, mainstreaming programs, hospitals for those with schizophrenic psychosis. Most juvenile criminals are institutionalized in state facilities intended more to punish than to rehabilitate. Many can't be turned around; the idea of near-universal rehabilitation is a liberal fantasy. But there are enough young convicts in whom the damage is situational that it is our moral obligation to treat them all. If we can redeem even 10 percent of would-be career criminals, we can reduce human suffering and economize on prosecution and prison. Jails draw on the popular belief that the more we punish people, the safer the country becomes. This resembles the assumption that the more you whip your children, the better they will turn out.

The three cardinal principles of imprisonment are deterrence, incapacitation, and retribution. Deterrence works to some degree; the prospect of jail can discourage those contemplating a crime, but it does so less than most of the general population thinks. The National Institutes of Health advised, "Scare tactics don't work and may make the problem worse."

Incapacitation works insofar as people behind bars cannot easily commit further crimes. But unless one plans to keep offenders in jail for life, the problem remains of how they will behave when they get out. In prison, first offenders learn criminal ways from more experienced peers. More than 80 percent of those incarcerated under age eighteen will be arrested again within three years of release. Once someone's been in jail, he's likely to be in repeatedly.

Retribution is a fashionable euphemism for *revenge*. Retribution is a way of indulging the victims; they feel powerless, and seeing their adversaries jailed or executed sometimes makes them feel empowered. That has a limited merit; interviews with people who have fought to have others put to death reveal that execution did not afford them the satisfaction they had anticipated.

Cora Nelson was verbally and physically abused as a child in rural Minnesota. Her early marriage—which produced two daughters, Jennifer and Mandy Stiles—was a disaster; in her mid-twenties, she developed cervical cancer and was told she would never again conceive. When she fell in love with Luke Makya, a handsome, alcoholic Native American, he didn't mind that they would be unable to have a family. Then, to the astonishment of her doctors, Cora became pregnant and delivered what she called her "miracle baby," Pete. For Jennifer, Cora's eldest daughter, her new half brother was "my living doll that talked and walked."

Pete loved his father, but could never rely on him. "There were times when it was going to be a bad day—but there were times when it was good," Pete recalled. "The first time I ever shot a rifle, we were aiming at pop cans in the water, and the first one I shot at, I hit. He just scooped me up in his arms, like he was so proud of me."

Luke, however, became increasingly alcoholic and vicious.

"The good man my mother had married, and that we all loved, ceased to exist," Jennifer recalled. Pete witnessed his mother getting hit and choked, and he was walloped too. Once, Luke crawled into Jennifer's bed and put his hand on her thigh; Jennifer, who had already been the victim of sexual abuse from a male babysitter when she was six, fought him off. "I have more good memories of this man than I do bad," she said, "but the bad ones are *so* bad."

One evening when Luke was drunk, he beat Pete badly, then drove off to hit the bars. For Cora, this was the end; she packed their bags and left with Pete, then six, and Mandy, who was a teenager; Jennifer had already moved out. Cora had Luke evicted and moved back home. Luke broke into the house, cut up Cora's dresses, and took his guns. Cora obtained an order of protection and filed for divorce. Pete would sometimes see his father on weekends, but Luke would usually be wasted.

Soon, Cora started dating Ethan Heinz, a bus mechanic. One week before Cora's divorce was supposed to come through, Mandy returned from school to find Luke at the kitchen table. She called Cora, who called the police, but Luke had fled before they arrived. Cora took the family to stay with Ethan. When they returned a few days later, they found the door open and called the police. Cora asked them to check the basement. "They go down, and he's in there," Pete remembered. "He's got a shotgun, a .22 rifle, and a .30-30 rifle. He comes out with the rifle in his hand, like he was going to shoot 'em. The gun was jammed, so he couldn't get a shot off—but they didn't know that. They shot him three times, and they killed him." Cora and her three children were upstairs.

Luke's plan had been to kill both Cora and himself. He had left his son a note, saying that what was to happen was not Pete's fault, and that if Pete should ever miss him, he need only "look at the constellation Orion, because that's me. Always the hunter, never the hunted." Pete said, "He had depression but wouldn't get help because he thought they'd make him give up his alcohol, and he loved his alcohol more than anything else. I wish so much he'd chosen me over alcohol. But he didn't."

After that, Cora would be fine some days, but on others, Pete recalled, "She just couldn't do much, and I'd have to take care of her a lot." That was a steep task for a grieving six-year-old—especially one who "felt like if I'd done something different, maybe he wouldn't have tried to kill my mom." Pete ached for the loss. "My father wasn't tall like me," he said to me. "But there's this jacket he had that fits perfectly. I wear it when I'm lonely."

The whole family went to live with Ethan. Jennifer had gotten pregnant in high school and dropped out after her daughter, Sondra, was born. When her relationship with Sondra's father ended, she and Sondra moved back in with the family. Jennifer developed chronic migraines. "I retreated to my dark room, for years," she said. "If Sondra didn't share a room with me, I don't think I would have done anything for her." Just as Jennifer had been Pete's childhood companion, so six-year-old Pete was now Sondra's.

But Pete was often sullen and withdrawn. In third grade he got annoyed at a girl and stabbed her in the thigh, deeply, with a pencil. He developed attention-deficit/hyperactivity disorder and had trouble in school despite his obvious intelligence. The family moved to a pleasant working-class suburb, and the counselor at his new school tried to combat Pete's inattentiveness with Ritalin. But his ADHD was mingled with serious depression, and Ritalin made him more agitated. Anti-depressants provoked hypomania in him. By then, his teachers had labeled him a troublemaker.

Pete rejected Ethan as a father figure; as time passed, he began to rebel against his mother as well. Cora found it difficult to discipline him. At thirteen, Pete broke into a store, stole some cigarettes, and was charged with a gross misdemeanor. A year later, he tried to walk out of the Mall of America with a shoplifted skateboard and briefly went to jail. By then, he was also getting in trouble for truancy. Cora requested a psychiatric consultation for him from her HMO, but Pete was denied treatment.

Soon thereafter, the nine-year-old daughter of Jennifer's best friend told her mother that Pete had forcibly kissed her and had rubbed her chest through her shirt; she insinuated that he had done more to Sondra. Jennifer's friend immediately called with the news. "I remember, vividly, throwing up right afterwards," Jennifer said. That night, she asked Sondra about it. "Full-on sexual abuse, starting when she was six," Jennifer said. "My baby brother, who I had taken care of, who I would have died for, had done this to my daughter." She called the police immediately.

The DA wanted Pete to be tried as an adult, even though he was only fifteen. Jennifer wrote a letter on his behalf, noting, "My brother needs to be punished, but even more, he needs help." Pete was sentenced to a program for sex offenders, where he was to serve almost two years, and would then remain on extended juvenile jurisdiction, which meant that any future offense would earn him twelve years in the penitentiary. While he was inside, he told his therapist that Sondra's father had abused her sexually before he had done so; an abuse expert who interviewed Sondra concluded that that was true. "It's weird—I was abused by the babysitter, then Luke; and Sondra was abused by her father, then Pete," Jennifer said. "They say lightning never strikes twice in the same place, but that's just not true."

Pete worked hard at the Hennepin County Home School, a facility for juvenile offenders in Minnetonka, Minnesota. While he was there, he cried about this father's death for the first time. He also told Ethan that he loved him. "He would not have opened up like that if he hadn't been forced to," Cora said. Pete also became interested in creative writing and produced a collection of sonnets, a startling accomplishment for a boy with ADHD. Pete is physically intimidating, but in prison he achieved a gentle quietude. As his release date approached, Jennifer said, "I miss him so much. Yet I feel guilty for missing him, because it's like I'm betraying my daughter." She looked earnest. "My brother will never have the opportunity to be alone with any of my children. But I want him back—I do."

The Home School set up apology sessions for Pete to meet with his mother, Jennifer, and Mandy. He did not see Sondra lest she be further traumatized. "My daughter says if Jesus Christ can forgive the sinners on the cross next to him, she can forgive Pete," Jennifer wrote to me. "I said to Pete, 'Prove that my faith in you is justified.' And he's done everything I asked."

She worried, however, that the full consequences of Pete's abuse might not surface until Sondra's adolescence.

A few weeks after Pete's release, the family celebrated Christmas together at Cora's, at Sondra's suggestion. By the time I returned to Minnesota the following May, new dynamics were in place. It was one of the first real spring days, a Saturday. Pete, Mandy's fiancé, and Sondra were playing football on the lawn, while the others cheered from the porch. Pete was seventeen; Sondra was eleven. I was momentarily shocked to see Pete tackle Sondra; one could sense no physical unease or emotional tension between them, which was unnerving. But the positive change in Pete was undeniable. "That sad kid who lived here is gone," Jennifer said.

Pete had made several visits to the Home School, and I asked why. "Inside, I got really close to this guy who vanished out of my life when he was released," he said. "That hurt me, and I was determined not to do that to the other guys. So I stop in once a month to see the people who helped me." Jennifer said, "He needed something more than we could give, and his way of crying out for help was through Sondra. It's almost like it had to happen—to save him, you know? Like poor Sondra was the sacrificial lamb." A year later, she wrote to me, "I was finally able to tell Pete this week that I forgive him. I couldn't do that until I was able to see for myself that he has changed. He is truly dedicated to living a productive life. My brother, for all his weaknesses, is an amazing young man. I'm so grateful that I'm able to see that."

Two years after I met Pete, Jennifer married; Sondra was a bridesmaid. It was an afternoon wedding, and as evening approached, Sondra drew a chalk hopscotch court in the driveway. After most of the guests had dispersed, the core group hopped through in wedding finery, including Pete. Pete had committed a crime of intimacy; his family had altered the nature of that closeness, but not its degree.

To immerse myself in the worldviews of juvenile prisoners, I took a position advising a theater project at the Hennepin County Home School. Minnesota is known for its strong focus on rehabilitative programs. With a population of mostly recidivist felons and a particularly strong program for underage sex offenders, the Home School presumes that punishment is accomplished by the lack of freedom accorded to inmates. The well-kept campus houses 120 juvenile felons at a time, with 167 acres of grounds. It offers full high school classroom work, with particularly strong arts and athletics programs. It also provides intensive individual, group, and family therapy, as well as a special program for substance abusers. Let it not be supposed, however, that it is all talk therapy and crafts. Freedom of movement is constrained; even using the bathroom requires permission. When necessary, units are put on lockdown, and inmates are placed under harsh restraints. Outbreaks of violence, although usually quickly contained, are not uncommon.

The Home School uses family therapy to resolve conflicts between inmates and their parents, to coach offenders on how to interact at home, and to train parents to exercise more effective control. Such methods may be crucial to breaking the kids out of a criminal identity, and to helping their parents see that their children's problems are not irreversible.

Karina Lopez came to the world in trouble and chaos. The third child of Emma Lopez, a Mexican-American teenage mother with a drug problem, she was born in St. Paul, Minnesota, and moved to Laredo, Texas, when she was a month old. Her father was already out of the picture, and all Karina knows about him is his name. Her mother was soon pregnant by Cesar Marego, a drug dealer fresh from prison, and headed to San Antonio, where she gave birth to Karina's little sister, Esmeralda. Whenever Cesar assaulted Emma, she would return to Minnesota with all four kids; then he'd come to take her back to Texas. By the time Karina was twelve, she had attended thirteen schools. The FBI was a regular visitor to their house; Cesar was serving a ten-year federal sentence when I met Karina.

When Cesar was incarcerated, the family's source of income vanished. Before his arrest, however, he had helped Emma quit drugs; she found a job as a waitress, and Karina had to take care of Esmeralda. She resented it. At thirteen, she began to rebel. "Most people that join gangs, it's because they have nobody who loves them, and that wasn't the problem," she said. "I had Mom, who loved me a lot. But we'd moved so much, and I never felt like I belonged anywhere, and a gang seemed like a solution."

For many years, Emma ran a cleaning service by day and waited tables by night, saving to buy a house. When she discovered that Karina was in a gang, she learned where its members met. At the appointed time, she broke into an abandoned house across the street. "I look across and these girls with guns are sitting in a circle," she said to me. "So I cross the street, bang on the front door, and say, 'Karina, you are coming home with me right now.' The whole gang is there; they could kill me. But I don't care. I wasn't having my baby in no gang."

"I didn't leave because of my mom, though that was a pretty weird scene," Karina said. "Gangs are pointless to me, period, but it's even more pathetic here in Minnesota. These people were riding the bus; they didn't even have money for drugs." Karina started hanging out with dealers; soon she was using regularly. "I was high for two years straight, every day," she said.

On November 22, 2002, Karina went with her aunt's boyfriend, Xavier, to pick up a horse saddle stuffed with four pounds of cocaine. Karina's name was not on the package; she was just helping a "friend." As Xavier drove off, she saw that they were being followed. "I'm snorting coke and snorting coke, and I'm fearless when I'm high. So we get on the freeway, and there are at least ten cars behind us, with the lights and everything. He's like, 'We're probably just speeding.' I was going crazy. So we started panicking." They took a highway exit that led to a dead end. "So it was meant to be," Karina said.

When Emma went to look for Karina, her first stop was the home of the "friend" to whom the package was addressed. When the police found Emma there, they connected her to the crime and arrested her. The police didn't believe a fifteen-year-old girl could have been operating independently at this level. Emma recalled, "I said to the cops, 'For ten years now I've had jobs, I've paid my taxes, I've sacrificed everything I knew how to give my kids a good life. You think I'd mess things up for them like this?'" She was angry for being wrongly accused, but she was mainly worried about her daughter. "I'm thinking, okay, I'm in trouble for what I didn't do and I hope I can get off," she told me, "but she's in trouble for what she did do and she's going to jail." Emma and Karina chose a lawyer from the Yellow Pages, unaware that they could have been represented by a public defender; meeting his bills, Emma fell behind on her mortgage, and the bank foreclosed on the house she had worked years to buy.

When Karina arrived at the Home School, her mother's case was pending. "I didn't care about being in myself, but my mom, my mom, I was so worried about my mom. This is my fault. What is my little sister going to do? My brothers? I mean, she was looking at a lot of years, and in federal."

Then one rainy day in May, a duty officer at the Home School told Karina to call her mother. "My mom never even told me about the court date, and she's like, 'Well, I went to court today. . . .'" Karina explained. "My heart dropped. She's like, 'It was dismissed.' I started crying and laughing at the same time. I got on my knees and I thanked God. 'Cause I prayed every day for my mom's case to be dismissed. It was about a thousand times more important than what happened to me. Now I can't wait to go home."

Visiting anyone else at the Home School, I felt the heavy hand of authority and the oppressive shadow of sorrow. Karina acted as though she had invited me over for fun, and her laughter bounced off the grim prison architecture. She uses foul language easily and apologizes for it charmingly, and points out the comical side of her own anguish. "I'm a different person, honestly. I'll always have my love for cocaine and weed, 'cause I just do. I'll miss 'em. But I won't use 'em."

When I first met Karina, she rhapsodized about being in

love. "My boyfriend, Rafael, he's been writing me every week since I've been locked up. And he went to all my courts." She'd met him when she was fourteen and he was twenty-one. "I know it's illegal, but mentally, I'm not a little girl." Our next visit was scheduled a few weeks later, but when I arrived at the Home School, the duty officer said she couldn't see me.

"On October fourth, I went on my home visit," she told me later. "Rafael came with my mom to take me back on Sunday. I gave him a kiss on his hand, because I couldn't climb into the back where he was, and that night I prayed, 'Take care of him.'" The next morning, when she was taking her high-school equivalency tests (GED) at an official testing site, she learned that Rafael had been shot on his way to work. Karina kept her face in her hands as she told me about it.

Karina's counselors were scared that she was going to relapse, but the tragedy had a galvanizing effect on her. A few weeks later, Karina made arrangements to finish her GED, which she passed; the day she left the Home School, she was offered two jobs. She remained close to Rafael's family, and her probation officer, impressed by her hard work and clean urinalyses, let Karina go to Mexico with them a few months later.

Karina moved on to a better-paying job at a bank. She was determined to buy her mother a house; to make her life a tribute to Rafael; to make good. "I just want to be happy, even if I'm by myself. I want to have all the material things I need, but I want to be a respected person. I don't want to be just Karina, who fucked up her life." Over the following two years, the girl who had never stayed in a school for more than a year stuck with her job at the bank and earned a promotion.

We kept in sporadic touch, and five years after her release, she wrote to me in an e-mail, "My daughter just turned two, and I turned twenty-two. This year was a roller coaster. I separated from her father, then got back together. My stepfather, Esmeralda's dad, was released after ten years, and went back to jail seven months later, so he's now looking at twenty-five years in prison at age sixty-three. The government should put more money into rehabilitating criminals so that they have a chance to turn their lives around. Most of us want to, if we can just figure out how."

The public endlessly debates what children and teenagers who have broken the law deserve and don't deserve: drug treatment, adult sentencing, mental health care, etc. Yet juvenile justice in the United Sates is largely a story of gross abuses. In 2003, an article in the *New York Times* described Mississippi's juvenile justice system: "Boys and girls were routinely hogtied, shackled to poles, or locked in restraint chairs for hours for minor infractions like talking in the cafeteria or not saying, 'Yes sir.'" A lawsuit brought against the operators of one center said, "Toilets and walls are covered with mold, rust, and excrement. Insects have infested the facility, and the smell of human excrement permeates the entire building. Children frequently have to sleep on thin mats that smell of urine and mold." Many children claimed to have been assaulted by guards; many were locked in their cells for twenty-three hours every day; infections caused by filthy conditions were rampant. Suicidal girls in Mississippi prisons have been stripped and put on lockdown in isolation cells with no light or window, and only a drain on the floor.

Offenders in other states don't fare much better. The US Attorney General's office found in Nevada that staffers were "punching boys in the chest, kicking their legs, shoving them against lockers and walls, slapping youths in the face, and smashing youths' heads in doors" and subjecting them to "verbal abuse in which their race, family, physical appearance and stature, intelligence, or perceived sexual orientation were aggressively attacked." A report by the Florida Inspectors General described how staff at a juvenile facility stood by as a seventeen-year-old begged for help and slowly died of a ruptured appendix. The list could go on and on.

It remains common to blame an abusive childhood environment for the rate of juvenile crime, and certainly criminality can be the upshot of fear, loneliness, hatred, and neglect. But this popular narrative of abuse and neglect was not the one I most commonly found. Even if they couldn't cope or were narcissistic, most of the parents I met in researching this chapter loved their kids. Most knew that it would serve their children's interests to avoid crime—or at least to avoid punishment. Many engaged in self-criticism and voiced a wish to make up for past deficits. Even among those who loved well, however, affection often did not seem to keep regular company with insight. Nonetheless, love is among the good medicines for crime and anger. A broken family is still a family, and a broken home, still a home.

Dashonte Malcolm, known to his family and friends as Cool, was sixteen when we met, a good-looking, well-spoken African American with a sense of humor about himself. He seems like a fellow you'd trust with your checkbook or your sister, so it was easy to believe that he was locked up because of someone else's bad behavior. "This is my first offense," he said, hanging his head, "and my last." While many of the kids at the Home School evinced embarrassment about the humiliation of being stripped of basic freedoms, Dashonte seemed genuinely remorseful about his crime.

Dashonte's father, a bus driver, had died of an alcohol-triggered stroke when Dashonte was five, and his mother, Audrey, had brought up her only son in the tough neighborhoods of South Minneapolis under the general patronage of her imposing father, the Bishop of Minnesota of the Pentecostal Church of God in Christ, with forty-four churches under his aegis—a man by whose air of grand authority I was always slightly awed. Audrey Malcolm is large and beautiful, with soft eyes and an aura of quiet dignity. She enfolds you in good cheer, although closer observation reveals that she is somewhat reserved beneath her outgoing manner. Dashonte describes his mom as his best friend; he told me he was thinking about having her face tattooed on his arm "so I'd always have her with me."

Audrey had moved a neighborhood away from the worst part of the ghetto to distance Dashonte from crime. "But there was always that thing picking at me, to go back to where the trouble was," Dashonte said. He described himself as "a badass" in school. In third grade, a new kid arrived at Dashonte's school: Darius Stewart from Tallahassee. Audrey didn't like Darius's influence, and she switched Dashonte to another school in sixth grade, to separate them. Two years later, Darius enrolled at the new school. When Dashonte was sixteen, Audrey bought him a car. Audrey was to buy Dashonte five cars before he turned eighteen. He wrecked three of them, and maintained that each of those crashes was the other driver's fault. Darius didn't have a car, and Dashonte took to giving him rides.

The offense that landed Dashonte behind bars was aggravated assault. He and Darius had picked up a girl at a bus stop, and wanted to go to a pool hall tournament that had a seven-dollar admission fee. Darius proposed robbing someone. Dashonte had a gun and they found a boy alone, threatened him, and took eighty dollars along with his jacket and sneakers. The news traveled around school after Darius wore the stolen clothing. Darius and Dashonte were arrested. "The detectives called and said, 'Aggravated robbery and assault.' I couldn't fathom it," Audrey recalled. She insisted that her son had never had guns—she searched his room from time to time and she knew. She walked into the Juvenile Detention Center, and Dashonte started crying. "I said, 'Cool, I might beat you half to death tomorrow—but I want to know tonight what happened,' she recalled. "So he saw that I was more with him than against him."

At the trial, Darius blamed Dashonte; Dashonte blamed Darius. I met them both and found Dashonte a great deal more likeable than Darius, but there can be no denying that Dashonte was the one with the gun. Both boys were sentenced to eight months at the County Home School. "I felt like, you've already humiliated yourself," Audrey explained. "My mom used to tell us, 'I don't care if you killed somebody. I want you to come home and tell me.' That's what I wanted Cool to hear: Whatever you do, you're my son. If it was murder, would I turn my back? No way. And I told him that." Audrey wrote Dashonte a letter every day, and closed each one, "Love you more than life itself. Mom."

There's a fine line between heroic love and willful blindness, and Audrey Malcolm has visited both sides of that line. "He said he didn't even think the boy they held up really took offense, because he was laughing at them through the whole thing," she told me. "Cool actually tried to give the money back, and Darius snatched it out of his hand." I wanted to believe what his mother believed, but both staff and other inmates told me that Dashonte was actually in the Bloods. When I mentioned the gang to Audrey, she said that Dashonte had always had a need to be popular, and pretended to be a gang member to get respect.

Shortly before Dashonte was released, I went with his mother to the Emmanuel Tabernacle Church of God in Christ. We arrived as people were streaming in, the women in bell-shaped hats that matched their dresses and handbags, their stilt-heeled shoes adorned with diamante butterflies and silk blossoms; the men in dandyish confections of suits, with pleats and gathered neckties. The atmosphere was warm and friendly. I greeted Dashonte's grandmother, Mother Forbes, the first lady of the church. There was already a man in the pulpit, and soon a woman got up and started singing, and before long, everyone was singing, accompanied by a Hammond organ and a drum set. First-time visitors to the church were asked to stand and introduce ourselves. The first woman who spoke up said, "I am on business in the Twin Cities and it is Sunday and I was not going to let this blessed day go by because without Jesus

I am nothing!" A second made a similar speech that ended, "I am here today to be brought out of sin! Hallelujah!" Then the microphone was passed to me. Meekly, I said, "I am here as a guest of Audrey Malcolm and Mother Forbes, and I am so moved by this congregation's faith." Everyone clapped.

I called on the Malcolms six months later. Dashonte was free; his grandmother came over, and the four of us had lemonade and carrot cake. I had heard that he still belonged to the Bloods, but, with his mother in the room, he described the fine life he had imagined for himself, with a wife and an office job. It felt more like tact than deception. "Gang life is always going to be on my mind," Dashonte conceded when I later spoke with him alone. You don't quit a gang in some grand ceremony; you let the affiliation peter out, often with ambivalence. I wanted to believe in Dashonte's resolve, but at that stage, his innocence felt like a flexible, daily decision.

Loyalty turned out to be Audrey's strong suit, and I came to love my visits with the Malcolms. Dashonte didn't quite get the white-collar job he'd talked about, but he managed to avoid serious trouble and did not return to prison. When he met a girl he really liked, he talked about her with joy; soon enough, they were engaged. In the end, his mother had believed him into becoming who he had sometimes pretended to be. Her gift for faith proved strong enough to achieve redemption not only in the next world, but also right here in this one.

In a sweeping survey of over two million American teenagers, one in four had used, carried, or taken part in an episode involving a gun or a knife in the previous year. Other sources suggest that as many as one in ten has physically assaulted at least one parent. About three million juveniles—a number greater than the entire population of Chicago—are taken into custody every year, and over two millions of these are arrested. Juveniles are more likely to be caught than are adult criminals; like any beginners, they are somewhat incompetent. About 70 percent are referred to juvenile court; about a third receive probation, and 7 percent are incarcerated or placed outside their homes. Arrest has become what one critic called "an extension of the principal's office."

Despite these high numbers, the rate of violent juvenile crime has gone down fairly steadily since 1994; the per capita rate of arrest for violent juvenile crime is about half of what it was then, and the rate of arrest for murder in this population is down by about 75 percent. The many competing explanations for this shift include economic growth through the new millennium; the end of the crack epidemic; the expansion of imprisonment, which keeps many would-be violent criminals off the streets; and changing methods of policing.

Kids who have committed crimes together reap different sentences according to the engagement of the family. One judge told me that she would always give less time to an offender whose parents appeared to be positive influences because "those kids might be able to learn, as opposed to destroying lives again." The thinking is sound, but the irony is inescapable: the deprivation that encouraged the child's criminality now lengthens his or her sentence.

Criminal behavior has been related to a genetic irregularity. The neuroscientist Avshalom Caspi at Duke University surveyed people with a genetic tendency toward violence who had had a nonviolent childhood and found that they had the usual odds of developing antisocial behavior; among those people in his study who had that gene *and* were beaten as children, 85 percent exhibited antisocial behavior. So the gene appears to confer not criminal behavior, but a vulnerability to develop such behavior. While family can be a negative influence, it can also be constructive.

A child whose family relationships are troubled is more likely to seek out a negative peer group than a well-adjusted child is, and at that point it is hard to say whether the child has been influenced by his friends or has influenced them. Mothers often told me, "Jimmy just got in with the wrong crowd"—and then I talked to the other mothers who claimed that Jimmy was the wrong crowd with whom their sons had fallen in. It seems noteworthy to me that, with a few exceptions, the criminals I met were not enjoying their own crimes; they were trapped in behavior that often made them as miserable as it made their victims. Criminality felt in many cases more like an illness than many of the "illnesses" I had set out to study. We "cure" disabled people who would prefer not to be cured, but we fail to treat some people with this condition who could recover and would like to do so.

Tall, handsome, tough, with close-cropped hair, Krishna Mirador had a way of wearing prison clothes that made them look like fashion. His English was heavily accented and sometimes hard to understand, and he would frequently ask me, "How you say in English?" as he groped for vocabulary. Born in south Los Angeles, he told me he had been abandoned at birth by a Latina mother whose name he never learned; he was raised by his father, Raul, who was only eighteen when Krishna was born, and who was a member of Sureños 13; the gang was the only family Krishna had ever known. When Krishna was eleven, his father was deported to Guatemala, but Raul knew a woman in Minneapolis who owed him a favor, and when I met Krishna, he had been living in her house for four years. He'd never found out why she was in his father's debt, and he didn't want to ask.

The weekend after I met Krishna at the Home School, a rather beautiful Irish-American woman in her mid-forties introduced herself as Carol and said, "My son Krishna wants to be in your research project." Then Krishna came into the room. "Hey, Mom, just give him your signature on the interview release form," he said in unaccented English. I stood there, astonished. Carol, who looked just like him, said how worried she was about Krishna, and I said that it seemed like he'd had a rough time after the hard childhood in Los Angeles. She looked at me as though I were slightly unhinged. "Krishna was born and raised in Duluth," she said.

Carol Malloy and Raul Mirador met in the late 1980s through Ananda Marga, which is sometimes called a cult, sometimes a spiritual movement, and sometimes a discipline. The group preaches unity and love but has also been accused of weapons smuggling. One of Ananda Marga's doctrines is "revolutionary marriage" in which people from completely different walks of life marry each other, thus breaking down bourgeois notions of class and nationality. Raul had visa problems, and

Carol's marriage was failing. Raul agreed to pay for her divorce if she would marry him.

They lived in Duluth until Raul moved them all to Guatemala when Krishna was five. Carol later told Raul she was going to divorce him unless he returned to the US with her; she was certain she could get custody of the children. When they returned, Krishna was ten; his sister, Ashoka, was eight; his brother, Basho, born in Guatemala, was four. Nine months later, Carol came home one day to an empty house. Raul had taken all three children back to Guatemala.

Carol served kidnapping charges on Raul through the American Embassy and eventually got custody in both countries. Raul went to jail, through Interpol, for kidnapping, but Carol didn't get the kids. "We presented the papers to Raul's parents. When we went in, the beds were still warm, but they were gone. The Mirador family had reabducted my kids." She left Guatemala in despair; two weeks later, Raul's parents paid someone off, and he was released.

Many years later, Krishna wrote to me, "I know my father loves me even though he seldom says it, and I know my mom doesn't even though she says it all the time. I haven't seen my dad have a girlfriend since my mom. He says it's because he doesn't have time, but I know it's because she broke his heart."

While Carol had her kids' pictures appearing on milk cartons as missing children, Krishna's grandparents hid him with cousins in LA for almost a year, and he joined Sureños. His first assignment, he told me, was to steal a car; then they gave him an Uzi with a full clip of ammunition and ordered him to take the car and "go get some rivals." He said, "I came back with no bullets left. When I felt that adrenaline pumping in my heart, I was like, yeah, this is *my* shit. This is *my* drug."

After nine months, Raul called Krishna back to Guatemala. A year later, when Krishna was thirteen, he and Ashoka came to see Carol in Minneapolis. When they arrived in Minnesota, she told them they weren't going back. "She didn't do it because she loved us," Krishna said. "She did it because she hates my father and it was revenge. She wanted a son so damn bad—I'm gonna show her how hard it is. I had to make her life hell for a little bit."

Their relationship, marked by rage and frustration on both sides, changed dramatically one evening when Krishna went to buy some marijuana and someone shot at him. He was fifteen. The police questioned everyone who was there, but detained Krishna in relation to the murder of a thirty-nine-year-old black man the preceding month. "Black gangs fight black gangs and Chicano gangs fight Chicano gangs," he said. "We like killing each other, I guess. So no way was this me."

But the police soon filed charges against Krishna. When Carol learned that her son would be tried in the adult system, she organized friends to write letters, protest, and pack the courtroom. She explained that Krishna had been kidnapped and was traumatized. For the first time in Hennepin County, a murder case stayed in the juvenile system. Krishna faced an uphill battle, but he was steely in his resolve, and the case was finally dismissed. By then he'd been in jail for seven and a half months.

Things did not go well when he came home. Anyone who came to the house with a blue kerchief—a Sureños symbol—Carol kicked out. Krishna said, "I think a mother should be until the end. Even if I was doing life in prison, she'd still try to be there for me. I was testing her." She replied, "Krishna says he wanted to make my life miserable, and that's why he kept himself in the gang. It's to see if I really love him. I don't think he planned it at all. The gang and the cult are the exact same: very hierarchical; rules; this small group of people dedicated to this pointless rigid structure and ready to die for it. He's recreating the childhood he hated."

At sixteen, Krishna was sent to a year at the County Home School, where I met him. "The gang has his back," Carol said. "Does anyone have your back? My medical insurance has my back. One thing he's proud of in the gang is that he tells other people what to do. He's always on that cell phone barking out orders in Spanish. I said to him, 'Look, I tell people all the time what to do, because I teach first grade. Would you consider it as an alternative?'"

But Carol also admitted that she is in part responsible for who Krishna has become, and she also thought that the complexities of being part white were too much for her son. "He's too scared to be himself. It's hard for mixed-race kids to stand up and say, I am neither here nor there; I am myself." In a letter Krishna wrote me, he said, "It would make sense to tell you who I am, even though sometimes *I* don't even know. Always classified as a 'spic' for my language, culture, looks, and demeanor, but always teased, ostracized, and not fully accepted by my Latino brothers for being a 'half-breed.'"

In the final month of his sentence, Krishna went out every day to a job, and could leave the premises in the evenings with a responsible adult. I took him to dinner. When we had sat up nights in the Home School, he would talk about how he wanted to go to college. Now, as he tucked into a sirloin, I mentioned that I had been interviewing Karina Lopez, and he laughed. "You heard her boyfriend died? My boys did that," he said, and actually thumped his chest. "I saw her the day it happened, in the med unit, crying her ass off. I laughed." Karina later confirmed the episode. "He didn't have anything to do with the murder," she said. "But he sure enjoyed it."

I told him that it was hard to reconcile all this with the boy full of dreams with whom I'd played Scrabble a few weeks earlier. "I love my hatred—it's so strong and sort of pure and real," he said. "And I kind of hate love, like I feel it's always false and disappointing, everyone saying they love me when they just want to control me. I love hatred and I hate love. So is that enough for me to be a psychopath?"

I had heard a great deal about Krishna's father, and wanted to see if Raul was the gentle sage of Krishna's raptures or the manipulative creep I'd heard about from Carol. Three years after I met Krishna, he was planning a trip to Guatemala. I proposed to his father that I visit at the same time.

Raul was warm and courtly and instantly likeable, a small man with thick black wavy hair. We stayed up talking late that night, and Raul returned over and over to the language of morality. "I can understand being willing to die, or to spend your life in prison, but not for a gang," he said. "Krishna needs a cause." He looked at me with sudden frankness. "Can you help him find one?" he asked.

The next night, with bravado, Krishna took me to a

gang-dominated part of the city, where he introduced me to the local Sureños. Everyone had guns and gang tattoos, and at one point we heard gunfire outside the room where we were gathered—and yet it felt weirdly like meeting some-one's fraternity brothers on a college campus. I understood for the first time how Sureños could feel both utterly dangerous and uniquely safe. The gang was itself a horizontal identity, and crime served a function in Krishna's life not unlike the role that Deafness or dwarfism played in other lives I'd examined, not unlike the role that being gay played in my own life. I kept remembering the letter in which Krishna had said he couldn't tell me who he was because he didn't know. His mother had attributed the confusion to being biracial, but it also reflected the question of whether he was his mother's son or his father's, American or Guatemalan, good or evil—a catalogue of duali-ties too long to enumerate. In that ugly room in an ugly neigh-borhood he knew exactly who he was, which allowed him to relax as I had never seen him relax before.

I had been surprised to be drawn to the world of the Deaf, but it was much stranger to be seduced by this world. And yet from the inside, gangbanging was hospitable. I knew that many of the people in that room had committed murder. They were kind to me, however, as a kindness to Krishna, a consideration for which he was clearly starved. That cordiality felt authentic and embracing. I had assumed that hanging out with the gang in the slums of Guatemala City would show me the toughest part of Krishna, but instead, it showed me the most vulnerable. Criminality is an identity, and like any other form of organized brutality—football, war, finanical arbitrage—it can beget great intimacy. There is a social imperative to suppress criminal behavior, but that should not preclude recognition of the identity. I deplore violence, but I recognize the military intimacy it allows men who have no other occasion to bond. Indeed, I recognize that the conquests by which the very map of the world is drawn derive from the loyalty and aggression of young men.

Krishna moved back to Minneapolis to live with his mother again, and the next I heard, he had been shot and was in critical condition; a month later, he got sixteen months for assault. The gang had disappointed him by then; one of the Sureños in the incident had turned state's witness. Krishna called Carol every week. "He calls me because he's allowed to," she said. "Where's the reality? I'd give anything to be able to find it. Even if it's ugly, really, really ugly, I could accept it, if I could only see it, even for a few minutes. That's my dream." She looked at me sadly. "Andrew, I know you better than I know my son," she said.

The next time Krishna was released from prison, he took his ACTs and sent the scores to several colleges, including UCLA, which was his first choice. But before his applications could be processed, he accompanied four fellow gang members on a drive that culminated in the shooting death of a member of the Vatos Locos gang. He was charged with aiding an offender for the benefit of a gang, pled guilty, and was sentenced to eight years in Minnesota's Stillwater maximum security prison.

There is a vast grayness to Stillwater. Krishna looked spruce whenever he entered the visiting room, but his idealist streak had dimmed. "I don't hate Carol anymore," he said to me one afternoon. "I used to think she was the one who had made me powerless, but now I think she loved me in whatever way she knows how. I just felt *so* powerless growing up, not getting to choose where to live, and I finally realized, I joined the gang so I could feel really powerful. And what's the upshot? I'm totally powerless again, right back where I started—only this time, I did it to myself."

Carol said to me a few weeks later, "He wanted to work with the oppressed, to be with his people, with the disenfranchised Latinos. But what has he done? He gets them to kill each other. He lands them in prison. The people he says are his people—they'd be better off without him." I asked if she thought she would be better off without him, and she said, "I've been without him the whole time. I don't really miss who he is at all. But who he was—I miss that person so much. And the person I thought that person would turn into, I miss him, too, with all my heart."

No other group of people has given me more confused information than these juvenile criminals. They didn't trust or like adult white male authority figures, and their knee-jerk lying and misleading was part of what had landed them in prison in the first place. More fundamentally, though, they didn't grasp their own reality.

Jail concentrates human emotions because it confiscates so many normal human actions and robs the inmate of so many ordinary decisions: what to eat, when to eat it, when to shower, and on and on. When you are not on the street, fending for yourself, running from crime to crime, taking drugs that banish the world, you are compelled into reflection. In this pensive state, prisoners dwell on love and hate, on reunion and vengeance. Virtually all the prisoners I met blamed someone else for their incarceration if not for their crime. They also long for the people who offer them comfort: a husband or wife, a boyfriend or girlfriend, the prisoner's children, parents whose love becomes a cherished souvenir of innocence.

The wrongs that some of these teenagers endured were far more real to them than the ones they'd inflicted on others. I met other kids, though, who seemed to have become criminals to give some objective weight to a previous and crippling sense of guilt. One boy I befriended at the Home School, Tyndall Wilkie, had a fight with his mother, a preschool teacher, when he was six and told the school nurse she had been abusing him, then repeated the story to the school social worker. She hadn't abused him; he just wanted to get her in trouble. Tyndall and his sister were put into permanent foster care; his mother was banned from teaching for five years. His whole life unfolded in the shadow of this error and his need for self-punishment.

Love is not only an intuition but also a skill. Therapeutic prison programs such as the Home School's provide structure and momentum for reflection, via group sessions, diaries, and letter-writing. Having a child at the Home School also provides learning opportunities for the child's parents. Prison defines parameters for affection that are easier for some people than the unmapped, everyday world. You come on visiting day. You stay the whole time. People who cannot achieve constancy from minute to minute can sometimes sustain it once a week. In some cases, this support would vanish when the child was released, but in others it functioned as training wheels: By the time the child's sentence was up, the parents were ready to perform their roles with new confidence and skill, unassisted.

Criminality appears to be more subject to resolve than many other conditions. No one can will his way out of Down syndrome, but some people can walk away from a criminal past. They usually require enormous supports to do so. Research on preventing crime points to a number of effective solutions, but we ignore most, writing off vast sectors of our society. Our lack of sympathy for these children keeps successful treatment out of their reach. Aside from the common prejudice that therapeutic interventions are soft on the criminal, the justification for withholding such treatments is that they are exorbitantly expensive. Neither justification has merit. The major financial benefit of therapeutic programs is curtailed recidivism. The cost of jailing a minor ranges from about $20,000 to $65,000 per year. A crime gives rise to enormous costs, including loss of property, trial expenses, health-care costs from injury, and psychological liabilities sustained by frightened victims. Bringing down recidivism even by a small percentage makes good economic sense.

Family interventions are the most productive. As with autism or Down syndrome, early intervention brings the best results. Study after study has shown that family therapies reduce recidivism. At-risk children whose families received no early therapy were 70 percent more likely to be arrested for a violent crime before they turned eighteen than those whose families received such therapy. These statistics have had little effect on how we deal with juvenile crime. Only one of ten juvenile prisons uses family therapies, and only about a quarter of these do so consistently. Basic family interventions can run anywhere from $2,000 to $30,000 per family served. One project showed that for new mothers deemed to be at risk of having a child who would commit crimes, every $1 spent on helping the mothers with parenting skills saved $7 in later costs associated with having children who committed crimes.

Moral questions loom large in any discussion of such treatments. What message do we convey if we respond to violent crime with therapy? If we opt for less prison time, more crimes will be committed by people who would otherwise have been locked up. We can't dismantle the justice system or knock out crime with kindness; fire is often needed to fight fire. At the same time, the overwhelming evidence is that punitive justice can be strengthened with therapeutic programs. To discard the prison system in favor of therapeutic interventions would be crazy; but a prison system that is used without therapeutic intervention, as in much of the country today, is at least equally crazy.

Families of criminals often struggle both to admit that their child has done something destructive, and to continue to love him or her anyway. Some give up the love; some blind themselves to the bad behavior. People who see and acknowledge the darkness in those they love, but whose love is only strengthened by that knowledge, achieve that truest love that is eagle-eyed even when the views are bleak. I met one family whose own tragedy had led them to embrace these contradictions more than any other, one mother whose love seemed both infinitely deep and infinitely knowing of a blighted person.

On April 20, 1999, Eric Harris and Dylan Klebold, seniors at Columbine High School in Littleton, Colorado, placed bombs in the cafeteria, set to go off during first lunch period at 11:17 a.m., and planned to shoot anyone who tried to flee. Errors in the construction of the detonators prevented the bombs from exploding, but Klebold and Harris held the whole school hostage, killing twelve students and one teacher before turning their guns on themselves. At the time, it was the worse episode of school violence in history. The American right blamed the collapse of "family values," while the left impugned violence in the movies and sought to tighten gun-control laws.

The number of people killed that day is generally listed as thirteen, and the Columbine Memorial commemorates only thirteen deaths, as though Klebold and Harris had not also died that day in that place. Contrary to wide speculation then and since, the boys did not come from broken homes and did not have records of criminal violence. The wishful thought of a world that witnessed this horror was that good parenting could prevent children from developing into Eric Harris or Dylan Klebold, but evil does not always grow in a predictable or accountable manner. As the families of people with autism or schizophrenia wonder what happened to the apparently healthy people they knew, other families grapple with children who have turned to horrifying acts and wonder what happened to the apparently innocent children they thought they understood.

The last Sue Klebold heard from Dylan, the younger of her two children, was "bye" as he let the front door slam on his way to school that April morning. In the middle of the day, Tom received a call about the shootings at school and learned that Dylan was a suspect. He called Sue. "I had a sudden vision of what he might be doing," Sue said. "And so while every other mother in Littleton was praying that her child was safe, I had to pray that mine would die before he hurt anyone else. I thought if this was really happening and he survived, he would go into the criminal justice system and be executed, and I couldn't bear to lose him twice. I gave the hardest prayer I ever made, that he would kill himself, because then at least I would know that he wanted to die and wouldn't be left with all the questions I'd have if he got caught by a police bullet. Maybe I was right, but I've spent so many hours regretting that prayer: I wished for my son to kill himself and he did."

That night, police told the Klebolds to leave their house—both so the police could turn it inside out, and for their own safety. The Klebolds went to stay with Tom's sister for four days, returning home on the day of Dylan's funeral. "We didn't really know what had happened," Sue said. "We just knew Dylan was dead, that he'd killed himself, and that he was involved with the shooting."

As Littleton's period of mourning began, a carpenter from Illinois erected fifteen crosses on a hillside near the school: one for each victim, including Dylan and Eric. "I was so buoyed by this," Tom said. "I wanted to be a part of the community. And I thought we could all grieve together." Sue remembered, "There were flowers, and Dylan's and Eric's crosses had as many as everyone else's." Then the parents of some of the victims destroyed Dylan's and Eric's crosses. The youth group at a local church planted fifteen trees, only to have some of the victims' parents arrive with a press escort to chop down Dylan's and Eric's trees. At the high school graduation a week later, there were eulogies for the victims, but the head of the school told friends of Dylan's and Eric's to make themselves scarce. Before long, reports referring to the incident started using the number thirteen rather than fifteen. "The shorthand was this," Tom said. "Thirteen people died. Two Nazis killed them, and the parents were responsible." Sue said reflectively, "I think the other parents believed they had experienced loss, and I had not, because their children were of value, and mine was not. My child died too. He died after making a terrible decision and doing a terrible thing, but he was still my child and he still died."

The Klebolds' lawyer had advised them not to talk to the press; their silence exacerbated the local hostility. "You'd read something, and you couldn't respond to it," Tom said. "It was just like constantly being hit, and being hit again," Sue said. "To me, the only way to heal this community was to try to have a one-to-one relationship with each of the victims. My journey is not complete until I can say to these people, 'If it would help you to talk to me, I'm here." She has never done it, because a counselor cautioned her that by contacting them, she might retraumatize them. "But I cried for their children just as I did for mine," she said.

Investigations over the ensuing months revealed an atmosphere of bullying at Columbine. "He and Eric didn't shoot us, and they didn't shoot up Kmart or a gas station; they shot up the school," Tom said. "The whole social pattern at Columbine was unfair, and Dylan couldn't do anything about it. That would cause enough anger in a sensitive kid to make him retaliate." Dylan had experienced significant humiliation at school, though he was six feet four and not easy to push around.

"I can never decide whether it's worse to think your child was hardwired to be like this and that you couldn't have done anything, or to think he was a good person and something set this off in him," Sue said. "What I've learned from being an outcast since the tragedy has given me insight into what it must have felt like for my son to be marginalized. He created a version of his reality for us: to be pariahs, unpopular, with no means to defend ourselves against those who hate us."

Tom, like Dylan, had been painfully shy in high school and felt that because of their similarities he knew Dylan instinctively; he can identify with how Dylan may have felt, but not with what he did. Sue sees a terrible confluence of circumstances, including depression, a school environment that caused rage, and an influential friend who had severe problems. "Dylan felt a little afraid of Eric, a little protective of him, and a little controlled by him," she said. "He was caught in something I don't understand. Yes, he made a conscious choice and did this horrible thing, but what had happened to his consciousness that he would make such a choice? The same pathology that killed and hurt all the others also killed my son."

From the day of the bloodbath, April twentieth, until the following October, the Klebolds knew few details about what had transpired, except that Dylan was at the shooting and supposedly committed suicide. "We kept clinging to the belief that he hadn't really killed anybody," Sue said. Then came the police report. "It just launched my grief all over again, because I didn't have denial anymore." Then they saw the "basement tapes" that Dylan and Eric had deliberately left behind, which reveal a Dylan spewing hatred, full of self-aggrandizing rage. "Seeing those videos was as traumatic as the original event," Sue said. "All the protective beliefs that we'd held onto were shattered. There wasn't hate talk in our house. I'm part Jewish, and yet the anti-Semitic stuff was there; they were going through every derogatory word: a nigger, a kike. I saw the end product of my life's work: I had created a monster. Everything I had refused to believe was true. Dylan was a willing participant, and the massacre was not a spontaneous impulse. He had purchased and created weapons that were designed to end of the lives of as many people as possible. He shot to kill. For the first time, I understood how Dylan appeared to others. When I saw his disdain for the world, I almost hated my son. For me, it's a smothering emptiness."

She added, "If I could say anything to a roomful of parents right now, I would say, 'Never trust what you see.' Was he nice? Was he thoughtful? I was taking a walk not long before he died, and I'd asked him, 'Come and pick me up if it rains.' And he did. He was there for you, and he was the best listener I ever met. I realize now that was because he didn't want to talk, and he was hiding. He and Eric worked together at the pizza parlor. A couple of weeks before Columbine, Eric's beloved dog was sick, and it looked like he wasn't going to make it, and so Dylan worked Eric's shift as well as his own so that Eric could have time to be with his dog."

In the writing Dylan and Eric left behind, Eric comes off as homicidal; his anger is all directed outward. Dylan comes off as suicidal; his energy fuels self-criticism. It's as though Dylan went along with the homicide for Eric's sake, and Eric with the suicide for Dylan's sake. Toward the end, Dylan was counting the hours he had left. "How could he keep it so secret," Sue wondered, "this pain he was in?"

Sue spoke of herself as a lucky person. "I was fortunate that Dylan did not turn on us. The worst thing he did to us was he took himself away from us. After Columbine, I felt that Dylan killed God. No god could have had anything to do with this, so there must not be one. When everything in your world is gone, all your belief systems, and your self-concepts—your beliefs in yourself, your child, your family—there is a process of trying to establish, who am I? Is there a person there at all? A woman at work asked me recently how my weekend was, and it happened to be the anniversary of the shootings. So I said that I wasn't doing so well and I told her why, and she said, 'I always forget that about you.' I gave her a hug and said, 'That's the nicest thing anyone has said to me in years.'"

When I mentioned to the Klebolds that I thought they spoke with an extraordinary clarity about their situation, in contrast to some of the other people I interviewed for this chapter, Tom said, "We are able to be open and honest about those things because our son is dead. His story is complete. We can't hope for him to do something else, something better. You can tell a story a whole lot better when you know its ending."

A few years after we first met, Sue said to me, "When it first happened, I used to wish that I had never had children, that I had never married. If Tom and I hadn't crossed paths at Ohio State, Dylan wouldn't have existed and this terrible thing wouldn't have happened. But over time, I've come to feel that, for myself, I am glad I had kids and glad I had the kids I did because the love for them—even at the price of this pain—has been the single greatest joy of my life. When I say that, I am speaking of my own pain, and not the pain of other people. But I accept my own pain; life is full of suffering and this is mine. I know it would have been better for the world if Dylan had never been born. But I believe it would not have been better for me."

Juvenile crime results from the interplay of the genetics, personality, and inclinations of the juvenile himself; the behavior and attitudes of his family; and his larger social environment. The idea of the bad seed appears to be outmoded, but some people seem to be born without a moral center, much as some people are born without a thumb. The genetics of decency are well beyond our primitive science, but despite boundless love and support, some people are geared toward violence and destruction, lack empathy, or have a blurry sense of truth. In most people, though, the criminal potential requires external stimulus to be activated; the intense, internally determined psychopath of the movies is unusual.

Yet much of the law is organized around the notion that young criminals are intractably bad. Moving cases from the juvenile system to an adult criminal court that can issue heavier sentences has become increasingly popular. Judges in overburdened adult courts often dismiss these cases, but sometimes they use adult sentencing guidelines; punishment therefore tends to be either negligible or far too severe. Further, judges may be more likely to direct into adult courts the cases of juveniles who are members of racial minorities, who do not present themselves well, or who appear not to have supportive families. In the 1990s, every state except Nebraska enacted legislation making it easier to try juveniles in adult criminal courts; the number of juveniles in adult prisons skyrocketed.

The first court specifically for juveniles was established in Illinois at the end of the nineteenth century, based on a subjective system of judging the character of young offenders. Through the early twentieth century, the courts conducted themselves like parents—with an all-powerful state acting outside the adult system of checks and balances. By the 1960s, reformers had begun to rise up against a capricious system. In 1967, in *In re Gault*, the Supreme Court examined the case of a young man convicted of making offensive sexual phone calls to a neighbor. The juvenile court judge committed the youth to a state school for up to six years—even though an adult found guilty of a similar offense would have gotten off with a fine of no more than $50 or two months in jail. In overturning the youth's sentence, the Supreme Court granted juvenile offenders the rights to receive a notice of charges, to consult a lawyer, to confront and cross-examine witnesses, and to invoke the privilege against self-incrimination. Then the Reagan administration pushed for a reversion to "get tough" policies. The states began to try juveniles as adults, enforced the death penalty for some juveniles, and saw a significant increase of juveniles in jail; by the late 1990s, almost half of convicted juveniles were locked up rather than in community or treatment programs.

Juvenile justice remains paternalistic. Police officers have discretion to dismiss detained youths, and many kids are sent home to their parents with a warning. Over the past twenty years or so, the left, led by the ACLU and similar organizations, has sought more due process and better-defined rights for young offenders, but the resulting formalization has deprived the system of its leniency; one recent survey showed that only a third of juveniles felt their attorney had helped them. The right, meanwhile, has pushed for harsher sentencing. The left wants children to have the rights of adults but not the responsibilities; the right pushes for exactly the opposite. The processing of cases is terribly slow, and juveniles may languish in detention for as much as a year pre-trial. Sentences are harsher than they were pre-*Gault*. As juvenile justice scholars Thomas Grisso and Robert G. Schwartz have said in *Youth on Trial*, "The adult-like procedures introduced by the left worked in spiral-like tandem with punitive measures introduced by the right to create an ungainly, harsh, and internally contradictory juvenile court."

Maturity does not arrive with adolescence. Biological evidence now demonstrates that the adolescent brain is structurally different from the adult one, which supports making a distinction between adult and juvenile crime. In the prefrontal cortex of a fifteen-year-old, the areas responsible for self-control are not fully developed; many parts of the brain do not mature until about age twenty-four. While the full implications of this variant physiognomy cannot yet be mapped, holding children to adult standards is biologically naive. On the one hand, kids who commit crimes are likely to become adults who commit crimes; but on the other hand, kids who commit crimes act on impulses because they are kids.

As many as three out of four incarcerated juveniles have a psychiatric diagnosis, as opposed to one of five in the general nine- to seventeen-year-old population. Some 50 to 80 percent of incarcerated juveniles have learning disabilities. Juvenile crimes are also associated with low IQ, impulsivity, poor self-control, deficient social skills, conduct disorders, and emotional underdevelopment. These predisposing characteristics are manifest terribly early. In one study, parents were asked to describe their toddlers; they were reinterviewed ten years later. Those labeled "difficult" as small children were twice as likely to have committed crimes as those labeled "easy." Of course, for every simple equivalence (difficult babies become lawbreakers), there is a parallel possibility (mothers who find their children disturbing bring up criminals).

Those who swing into full-fledged delinquency before age twelve are highly likely to become chronic adult offenders and are much more likely to commit violent crimes than are those whose behaviors kick in later. This may reflect habit; the norms of your childhood are particularly hard to buck. It may also be that some children who are troublesome early have that missing moral thumb and are manifesting something fundamental to their personality. If a child's delinquency stems from habit, then early interventions to break those habits might be effective. If it's genetic, then such interventions are much less likely to succeed.

In the chapter on schizophrenia, I noted how many schizophrenics are in jail; in researching this one, I learned how many people in jail suffer from some vague mental health diagnosis. Incarcerating mentally unstable people with the larger prison population may exacerbate criminals' destructive behavior. Carol Carothers, executive director of the National Alliance on Mental Illness Maine, has said, "It's hard to imagine a worse place to house a child that requires services for their mental illness."

Since the day in December 2012 when Peter Lanza's son Adam killed his own mother, Nancy; himself; and twenty-four young children and two adults at Sandy Hook Elementary School, strangers from across the world have sent Peter thousands of letters and keepsakes: bibles, teddy bears, homemade toys. People sent candy, too, but Peter said, "I was wary about eating anything—there was no way to be sure it wasn't poisoned."

An accountant who is a vice president for taxes at a General Electric subsidiary, Peter hadn't seen his son for two years at the time of the Sandy Hook killings, and, even with hindsight, he doesn't think that the catastrophe could have been predicted. But he wishes he had pushed harder to see Adam. "Any variation on what I did and how my relationship was had to be good, because no outcome could be worse," he said.

Born in 1992, Adam Lanza didn't talk until he was three, and he always understood many more words than he could speak. He showed such hypersensitivity to physical touch that tags had to be removed from his clothing. In preschool and at Sandy Hook, where he was a pupil till the beginning of sixth grade, he sometimes smelled things that weren't there and washed his hands excessively. Diagnosed with sensory-integration disorder, Adam underwent speech and occupational therapy in kindergarten and first grade. Still, photos show him looking cheerful. "Adam loved Sandy Hook school," Peter said. But Adam struggled with basic emotions, and received coaching from Nancy, who became a stay-at-home mother after Adam was born.

Peter and Nancy's marriage began to unravel. Peter moved to Stamford, nearly an hour from Newtown, but still saw Adam and his brother every weekend. When Adam began middle school, the structure of the school day changed; instead of sitting in one classroom, he had to move from room to room, and he found the disruption punishing. His mother Xeroxed his textbooks in black-and-white, because he found color graphics unbearable. He quit playing the saxophone, stopped climbing trees, avoided eye contact, and developed a stiff, lumbering gait. "It was crystal clear something was wrong," Peter said. "You could see the changes occurring." It is hard to be sure whether new problems were setting in or old ones were becoming more apparent.

Many of the symptoms that afflicted Adam are signs of autism that might be exacerbated by the hormonal shifts of adolescence. When Adam was thirteen, Peter and Nancy took him to a psychiatrist, who gave a diagnosis of Asperger syndrome. But Adam would not accept the diagnosis. The psychiatrist recommended homeschooling, arguing that the disadvantages of sending Adam to a regular school were worse than those of isolating him from his peers. From eighth grade on, Nancy taught Adam the humanities and Peter met with him twice a week to handle the sciences. Adam displayed what his father described as "the arrogance that Aspies can have." Adam wrote that he was "not satisfied if information related to me is not profound enough." He went on to discount his parents' teaching, asserting that he had taught himself chemistry.

When Adam was fourteen, Peter and Nancy took him to Yale's Child Study Center for further diagnosis. The psychiatrist who assessed Adam recorded that he was a "pale, gaunt, awkward young adolescent standing rigidly with downcast gaze and declining to shake hands." He also noted that Adam "had relatively little spontaneous speech but responded in a flat tone with little inflection and almost mechanical prosody." Many people with autism speak in a flat tone, and avoiding eye contact is common too, because trying to interpret sounds and faces at the same time is overwhelming. He reported, "Adam imposes many strictures, which are increasingly onerous for mother. He disapproves if mother leans on anything in the house because it is 'improper.' . . . He is also intolerant if mother brushes by his chair and objected to her new high-heel boots, because they were 'too loud.'" The psychiatrist was concerned that Adam's parents seemed to focus on his schooling, and said that it was more urgent to address "how to accommodate Adam's severe social disabilities in a way that would permit him to be around peers." He concluded that Nancy was "almost becoming a prisoner in her own house."

"Adam was not open to therapy," Peter told me. "He did not want to talk about problems and didn't even admit he had Asperger's." Peter and Nancy were confident enough in the diagnosis that they didn't look for other explanations for Adam's behavior. In that sense, Asperger's may have distracted them from whatever else was amiss. "If he had been a totally normal adolescent and he was well adjusted and then all of a sudden went into isolation, alarms would go off," Peter told me. "But let's keep in mind that you expect Adam to be weird." Still, Peter and Nancy sought professional support repeatedly, and none of the doctors they saw detected troubling violence in Adam's disposition.

Peter gets annoyed when people speculate that Asperger's was the cause of Adam's rampage. "Asperger's makes people unusual, but it doesn't make people like this," he said, and expressed the view that the condition "veiled a contaminant" that was not Asperger's. Both autism and psychopathy entail a lack of empathy. Psychologists, though, distinguish between the "cognitive empathy" deficits of autism (difficulty understanding what emotions are, trouble interpreting other people's nonverbal signs) and the "emotional empathy" deficits of psychopathy (lack of concern about hurting other people, an inability to share their feelings). The subgroup of people with neither kind of empathy appears to be small but dangerous.

By 2008, when Adam turned sixteen and was going to school only for occasional events, Nancy's e-mails to Peter described Adam's escalating misery. "He had a horrible night. . . . He cried in the bathroom for forty-five minutes and missed his first class." Two weeks later, she wrote, "I am hoping that he pulls together in time for school this afternoon, but it is doubtful. He has been sitting with his head to one side for over an hour doing nothing." Nancy regularly asked Peter not to come when Adam was having a "bad day," but her correspondence shows no sense of crisis commensurate with the Yale assessment. Peter had begun to feel distanced by the intensity of Adam's relationship with Nancy. His approach to parenting was as docile as Nancy's was obsessive. She indulged Adam's compulsions. "She would build the world around him and cushion it," Peter said. All parenting involves choosing between the day (why have another argument at dinner?) and the years (the child must learn to eat vegetables). Nancy's error seems to have been that she always focused on the day, in a ceaseless quest to keep peace in the home she shared with the hypersensitive, controlling, increasingly hostile stranger who was her son. Her willingness to indulge his isolation may well have exacerbated the problems it was intended to ameliorate.

In the fall of 2009, Adam developed his private obsession with killing. He started editing Wikipedia entries on various well-known mass murderers and seems to have been eerily well informed. Although there were still no outward signs of violent tendencies, he was becoming ever harder to deal with. Schoolwork often triggered a sense of hopelessness. "He was exhausted and lethargic all day, and said he was unable to concentrate and his homework isn't done," Nancy wrote. "He is on the verge of tears over not having his journal entries ready to pass in. He said he has been wondering why he is 'such a loser' and if there is anything he can do about it."

Adam always had aspirations beyond his abilities. His list of colleges started with Cornell, for which he clearly didn't have the academic record. Adam and Peter concluded that he would take classes at Norwalk Community College, near Stamford, before attempting campus life anywhere. Adam wanted to take five classes, but Peter suggested two classes that they could work on together. Peter went to pick him up for a weekend visit, and Adam refused to go. Peter said, "Adam, we've got to figure out a system so I can work with you." Adam was angry. "It was, like, 'I'm taking the five classes. I'm taking them,'" Peter said. It was September 2010: the last time Peter saw his son.

Earlier that year, Nancy had written, "He does not want to see you. I have been trying to reason with him to no avail. He is despondent and crying a lot and just can't continue." Nancy surmised that Adam resented Peter's warning about the heavy course load. I wondered how Peter had felt through this period. "Sad," he said. "I never expected that I would never talk to him again. I thought it was a matter of when."

In early 2012, Nancy said that Adam had agreed to see Peter in the spring, but nothing came of it. Nine months later, Peter protested that Adam never even acknowledged his e-mails. Nancy wrote, "I will talk to him about that but I don't want to harass him. He has had a bad summer and actually stopped going out."

About a week before the shootings, Nancy reportedly told an acquaintance, "I'm worried I'm losing him." But losing him seemed to be a matter of his withdrawal, not of violence. The state's attorney's report says that when Nancy asked Adam whether he would feel sad if anything happened to her, he replied, "No." Peter does not think that Adam had any affection for him either by that point. He said, "With hindsight, I know Adam would have killed me in a heartbeat, if he'd had the chance."

Scientists are sequencing Adam's DNA to see if they can find anomalies that might explain what was broken in him. And yet, if someone has committed heinous crimes and is then found to have bad genes or a neurological abnormality, should we presume that biology compelled him? It's a circular argument that conflates what describes a phenomenon and what causes it. Everything in our minds is encoded in neural architecture, and if scanning technologies advance far enough we'll see physiological evidence of a college education, a failed love affair, religious faith. Will such knowledge also bring deeper understanding?

The psychiatric profession doesn't consider mass killers to be necessarily insane, which distresses Peter. For him, the crime defines the illness—as he said soon after we met, you'd have to be crazy to do such a thing. He found the idea of Adam's not being insane much more devastating than the thought of his being insane. James Knoll, a forensic psychiatrist at SUNY, has written that Adam's act conveyed a message: "I carry profound hurt—I'll go ballistic and transfer it onto you." That's as much motive as we're likely to find.

Old friends have been unflagging in their support, but Peter said he thought he might never make new friends again; "This defines who I am and I can't stand that, but you have to accept it." I wondered how Peter would feel if he could see his son again. "Quite honestly, I think that I wouldn't recognize the person I saw," he said. "All I could picture is there'd be nothing there, there'd be nothing. Almost, like, 'Who are you, stranger?'" Peter declared that he wished Adam had never been born, that there could be no remembering who he was outside of who he became. "That didn't come right away. That's not a natural thing, when you're thinking about your kid. But, God, there's no question. There can only be one conclusion, when you finally get there. That's fairly recent, too, but that's totally where I am."

Transgender

WESTERN CULTURE LIKES BINARIES: LIFE FEELS less frightening when we can separate good and evil into tidy heaps, when we split off the mind from the body, when men are masculine and women are feminine. Threats to gender are threats to the social order. If we tolerate people who want to chop off their penises and breasts, then what chance do we have of preserving the integrity of our own bodies?

The term *transgender* includes anyone whose behavior departs significantly from the norms of the gender suggested by his or her anatomy at birth. The term *transsexual* usually refers to someone who has had surgery or hormones to align his or her body with a nonbirth gender. The term *transvestite* refers to someone who enjoys wearing clothing usually reserved for the other gender. Though the terms get used in a variety of ways, *transgender* and its abbreviation, *trans*, are the most widely accepted in the trans community. A *transman* was born with female anatomy and lives as a man; a *transwoman* was born with male anatomy and lives as a woman. *Intersex* describes people who are born with ambiguous genitalia or are in some other physical way both male and female from birth. *LGBTQ* is the abbreviation often used to refer to the larger group of people—lesbian, gay, bisexual, transgender, and queer—who are fighting for expanded civil rights.

It is a poverty of our language that we use the word *sex* to refer both to gender and to carnal acts, and from that unfortunate conflation springs much of the disgust around the notion of transgender children. Being trans is taken to be a depravity, and depravities in children are disturbing. But trans children are not manifesting sexuality; they are manifesting gender. The issue is not whom they wish to be with, but who they wish to be. As Aiden Key, a trans activist, put it, "My gender is who I am; my sexuality is who I bounce it off of." This is an essential distinction. Yet teasing out the complexities of transgender identity reveals how often these things can be confused. *Gay* and *trans* are separate categories, but a grayscale runs between them. Making the distinction is especially hard in childhood. One mother described being asked by a male friend whether her boyish daughter was gay and saying, "She's four—I don't think she's got sexual desires yet." But such children may be demonstrating qualities associated with subsequent patterns of attraction; they may, in effect, be pre-gay.

In 1987, Richard Green published his influential *The "Sissy Boy Syndrome" and the Development of Homosexuality*, in which he followed a group of forty-four feminine little boys for fifteen years. Only one transitioned; most turned out simply to be gay. Sexuality and gender are independent yet entwined. Because cross-gender expression is much more common among gay people than it is among straight people, prejudice against such expression is a gay issue. Gay, too, is an identity—not just something you do, but something you are. Those who are ignorant about homosexuality and transgender culture tend to confuse them with reason: homophobia has always targeted gender nonconformity.

The political liberty of transgender people has been ingrained in the battle for gay and lesbian rights. There are far more gay people than trans people, and the trans movement needs numbers behind it, but the conflation of the two issues nonetheless causes confusion. Some gay people think their trans brothers and sisters are in the same situation as themselves only more so, and become passionate advocates on their behalf; others find the trans community embarrassing and attempt to dissociate themselves.

Gender dissonance can manifest extremely early. By age three or four, sometimes even younger, children may notice an incongruity between who they are told they are and who they sense they are. That discrepancy has been called gender identity disorder, or GID. In early childhood, gender nonconformity is often tolerated, but by seven or so, children are pushed into gender stereotypes. Trans children may respond to such pressure by becoming anxious and depressed. Telling their parents is usually terrifying for them. "If you don't let them transition, their internal energy is fully occupied with gender identity, and this keeps them from reaching their developmental markers," said Stephanie Brill, founder of the counseling entity Gender Spectrum, and author, with Rachel Pepper, of *The Transgender Child*. "Often with transition, children's learning disabilities and other diagnoses resolve themselves because the mind and heart are not so occupied with this central problem."

Even twenty years ago, most transsexuals sought to move completely from one gender to the other. Nowadays, the categories are blurred. Some live *stealth*, meaning that everyone around them believes that they were born into the gender they inhabit. Others live openly as transmen or transwomen. Many spend some time stealth and some openly trans. Some people are *genderqueer*, identifying as neither male nor female. Others are *gender fluid*: male some days, female other days, and sometimes neither, or both. Some suffer from *gender dysphoria*—a deep misery about the body into which they were born—but others reject the darkness of that term.

People in any of these categories may or may not have had surgery, be taking hormones, or have had a variety of other physical interventions. Lynn Conway, a computer engineer who has analyzed recent data, has estimated that there are between thirty-two thousand and forty thousand postoperative transwomen in the United States, but said that only one of five or ten people who experiences intense discomfort with birth gender pursues genital surgery. The National Center for Transgender Equality estimates that for up to three million Americans, in journalist Barbara Walters's words, "What's between their legs doesn't match what's between their ears."

Scientists, psychologists, clergy, and academics argue about whether bodies should be altered to accommodate minds, or minds to accommodate bodies. Some believe that all people who vary from gender norms can, with psychiatric treatment, live contentedly in their birth gender. Others presume that the role of medicine is to facilitate transition and believe in using hormones and surgery to do so. Parents are in a bind, familiar throughout this book, between cure and acceptance. Advocates for therapy insist that people live better in unmutilated bodies and that medical corrections involving pain, risk, and expense should be options of last resort. Opponents contend that discouraging transgender people from inhabiting their real selves is a prescription for despair, often for suicide.

Twenty-seven weeks pregnant as a single mother, Venessia Romero was rushed to a Denver hospital, where she gave birth to a girl and a boy. The girl looked fairly strong, but the boy was less than a pound and a half and covered with fuzz, his organs visible through his unformed skin. Because the girl was stronger, they treated her first. She died within minutes. The boy survived.

Within a year, Venessia met and married Joseph Romero, an air force sergeant. The baby's father had never even seen him; Joseph adopted him and changed his name to Joseph Romero II, called Joey. When the baby was twenty months old, the family was posted to the US Air Force base in Okinawa, Japan. "The baby would cry all the time," Joseph recalled. "But not 'I want food,' 'I want to be changed.' It wasn't a physical need, and we had no way to console him. The temper tantrums were so bad that we couldn't take him out in public."

Over the next four years, Joey was diagnosed with ADHD, depression, anxiety, attachment disorder, and asthma. At three, he was on fourteen medications. "We had a child who never smiled," Venessia said. "All the time we were cooing, 'Oh you're such a good boy, such a beautiful boy.' Boy, boy, boy. Every time I put shoes on him, they were little boy's shoes. A little boy's jacket." Joey was already interested in wearing girlish outfits; Venessia thought he was probably gay and worried about how that would go over with her military husband.

The Romeros had access only to military doctors, who were cautious of a diagnosis that the military does not welcome, but one finally told Venessia, when Joey was five, to look up GID online. "It was making him squirm just to say that, like his rank was going to fall off," Venessia said. "I had never even heard the word *transgender*. I was hugely relieved. Other people go through this?" Kim Pearson—herself the mother of a transgender child and one of the founders of Trans Youth Family Allies (TYFA)—found Venessia online. "She carried me to a forum with other parents," Venessia said. "I cried with gratitude."

The revelation threw Joseph Sr. into an abrupt and severe depression. Venessia started to call her child Josie. "Josie wouldn't go outside unless she could go in her girl clothes. I had to decide then, was I willing to leave my marriage to protect Josie? Well, to make Josie be a boy is asking her to commit suicide." By this time, Venessia and Joseph had adopted a younger daughter, Jade, from China. "I'm willing to give Joseph up, and I'm willing to walk away from Jade, which was incredibly hard. But Josie was five and had already paid enough penance for ten lives." While Venessia was making these calculations, her husband gradually came around.

When I first met Josie, she was eight, and she said, "I'm a girl and I have a penis. They thought I was a boy until I was six. I dressed like a girl. I said, 'I'm a girl.' They didn't understand for the longest time." Josie was increasingly assertive about her need to be a girl all the time, so one day Joseph agreed to take her to school on the base in a denim skirt with a pink rabbit on it, and pink leggings underneath. The kids were mostly accepting, but their parents were another story. "The next day there was a screaming crowd outside Josie's classroom door," Venessia said. "People were throwing things at our house, calling us child molesters. Little girls screaming, 'You're a fucking faggot.'" The wife of the judge advocate general on base started a petition to remove Josie from school. "It was awful when everyone found out I was a girl," Josie remembered. "My neighbor Isabelle said she was going to call the police and put me in jail. It made me sad. I thought she was my friend."

Venessia allowed Josie to choose her clothes. "She wouldn't go outside without a skirt on," Venessia said. "But she's got the biggest smile on her face. Well, I'm going to smile too. So I did. I was holding her hand tighter than usual, but she just kept on marching." Before long, Venessia and Joseph had taken her off all her medications. Her asthma, depression, anxiety, and attachment disorder were all gone. But the military told the family to get out of Okinawa, claiming they could not protect Josie; they were reassigned to a base in the Arizona desert.

Venessia didn't want Josie at another military school. She located a public school in Tucson with a liberal-leaning principal and enrolled both daughters. But Josie's teacher refused to call her by a female name and told Josie that Venessia was a "mean mommy" who was forcing her to live as a girl when everyone could see she was a boy. "She was an awful, rude teacher, who didn't want me at her school," Josie said. "I got so angry and frustrated." Josie complained of stomachaches and headaches and fought every day against going to school.

The Romeros moved to another town. Fearing for Josie's safety, they installed alarm wiring on the windows and doors and bought a Great Dane to intimidate attackers. Venessia sent an e-mail to the principal of the local public school that began, "I'm the proud mother of an eight-year-old transgender daughter." His head of human resources said, "We follow state laws, and there are no antidiscrimination protections for your child here." In November, Venessia placed her daughters at a Waldorf school, but at $20,000 per year, it was impossible on an air force salary. The only option left was homeschool. Josie said, "I miss going out." Joseph said, "The isolation is the price we pay to shield her from a world that could harm her."

Isolation is not the only difficulty. "I always have the penis problem," Josie said. "I want to get rid of it. But I think it will hurt. They said I have to be a certain age to take my penis off, when I'm more like fifteen." Venessia said, "Eighteen. But you'll be able to take estrogen and grow boobs sooner than that." Josie explained, "When I'm a mommy, I'll adopt my babies, but I'll have boobies to feed them and I will wear a bra, dresses, skirts, and high-heeled shoes." She seemed equally definite when she told me that she wanted to marry someone with rainbow-colored hair who was beautiful on the inside and the outside. "We'll get a baby here in Arizona, and then go live in whatever state Jade is in so we can be next-door neighbors," Josie said. "We'll live in a tree house. I'll grow my hair all the way to California."

Venessia plans to give Josie puberty blockers, which stop the production of testosterone and estrogen. "She won't have testosterone ravaging her body," Venessia said. "So she'll never get an Adam's apple or facial hair. She'll never look like a man in a dress." Venessia found a doctor in Tucson who was willing to work on this protocol. Joseph persuaded the department of records to issue a new birth certificate for Josie, with her correct name and gender. But Venessia also deliberately kept toys for boys and girls around the house, saying, "I don't want her to feel like she has to prove she's a girl by playing with Barbies all the time."

Most trans children I encountered were living stealth. I was struck that many of these kids had gone from one discrepancy—living in an anatomical gender that was anathema to them—to another—living in a gender that did not match their body. Josie's openness had come at a high cost, but she struck me as more truly free than many other trans children. Josie has become an activist. When I met her, she had just been filmed by National Geographic for her second documentary; she has met with members of Congress and the governor of Arizona. "Josie's very fragile, very emotional," Venessia said. "But Josie wants to change the world."

Gender is among the first elements of self-knowledge. This knowledge encompasses an internal sense of self, and often a preference for external behaviors, such as dress and type of play. Gender identity's causes remain obscure. Heino Meyer-Bahlburg, a professor of psychology at Columbia University who specializes in gender variance, described numerous possible biological mechanisms, and said that as many as four hundred rare genes and other biological phenomena may be involved: genes associated not with hormone regulation, but with personality formation. Like autism, gender nonconformity seems far more prevalent than ever before; as with autism, whether the condition is actually more frequent or simply more recognized is unclear.

Nongenetic biological arguments are confusing. A synthetic estrogen drug developed in 1938 and used until the early 1970s to prevent miscarriage has had many adverse effects on both males and females exposed to it in utero. A 2002 survey of children born to women who took the drug found an extraordinary 50 percent rate of transgenderism. This supports the hypotheses that gestational hormone levels can trigger cross-gender identity. Scientists have also expressed concern about endocrine disruptors (EDCs), a class of chemicals found in everything from food to floor polish to packing materials. EDCs are known to be responsible for an increasing incidence of deformities in amphibian reproductive systems; researchers have speculated that they might be responsible for the increasing incidence of genetic abnormalities and atypical gender identity in human beings.

Being trans is without question atypical; the relentlessly debated question is whether it is also pathological—a condition that needs to be fixed. Gender identity disorder was introduced as a medical category in 1980. Boys diagnosed with GID commonly prefer feminine clothing and hairstyles, often are mothers when they play house, avoid rough-and-tumble play and athletics, and are interested in female fantasy figures like Snow White. Girls diagnosed with GID often have intensely negative responses to being asked to wear dresses, prefer short hair, are often mistaken for boys, seek out rough-and-tumble play, enjoy sports, and choose male fantasy figures like Batman. Such preferences are not uncommon in people who will go on to be gay, but they are usually more vehement and persistent in people who are trans. In an age when women can work in construction and men can marry other men, the notion of a medically enshrined "Batman vs. Snow White" classification of gender identity seems overly simplified, yet it still has currency in the medical literature.

Whereas most children will play at an early age with toys suitable to either gender, trans kids often refuse the toys associate with their natal sex. Natal males become more female than most females, while natal females become more male than most males. Adults with GID show clinically significant distress or impairment in social and occupational functioning. Some children who have gone undiagnosed will manifest the syndrome during puberty or afterward; conversely, only a quarter of children given a GID diagnosis will show full cross-gender identification in adolescence. In other words, sometimes their play means nothing about their future identity and sometimes it means everything. This is why decisions about how to raise them are so fraught.

Many professionals who work with trans children believe that the society at large is failing them. Kelly Winters, founder of GID Reform Advocates, has written, "Behaviors that would be ordinary or even exemplary for gender-conforming boys and girls are presented as symptomatic of mental disorder for gender-nonconforming children," meaning that what is deemed healthy in a girl is considered a symptom of psychiatric illness in a boy. Activists have spoken of the GID diagnosis being used not only to prevent natal boys from identifying as girls and natal girls from identifying as boys, but also to stigmatize or prevent effeminate homosexuality and butch lesbianism. Stephanie Brill added, "A male child who says, 'I must be a girl because only girls want to do these things,' is not showing evidence of being transgender; he's showing evidence of sexism."

Other activists, however, rail against the possibility of losing the diagnostic category. In *The Riddle of Gender*, Deborah Rudacille writes, "The diagnosis legitimizes the range of hormonal and surgical interventions that have provided relief to thousands of transsexual and transgendered people." The harm of eliminating the GID diagnosis from *The Diagnostic and Statistical Manual of Mental Disorders* (DSM) is potential loss of access to care. The harm of continuing to list it as a mental disorder is social stigma. The real task is to increase access to care and reduce discrimination. The quandary echoes the experience of deaf people and dwarfs, who may not care for the disability label yet need it to secure accommodations and services.

Surgical and endocrine interventions for transgender people, however, are seldom eligible for reimbursement and tax deductibility. Many transgender people would like to see their condition classified as a physical and not a mental health condition, which would resolve the problem. Others maintain that trans, like pregnancy, is a medical condition but not a disease.

As long as GID is classified as a mental illness, professionals will try to cure it, and parents will refuse to accept it. Edgardo Menvielle, a psychiatrist at Children's National Medical Center, said, "The goal is for the child to be well adjusted, healthy, and have good self-esteem. What's not important is molding their gender."

Most Deaf people don't take exception to being called *deaf*; most people with intellectual disabilities raise no objection to the term *Down syndrome*; yet *gender identity disorder* infuriates the people it describes. Most conditions in this book entail a positive model of identity and a negative model of disorder. While no one wants to be put in a stigmatized diagnostic category, most people fight the stigma rather than the category. Those who think of deafness or autism as identities can do so even if others call them disorders. GID suggests not simply that trans people have a disorder, but that their identify itself *is* the disorder. This is a dangerous standpoint. We all have multiple identities, and most of us regret some of them, but identity is who we are. The GID designation bespeaks an agenda of terminating identity. You can seek better ways to manifest identity, but you can't ask any class of people to discard their identity itself. The twentieth century reached its lowest point with attempts to free the world of Jewish identity, Tutsi identity, Bosnian identity, or the many identities that communism suppressed. The practice of obliterating identities does not work at this macro level; it does not work well on the micro level either.

Bettina and Greg Verdi both come from traditional Italian Catholic families in the Northeast. Greg works as an airline ground mechanic and Bettina as a preschool teacher. When Greg was hired by Lockheed Martin, they moved south of Atlanta. Their second child, Paul, preferred pink toys at three months; at two, he would drape a shirt over his head to mimic long hair, and wear one of Bettina's tank tops as a gown. When he was two and a half, Bettina agreed to get him a yellow flowered dress at a garage sale. "I figured at home at play time, what's the harm," Bettina said. Greg was not entirely comfortable with the dress, but like Bettina, he assumed it was a phase.

At five, Paul said to Bettina, "Mom, I want to go to school as a girl, dress like a girl, have a girl name, have girl toys. I want to be a girl." Bettina was terrified. They went back to their pediatrician and asked what he thought about GID; he told them "those children" mostly committed suicide, so they should go to the Christian bookstore, read up on it, and pray. Bettina found a therapist in Atlanta, and made an appointment to go in with Greg. "I was prepared to make this happen without Greg," Bettina said. But on the drive home, Greg said to Bettina, "Okay, let's do it."

Bettina went to see the religious education director at her Catholic church. "I was so emotional about it. She was like, 'Okay, do you want her to attend as Paula? We'll just change the paperwork.' So we transitioned at church." Next, Bettina told the school, and the principal said, "We provide a safe, friendly environment for all our children, and yours is no different." Paula would have to use the nurse's bathroom, but otherwise, she would just be Paula. Bettina's family was supportive from the start. Greg's parents, already in their eighties, accepted it the first time they saw Paula.

But the Verdis did not reckon with her community. "Suddenly, we're in the Bible Belt," Greg said. Bettina notified the neighbors. "I had gone to the bus stop with this one guy every morning for two years, and I felt like he was my friend," she said. "The first week of school he would meet me at the end of his driveway with papers he downloaded about how evil this was." One brother and sister put their hands on Paula's head on the school bus and prayed to turn her back into a boy. Bettina went to see the mother of the praying kids. "She's telling me,

'God doesn't make mistakes.' I'm telling her, 'Look, if God doesn't make mistakes, then your son doesn't have a vision problem and doesn't need glasses.' 'Well, that's not the same thing.' 'Why is it not the same thing? It's a body part. What's the difference?' I just said, 'Look, you're a really good mom, and I know in my heart of hearts, if you were in my shoes, you would do the same thing. You would listen to your child and make your child happy.'"

I first met Greg and Bettina at a trans conference in Philadelphia, when Paula was six; soon, a beautiful little girl came over with Greg's courtly parents, who presented the deceptive air of having attended trans conferences for decades. Paula shook my hand, a little somberly, and then skipped down the hallway, her grandparents in pursuit. Bettina said, "This conference is more for us than for her. She knows what she's doing. We're clueless." Bettina and Greg showed me the "safe folder" they take with them at all times. Many parents of trans kids keep one: paperwork to be shown in the event of trouble, as law enforcement and the medical system can be unfamiliar with or hostile to gender variance. A folder may include letters from the child's pediatrician and a psychotherapist confirming the child's gender identity; letters from at least three friends or family members and, if possible, a pastor or minister or other prelate that testify to the parents' sound parenting skills; videos or snapshots of the child displaying atypical gender behaviors throughout life; copies of birth certificates, passports, and Social Security cards that reflect a change of gender or name; a home study documenting family stability, if available; and a Bureau of Criminal Information analysis that shows that the parents are not child abusers.

I asked whether Bettina's advocacy perspective made it easier for her than for Greg, or the other way around. Greg began crying. "I just struggled," he sobbed. "Because it was my little boy. I want my child to be happy. But I found the pictures of us as a family before all this, and I miss that little boy. Just once in a while, it still hurts." I asked Bettina whether she ever felt that way. "No," she said, after a minute's thought. "What I regret is that time with Paula that I didn't have. I missed my daughter's infancy, spending all my energy on someone else who never existed."

The idea that the child's gender-inappropriate behavior is caused by the parents determined treatment for most of the twentieth century. In the 1940s and fifties, the psychologist John Money believed that health required strong gender identification. Girls should be encouraged to be girlish, and boys, boyish. Money's theory was explicitly tested on David Reimer, one of identical twins whose penis was burned off during a circumcision. Money proposed to Reimer's parents that they raise him as a girl, oversaw infant sex-reassignment surgery, and instructed them to give him only girlish clothes and toys. The parents were told that they must never tell David what had happened.

For years, Money published fraudulent articles about the great success of this experiment, thereby encouraging others to attempt similar therapies, which damaged thousands of people. Only in the late 1990s did David Reimer give an interview to *Rolling Stone*, which eventually grew into the book *As Nature Made Him: The Boy Who Was Raised as a Girl*. Reimer's childhood was filled with rage and misery; he insisted on urinating standing up and despised Money and all the dolls and frilly dresses that were forced on him. His behavior became so violent that his parents finally broke down and told him the real story when he was fourteen. Reimer had penile reconstruction and lived as a man in later life, but the damage done was enormous, and he committed suicide at thirty-eight.

Recent science suggests that successfully raising genetically programmed boys as girls is almost impossible. A study from Johns Hopkins looked at children born with a condition in which they have XY (male) chromosomes and testes, but no penis—who were castrated and assigned female gender at birth. Many chose to live as boys or men as they grew up and all had typical male interests and attitudes. Their male identity and gender role developed despite an environment that told them they were female. Reparative therapies for gay people are now deemed unethical by most professionals, but whether reparative therapies for trans people should be regarded the same way is widely debated.

Kirk Murphy was treated for childhood effeminacy at UCLA in the 1970s under the auspices of the same theoretician who developed the reward-and-punishment behavioral treatments for autism to which some autistic people have objected. Kirk's mother was coached to reward him for masculine behavior and to punish feminine behavior. Though he became so upset during these sessions that he would scream, his mother was reassured that she was doing the right thing. At home, a token system was put into play. He was given blue chips for masculine behaviors; a certain number of these meant he got a treat. He received red chips for feminine behaviors and was beaten by his father with a belt when he had too many of them. The effeminate behavior eventually ceased, and for years the work was written up as a success.

Kirk joined the air force and lived as a masculine man—until he hanged himself in 2003 at the age of thirty-eight. His mother and siblings went public to talk about how the therapy had destroyed him. His sister said, "He was gay, and he committed suicide. I want people to remember that this was a little boy who deserved protection, respect, and unconditional love. I don't want him to be remembered as a science experiment." Phyllis Burke's *Gender Shock*, published in 1996, documented with considerable horror that techniques like those that destroyed Kirk Murphy were still in use—and still receiving government funding. Indeed, some are in use even as I write.

While wealth and education do not guarantee families of trans kids an easy time, poverty increases the chances of everything going horribly wrong. Indigence exacerbated the difficulties for Hailey Krueger and Jane Ritter. Each had lived a long secret life. Neither wanted to admit to her mother that she was a lesbian, and both married men. Their impoverished marriages were full of lies and abuse and dysfunction. Hailey had dropped out of school in Kansas in the ninth grade; Jane had completed high school in Missouri, but had no professional qualifications. Jane had an adolescent daughter; each had a young son. Hailey was femme, and Jane was butch, and they met in a homeless shelter in Wichita, Kansas.

Hailey's husband was given to cross-dressing, but only at home and in complete privacy. Soon after marriage, they had a son, whom they named Jayden. "My child was always embarrassed of down there," Hailey said. "He was always trying to hide it, even when he was a baby. He sat down to pee, and wiped, like a girl." At five, Jayden declared that his name was Hannah, after Hannah Montana, the Disney girl who lives as a normal teenager by day and a rock star by night; that story of opposite selves in a single person had resonance for many trans kids I met who were leading a double life.

Jane said, "The first time I met Jayden, in the shelter, age six, I honestly thought it was a girl." After a few months, Hailey and Jane moved out to a trailer with Jayden, and Jane's kids, Bryan and Lillian. "Jayden had just had enough of hiding," Hailey said. "We settled in, and he says, 'Mamma, can I put my bra on?' I said, 'Go ahead. No one can see it.'" Jayden told Jane he had something to tell her. "He goes, 'I got a bra on,'" Jane said. "I said, 'Okay.' He was like, 'You're not mad?' I said, 'No, baby, because Mama Jane thinks that everybody needs to be themselves.' His face lit up, and he was so happy." It wasn't long before Jayden started introducing himself to other children as Hannah. His father was horrified.

Jane found a job at MacDonald's, and Hailey, at Dollar General. They moved into a depressed area of Wichita. By the time Jayden was seven, he was sporting fingernail polish at school. "The school would bring it up, and I'm like, 'Kids will be kids,'" Hailey said. "Then he started wanting to grow his hair out. He wanted a pair of tights, makeup. He cried a lot, wanting to go to school as a girl." As soon as Jayden came home, he'd put on girl clothes. One night, he said to Jane, "I'm so mad at you." Jane said, "Why, baby?" Jayden said, "Because you're able to be who you are. And I can't." Jane said to me, "That just about broke my heart."

The school wanted Jayden in therapy, but Hailey and Jane didn't want him to see someone who would, as Jane put it, "deprogram" him. They had never heard the word *transgender*, had no idea that there were other children like Hannah. They learned of a sixty-five-year-old transwoman, Leona, who ran a support group who in turn introduced them to the Metropolitan Community Church (MCC), the LGBTQ-positive denomination to which she belonged, and to her pastor, Reverend Kristina Kohl. MCC was the first public place where Hannah presented herself as a girl.

When Hannah entered first grade, pressure mounted from the school for her to act more like a boy; pressure mounted from Hannah to go to school as a girl. Leona said to Hannah, "For your safety, it's best for you to live a double life right now." Kristina Kohl said, "All her life, she'll have to make concessions. We all do." Hailey and Jane had three meetings at school to discuss the situation. "I told Jayden, 'If you're purple, and you're the only purple person in this world, I'd love you to death,'" Hailey said. "'But you cannot be Hannah at school.'" Jane said, "Hannah was calling herself a freak. It upset me so bad. I said, 'Hannah, please do not use that word. You are not a freak.'"

On February 24, 2009, Jane got Hannah ready for school. "I gave her a hug and a kiss, and I said, 'I got a surprise when you get out of school. We're going to eat pizza and go bowling.'" At one thirty, a social worker called Hailey. "I've got your child," she said. "You have a court date Tuesday at eight thirty in the morning." The social worker had interviewed Jayden at school and asked what he would wish if he had three wishes. Jayden said, "Change all my boy clothes into girl clothes; me be a girl; my boy body parts be girl body parts." The social worker presented this as evidence that Hailey and Jane had "convinced" their child that he was female. The paperwork noted that Hailey had a female partner, and that her child was therefore subject to "more confusion and social difficulties than other children." The judge ruled that Hannah be placed in a foster family with "healthy parents."

Kristina became the moms' chief advisor. "Hailey and Jane are educationally challenged; they come out of generational poverty," she told me. "The kids hadn't been to a dentist or a doctor, didn't have shoes that fit. It's not simple. But they love those kids, and Hannah absolutely loves her home." Hannah's foster family would not allow Hannah to use her female name, wear female clothes, or do anything else outside masculine norms. On Hailey and Jane's first supervised visit there, Hannah said, "If I have to be a boy to go home, I will. I'll do anything to go home."

Social and Rehabilitative Services of Kansas (SRS) was now in charge. It can be hard to tease the transphobia apart from the homophobia. SRS continued to say in court, "We're not giving this child back to lesbians." SRS finally appointed a therapist, Mia Handler, for Hannah and her mothers. They all loved Mia. Hailey said, "We brought some dresses to Hannah in therapy, because Mia said that she could wear them. Hannah was, 'Oh, I don't want to do it in case my foster parents find out.'" Hailey wept openly. "Hannah is that scared. She was like a bird being able to fly, okay? Free. Now, even with us, it's like she's caged."

Hailey and Jane are allowed to attend Hannah's baseball games. "At the ball park, she says, 'Mama, can I wear your pink sandals to the picnic table?'" Hailey said. "I want to just sit there and scream, 'What's it going to hurt for my child to put my flip-flops on?' But they told me no. So I have to abide by that." Following these rules seems like the best way to get Hannah back, and may help Hannah get by in Wichita. But it teaches troubling lessons. "In therapy, she said she was tired of the double life," Hailey said. "Then she said, 'But I have to do it because I'm a bad person.'"

When I met Hailey and Jane, Hannah had been away for seven months. The women saw Hannah for an hour of therapy and one two-hour supervised home visit each week. They were not allowed to phone or message her, and she was not allowed to phone or message them. It was Hannah's eighth birthday, and Hailey and Jane had done their best to make it festive. "I had a little present," Hailey said, "and I gave it to Hannah and said, 'Here you go, baby boy.' She just looked at me like, Mama, do you not accept me anymore? So the social worker walked out for a second, and Hannah looked at me real quick and said, 'You mean "baby girl"?' I said, 'When these people are around, I can't say that.' I felt so low." Jane said, "How can you just tell this child, 'Okay, here and here you can be yourself, but out here you can't be yourself'?" Hailey said, "I don't know what I'm supposed to say and what I'm not. My biggest fear is of getting her back and then just losing her again. It will definitely be very dangerous for her and for us if she's herself."

Natal males who become females are often unconvincing as women because of their height and the thickness of their bones; however, their postoperative genitalia, sexual response, and urination patterns can be almost identical to those of genetic females. Natal females who transition can usually pass in public once they develop facial and body hair, deep voices, and, in many cases, male pattern baldness, but their sex organs are noticeably different from the genuine article; most cannot urinate while standing up, and none can achieve a male orgasm.

It takes little injected testosterone to overwhelm a genetic female's estrogen. To overwhelm a genetic male's testosterone is a much bigger project. Many endocrinologists recommend that genetic males undergo gonadectomy—removal of their testicles—as early as possible to avoid the health risks that accompany such high levels of estrogen. In both male-to-female and female-to-male transitions, some people pursue multiple procedures to make the switch feel complete to them, including feminizing facial surgeries and breast augmentation for transwomen and double mastectomies and hysterectomies for transmen.

Prepubescent transgender children with supportive families may avoid some physical difficulties of transition through the use of hormone blockers, which suppress puberty. This therapy may start as early as age ten for girls and twelve for boys. The treatment buys families time; if the child is indeed transgender, puberty blockers can save him or her from going through the "wrong puberty" and may remove the need for many surgeries in later life. Girls do not develop breasts, widened hips, female fat distribution, or active ovaries. The estrogen surge that limits female height does not occur for them, so they grow tall. Boys who are treated with puberty blockers do not develop facial or body hair; their voice does not deepen and their Adam's apple doesn't grow; bones do not thicken, shoulders broaden, or hands and feet enlarge. Estrogen supplementation can be timed to limit their height.

The androgyny of childhood can be prolonged. If someone goes off puberty blockers without starting cross-sex hormones, the deferred puberty of his or her natal sex will begin within a few months and will follow its natural course. Cross-sex hormones will initiate the puberty of the person's affirmed, chosen gender. Most children who start with puberty blockers choose to remain on them until they obtain gender reassignment surgery between eighteen and twenty-one.

Parents often oppose puberty blockers because of the young age at which they are introduced. "Parents say, 'I'm not ready to deal with this yet,'" Stephanie Brill said. "But they are dealing with it. Badly." The underlying fallacy is that slowing transition is cautious, and accelerating it is rash. There is some concern that starting children on blockers will cause some who are just going through a phase to make it permanent; they may be too embarrassed, scared, or confused to revert if they think that they've made a mistake. Rushing a child into transition in which he will be trapped for the rest of his life would be a terrible mistake; however, forcing a child who is firm about his or her own identity to go through puberty and develop a body that will never match who he or she knows himself or herself to be, even after multiple, expensive, traumatic surgeries, is equally troubling. Also troubling is the fact that American insurance plans seldom cover the use of puberty blockers. Their high cost creates a class divide between transgender youth whose parents are willing and can afford it, and all others.

Many parents are willing to do what it takes for their children to be happy, but it isn't always possible to know what it takes. Dramatic physiological interventions to make it possible for a child to express his or her authentic identity can seem like a technological madness. But one has to wonder if it is more of a technological madness than the cochlear implant. Many people outside these horizontal identities categorize that intervention as a way to normalize an abnormality, and sexual reassignment interventions as a way to indulge one. It is instructive to note, however, that whereas the protest *against* cochlear implants comes from the marginal identity group, the demand *for* trans surgeries comes from the marginal identity group.

The debate over gender identity was once framed as a nature-nurture divide; nowadays, it's an intractable-tractable divide, which is equally hard to call. Clearly nature is involved, but the question remains whether nurture enables it, and whether it can and should disable it. The answers are frustratingly vague. Transitioning is still bound up with the medical and therapeutic communities. In the best cases this means responsible professionals can separate the fears and desires of the parents from those of their offspring and distinguish between an essential desire that will never change and a transient neurosis. That can, however, be daunting.

In his own practice, Columbia University's Heino Meyer-Bahlburg believes that transition is best avoided if possible. "It's terrible to mutilate a healthy body and make someone infertile," he said. He believes in a centrist treatment. "We try to introduce them to more of their same-sex peers," he said, "and if their fathers have already turned into sissy-boy-hating, distant fathers, as happens in this homophobic country, we try to get them to reengage positively and develop a relationship. Many of these children become more comfortable in their birth gender, and even if they don't they can have a broader circle of friends and experiences." That said, he has also put children on puberty blockers as early as eleven. "Sometimes, I help patients make the change, and sometimes, in a noncoercive fashion, I try to stop them from doing so," he said. "It's only based on my own intuition; I have no formula."

Members of the trans community often fear therapists who steer children away from their true selves; parents are more likely to fear that their children will have surgery and come to regret it. It is impossible to know how many people who have transitioned socially but not physically have transitioned back. We do know, however, that as many as one in a hundred people who have had sex-reassignment surgery wish they had not done so. Such stories are used to discredit the trans movement as a whole. Cases of profound postsurgical regret make headlines, while much less space is given to people who would have been much happier with a full surgical transition but were never able to achieve one. Mistakes will be made in both directions, and lives can be ruined either way. It is terrible to perform unnecessary surgery on a healthy body, but it is also terrible to deny relief to a mind that knows itself.

Far more boys are referred for treatment for GID than girls. However, this does not mean that more natal boys have gender-atypical behavior than natal girls, only that they worry their parents more.

Tony Ferraiolo showed such pronounced masculinities all his life that doctors who examined him when he was still called Anne thought he must be intersex. When I met him, Tony was in his forties. His father had not spoken to him in five years; his mother saw him occasionally and continued to call him Anne. "They're missing out on a really cool guy," Tony said to me.

At age five, Anne and her twin, Michelle, were playing football with their brothers, Frank and Felix, and Anne took her shirt off. Her mother said, "Girls don't take their shirts off." Anne began to cry, and said she was a boy. "She never played with dolls," Tony's mother, Big Anne, remembered. "She never wore a dress. She wouldn't carry a pocketbook. I surmised she was going to be a lesbian." Three early behaviors are often taken as indicators of fixed identity: what underwear the child selects; what swimsuits the child prefers; how the child urinates. "I remember trying to stand up and pee as a little kid," Tony said. "I never wore girl underwear or bathing suits. I didn't even know that people had intercourse, but I knew that my gender was male."

When Anne was in fifth grade in a New Haven elementary school, the teacher asked what each pupil wanted to be when he or she grew up, and Anne said she wanted to be a boy. The class erupted in laughter. By eleven, she was self-injurious. "You've got a little kid that's outside for recess, taking a piece of glass, cutting themselves," Tony said. "I'd gouge and gouge, then take dirt and try to get an infection, to hurt myself as much as I could. My parents knew it. No one did anything." Anne's sister, Michelle, identified as a lesbian early on, but she was a jock, as popular as Anne was marginalized.

Anne's father, Anthony, was abusive, and Big Anne, addicted to Valium, was passive in the face of that. Adolescence is a trauma for most trans people, and for Anne, doubly so, as she had organic surges of both male and female hormones, despite showing no anatomical or genetic markers for intersex. "My facial hair and boobs are growing at the same time. What the hell's going on here?" By the time Anne was thirteen, she was shaving every day. "I took up drugs and drinking; I was suspended more than I was in school." Her father often refused to speak to her; when she was sixteen, he threw her out of the house. She walked fifteen miles into New Haven and moved in with a girlfriend; when that arrangement failed, she was homeless for a month. "Then I called my mother and asked to go back home," Tony recalled, hanging his head. "I went back into the bullshit."

Through her twenties and thirties, Anne was a club promoter and threw huge parties for hundreds of lesbians; she started a band called Vertical Smile. But she never felt like a lesbian. She started using *Tony*, spelled "Toni" in a concession to the family. "I used to pray to God that I was a butch lesbian," Tony said. "But a butch lesbian wants breasts and a va-jay-jay. A transgender person wants a penis." In his mid-thirties, Tony was in a car accident, and received an insurance settlement. His family suggested he buy a house. He spent the funds on a double mastectomy.

Tony was not interested in so-called bottom surgery—a reworking of genitals. "That part of my body isn't public, so it was never an issue. The boobs were public. When the doctor unbandaged me, my knees just buckled. When I took my girlfriend, Kirsten, to the beach, I said, 'I'm experiencing everything for the first time.' I haven't shaved since. I fuckin' love my goatee. When I look in the mirror, I see the person that was always supposed to be there. I used to take sleeping pills so I wouldn't have to live much of my life. Now all I want is to stay awake." When I saw Tony, he'd lost more than sixty pounds. "You can't love your body if you hate your body. Now, I eat healthy. I work out."

Tony's younger brother, Felix, said, "My sister's my brother now, and I've never seen him happier in my life." His kids switched very naturally from "Aunt Toni" To "Uncle Tony." Tony's father and his brother Frank were not supportive. Big Anne was distraught, and did not see Tony for a full year after the surgery. "Then she just said, 'Well, I'll come over,'" Tony said. "I thought, is she going to open the door and pass out? So, she came in and she was like, 'Oh, my God, you look just like my dentist.'"

When I asked Big Anne if she could see that Anne had become Tony, she said, "Once in a while, I say, 'Tony,' but mostly, it just comes out, 'Anne.' Really down deep, it's my daughter. When I look at 'him,' I still see her." She turned to Tony. "You always had that angry something that was bothering you inside. But I didn't know anything about this back then. I was stupid, in a way." Tony put a hand on her arm. "I don't think you were stupid," he said. Big Anne said, "I watched things on television about it. I started understanding more; it's not that you wanted to be this way." She turned to me and said, "Her being unnatural, I was upset by it at first. But I understood more how they felt inside. Now she does all this activism. That's very good." She turned back and forth. "You're still my child," she said to Tony. "I still love her," she said to me. "You know what I mean. Him?" I asked Tony whether he minded being called "Anne" and "she." He said, "Andrew, she thinks I'm a straight girl going through a phase. But I had to realize that my mother's my mother. My mother can call me 'them,' and it wouldn't bother me."

Big Anne's quiet acceptance of and palpable love for her child are in her own mind subsidiary to the splintering that Tony's transition introduced into her family. She responded to most of the questions I asked her about herself with information about her husband; her effacement of Tony echoed her self-effacement. When I asked how she had felt about Anne's being gay, she said, "My husband accepted her being a lesbian." She turned to Tony. "He knows that you should have been a boy, but he still says, 'Why couldn't she just stay a lesbian like everybody else?'" Tony said to his mother, "You have risen to the occasion. You come and see me. We talk." Big Anne sighed and turned to me. "My husband went to his mother's sister, who's ninety, and she started crying, 'She's still your child. You go see her. You'll get used to it.' Then the priest said, 'Go see him. He's your son. Tell him that it bothers you, but talk to him.' But he never did."

I was surprised that Big Anne had agreed to talk to me. Tony had told her to watch an *Oprah* special about trans kids; she called him and said, "I'll meet with Andrew, if you like. That was you. I'm sorry. I didn't know." Tony explained, "Nobody fuckin' knew in the seventies. My mother's a nice lady. She has a good heart. But this is big." I asked Big Anne what her husband would say when she arrived home. "He'll ask how she is," she said. "He misses her."

Tony's natural hormonal balance—whatever caused him to grow facial hair—has been sufficient, and he does not take testosterone. Like all trans people, Tony is often asked about his genitalia; he takes it as a question about his strap-ons. "A lot of people ask, 'Do you have a penis?' My answer is, 'I have five.' I just go to the next question. 'Does your girlfriend know you're trans?' I'm like, 'Love is honesty. I'm not ashamed of who I am.'" When Big Anne had confessed, during our conversation with Tony, that she still worried everything was her fault, her son had responded, "It's nobody's fault. But I have to tell you that if it was your fault, I would thank you. Because my transition is the best thing that ever happened to me." Then Tony laughed. He said, "Life isn't about finding yourself; life is about creating yourself."

Parents are right to fear for their transgender children. The level of prejudice against them is unimaginable for those who have not encountered the problem. In 2009, the National Center for Transgender Equality and the National Gay and Lesbian Task Force published a large survey of transgender people from every state and territory of the United States, with ethnic distribution roughly comparable to that of the general population. The online distribution of the questionnaire meant that it was skewed toward relatively privileged subjects. Four out of five people surveyed had been harassed or physically or sexually attacked in school, almost half by teachers. Although almost 90 percent had completed at least some college, compared to less than half of the general population, they were twice as likely to be unemployed. One out of ten had been

sexually assaulted at work, and almost as many had been physically assaulted at work. A quarter had been fired for gender
nonconformity. They experienced poverty at twice the national
rate. One out of five had been homeless; a third of that group
had been refused entry to a shelter because of their gender. A
third had postponed or avoided medical care due to disrespect
or discrimination by providers. More than half of trans youth
have made a suicide attempt, as opposed to 2 percent of the
general population. The rates of substance abuse and depression are staggering. Some 20 to 40 percent of homeless youth
are gay or trans, and more than half of trans people of color
have supported themselves by streetwalking. One sex worker
in a shelter for trans kids in Queens, New York, said, "I like the
attention; it makes me feel loved."

Severely disabled children, autistic children, schizophrenic
children, criminal children—many of these are at greater risk
of death than a conventionally healthy child, but parents of
trans kids and the kids themselves are uniquely poised between
two equally terrifying possibilities: If the child is not able to
transition, he or she or they may commit suicide; if the child
transitions, he or she or they may be killed for having done
so. Since 1999, more than four hundred trans people have
been murdered in the United States, and Transgender Day of
Remembrance puts the rate of fatal hate crimes at more than
one a month. Worldwide, a transgender person is murdered
every three days. Many of them are minors.

Anne O'Hara grew up in a small town in Mississippi. Both her
parents were addicts, and Anne stole food to feed her sister and

brother. "We were dirty," she recalled. "People didn't talk to us." The first person on either side of her family to finish high school, Anne graduated as class salutatorian, then attended Mississippi State University in Starkville. She lived in her car for a year, working at Subway and washing in their bathroom; it took her eight years to get through college, but she made it. She earned a certificate in special education. Anne moved back home, found a job at a school just across the border in Tennessee, and married Clay, a man she'd known all her life, who worked in a local plastics factory. Anne set out to change how special education was delivered in rural Tennessee. By the end of a decade, she had succeeded in mainstreaming all of her students from second to fourth grade for science and social studies; some were being invited to parties by nondisabled students.

Anne and Clay, unable to conceive, signed up to adopt. On the day Anne's father died, several hundred miles away, three boys unknown to Anne were taken into state custody. Marshall Camacho, Glenn Stevens, and Kerry Adahy had lived with their mother until she was arrested for child abuse. The police had found the children—then ages three, four, and five—drugged with their mother's antipsychotics, which she used to sedate them rather than herself; she kept them tied to a pole, and fed them nothing but cereal. The state placed the boys with a foster family, and enrolled Marshall in the school where Anne taught. Anne assumed that while some of his problems were biological, others were the result of abuse, and she was determined to sort them out. She argued against medication until every behavior management strategy had been tried. "He went from having a fifty-five IQ and being extremely violent and not talking, to a first grade boy who could read and write with an average IQ," she said.

Marshall had been in Anne's class only a few weeks when the social worker in charge of his case told her that the three brothers were to be separated, because Marshall, half-Mexican, and Kerry, half-Cherokee, looked dark, and wouldn't interest white families. Anne said, "What would I need to do to keep them together?" The next day, Friday, she found out she'd need to move just across the border to Tennessee, because the foster care system would not allow the kids out of state. The social worker expected Anne to balk; instead, Monday afternoon, Anne and Clay found a new house. They moved in two weeks later, were given the kids, and started adoption proceedings. "A two-year-old will grab everything, and rip it in half or drop it or roll it," Anne said. "Nothing is safe. Marshall was doing that at six, but he was angry. So it was just a matter of letting him lick and touch and drop and tear until he got all of that out of his system. It took a year. Glenn had a fascination with putting things in different holes of his body." Kerry had a very feminine manner, which was the least of Anne's worries.

The boys hid things under their beds and mattresses. If Anne was missing fried chicken or macaroni and cheese, she would go into their room and retrieve it, but objects she would just leave alone. She noticed that Kerry was often hiding girl things, lifted from the houses of his cousins. "You can't attack a child who's taken something like that," Anne said. "I'd say, 'Oh, Alicia lost her such-and-such, and she would love to have it back.' A few days later, it would be back at Alicia's house. Kerry didn't want to make anyone else sad; he just wanted pretty things." The other kids at school tormented him. In second grade, he stopped doing homework. "About a month before the end of school last year, he was sitting on the front porch, with his little knee propped up under his chin," Anne said, "And he said, 'I wish I was a girl.'"

Anne called several local psychologists before finding Darlene Fink in Knoxville, a transgender activist and therapist. After Darlene diagnosed Kelly with GID, Anne spent two solid days researching the subject. "Then we went to Walmart and bought clothes, purses, fake jewelry, and a Barbie doll," Anne said. "Different colors of lip gloss. She was so excited. Then it was, 'I want to change my name.'" The change was palpable. "She was the child I wanted to raise, the happy one who's comfortable in her own skin."

Anne went to tell the principal at school. "I had already talked to two teachers, and after I'd explained for half an hour, they were fine," she said. Anne felt confident; Anne felt beloved. "In our town, people would come over for dinner; they'd invite my kids to birthday parties; I made friends with people on the block. I had a church. I really thought that we were part of the fabric of that community. Well, it turns out, I really didn't even know what that fabric was made out of."

The day after Anne went to the school, the phone calls began. "I didn't recognize the voices," Anne said. "They were going to gut her. They were going to cut off her genitals and treat her like the woman she wanted to be. They were going to snatch her from school or in a parking lot, and I would never see her again. Some of them were going to raise her up right. Some of them were going to kill her." Anne was at a loss. "She's eight,"

Anne said. "She's the tiniest kid in class." When Anne tried to go to the school the next day, the janitor she'd known ten years wouldn't let her in the building. Her pediatrician asked her to see him in his office. "He had been sitting around the country club pool, with the other people from the Baptist church. He said, 'People are not talking about *if* they're going to hurt you and Kelly. They're planning *when* and *how* and *what they're going to use* to do it. You have to put your child in a foster home somewhere else, or he's not going to live till the next school year.'"

Anne was reeling. She went home, loaded the shotgun, and slept in front of the door. "I'm getting cell phone calls from neighbors saying, 'Anne, there are people parked in front of your house, and they're peeking over the fence.' Of course, they didn't know yet. Those phone calls stopped when the gossip reached them."

Anne met a mother online who said that things were better in the big Southern city where she lived. Anne decided it was as good a destination as any. She sold whatever she could online. "I let it be known I was armed," Anne said, "and that I would kill anyone who stepped on my porch. The phone calls continued and I told them, 'We're no threat to you. We're leaving.' I put the kids in the van with as much stuff as I could, and left. Everything fit except the dog." Clay stayed behind because he needed to keep his job. A few days later, he came home to find that a crowd had disemboweled the dog, and nailed its remains to a fence. "It was just a message to us not to ever come back," Anne said. "We never will. I'll never see the town I grew up in again, either, because I'm not telling anyone from that whole area where I've gone. I'll never see my mother or my sister."

Anne began to cry as she recounted all this. Shaking slightly, she said, "I knew I was a lesbian when I was fourteen years old, and I kept that to myself for twenty-one years. I married to fit in and be wanted and keep my home and family and church and everything that was important to me. It wasn't worth it to give all that up to be myself; I preferred to live a lie. I gave it all up in a month for Kelly. That's how important she is. I came out to Clay two days ago." Anne's fear was that Clay would say she and her lesbian ways had done this to Kelly; Clay's fear, as it turned out, was that Anne would think this had happened because he wasn't a good father. "It boiled down to, neither of us is guilty," Anne said. "He just said, 'Well, that explains a lot.' We're better friends now than we've ever been."

Daily life remains difficult. For the first week, Anne didn't let the kids outside, in case they'd been followed, and even now, she doesn't let them out of viewing distance. Teaching jobs require references, and she doesn't want anyone from her new town to be in touch with anyone from the old one, so she can't work in her field. Anne had to work with the kids on not blowing Kelly's cover. Marshall and Glenn both complained that they didn't know how they could keep it all a secret, and what if people asked them? So Anne said she was going to do an exercise with them. She told them all to sit together right inside the trailer door while she went outside for a few minutes. Then she walked in, flung open the door, and said, "Hi, kids. I'm Anne O'Hara, and I have a vagina." They all ran away screaming, as she'd known they would. "No one wants to hear that," she said. "It's not secret. It's private. Kelly's anatomy is private too."

As long as Clay keeps his factory job, they have insurance

to pay for the kids' medications. Other than that, his salary pays for his life in Tennessee. Anne is living on the money from selling the lawnmower and the four-wheeler, and on the assistance check she receives for having adopted special needs children. "We get about $1,900 per month," she said. "Living in this trailer, rent and utilities is $900 per month. I spend about $100 a week on groceries and about $25 a week on gas. We have a lot of Tuna Helper, pea soup, bagels, and yogurt."

Anne has another safe place in mind if things fall apart where she is. She's figured out exactly how she'll move and what she'll do. When I suggested that she talk to school administrators about why she couldn't provide references for a new teaching job, she replied, "I will work at a gas station before I tell anyone my child is transgender." We walked up through the trailer park to meet the school bus. Three exuberant children bounded out and ran to hug Anne. She stood there, so soon after our long, tearful talk, wrapped in all those young arms, and she burst out laughing. "It's funny how your priorities change," she said. "I've got this happy little girl. When she gets off that bus and you see this happy little face, you've got the whole world right there. I haven't given up one thing that's worth that."

Later, she explained, "I don't love my daughter less for mourning over what I've lost. But I miss my mom. I miss my sister. My daddy's grave is back there, and I just have to hope other people are putting flowers on it. I miss my dog. I miss my students. I feel really guilty because I'm still hung up on all this stuff that we left behind. I should just let that go. But it makes me so angry that these people have taken our lives from us."

Then Anne smiled again, as though she couldn't really help herself. "You can't grieve all the time when you've got your kids," she said. "You see how far they've come, and they reach you right in your heart. That moment when they come off the bus is one of my best moments. My other is when they get up in the morning, and they collide on top of me. So, regret? No. I miss the things that were in the old life. But if I knew this was going to happen, I would still adopt Kelly. I'm the lucky one. Because, honestly, if it weren't for Kelly coming into my life, I would have never have entered this bigger, more beautiful world, where I've met you and so many other wonderful people. I would still be married to a man for the next twenty years. I mean, if you just look at it, Kelly has brought more blessings into my life than I could possibly give back to her."

Playfulness about gender is much more commonplace than it used to be. "To some extent, transgenderism has become a fad," Meyer-Bahlburg said. This observation conformed with my experience. I met people on college campuses who were defining themselves as genderqueer to express revolutionary feelings, or to communicate their individuality; they were gender fluid—sometimes male, sometimes female—without being gender dysphoric, or miserable in the body to which they'd been born. This phenomenon may be culturally significant, but it has only a little bit in common with the experience of people who feel they can have no authentic self in their birth gender.

Belonging is one of the things that makes life bearable, and it can be tough to look at a binary world and choose against both sides. A therapist who works with children with various challenges told me that it's much harder to be ambidextrous than it is to be left-handed. Sometimes, idiosyncrasy can be a pose, membership in the smaller club of the anticlub, but often it occurs not because genderqueer is a cool thing to be, but because nothing else fits. Such experiences express the wide vision that lies outside of belonging.

Changing social mores and advancing science have caused us to question the basic structuring principles of human society. Genesis describes a world born in categories. God made grasses and trees, then whales and fish, then fowl and birds, then cattle and creeping things and beasts, then human beings to have dominion over all the rest. "Male and female he created them," says the verse. In the great creation story, humans and animals occupy categories that can never cross, as do men and women.

In the twenty-first century, new arguments are afloat that some men are women, that some women are men, that some human beings are persons but are neither women nor men. Globalization has blurred national identity, and intermarriage has compromised racial identity. We like categories and clubs as much as we ever have; it's only that the ones we thought were sacred and unbreakable turn out not to be, and others that we never imagined are taking their place.

When Carol and Loren McKerrow met, she was runner-up for Miss Texas and he was completing his training in ophthalmology outside Fort Worth. When they married, he took her home to Helena, Montana. They adopted their son Marc because they thought they were unable to conceive. However, Carol became pregnant with Paul, later Kim, about the time they brought Marc home; Carol gave birth to another son, Todd, a couple of years later. Marc had behavior problems. "Whenever school called," Carol recalled, "it was an awards ceremony, academic or athletic, for Paul, or to tell me Marc had been suspended." While all the anxiety was focused around Marc, Paul was secretly struggling with gender. "I had a paper route when I was ten," Kim remembered. "It was very early. I used to crossdress because I didn't think anyone would see me. Then I would throw away the clothes and pray that some power could dispel this thing that was making me unlike anyone else I knew of."

Paul became a great athlete and was quarterback on his high school football team. "That was the recipe to be normal, and a way to shut off your brain," Kim said. "If you're uncomfortable with your body, you want to control that body, and sports are a really good way to do it." Paul was valedictorian and class president at Helena High, where he was voted most likely to succeed.

Paul went on to University of California–Berkeley and spent his junior year, 1988, abroad. "Everybody else is going to Florence or Paris," Kim said, "I'm going to Norway because I'm just going to hide in a long, dark winter, read Beckett, drink blackberry tea, and starve. I went thinking, 'I'm going to stop this.' A couple of months into it, it was like, 'I can't stop this.'" Some people give a single date for their transition; Kim described hers as happening from 1989 to 1996. She moved to San Francisco and saw old friends and family as little as possible; the only person from her previous life who knew was her brother Todd, who was openly gay. He was easygoing and had come out without much drama, but Kim kept even him at arm's length.

Kim was the most generic name she could think of, and she changed her last name to *Reed*, her old middle name, to make a fresh start. Even so, Kim felt awkward and artificial; it took five years for her to start hormones.

"I wasn't sure who I was," Kim said. "I wasn't even sure gender was the gateway. It's awfully complicated, awfully expensive, awfully isolating, and the practical angle alone is very difficult." Today, however, Kim has an unaffected femininity. Once when I was out with her, someone came up to her and said, "My friend is struggling with transitioning. You're so relaxed; how did you learn all these gestures?" Kim said, "When I was making the switch, I was too conscious of how I moved, and it wasn't until I began to forget about it that who I really was started to take over."

Kim, still Paul to the family, would talk to her mother on the phone, but for almost five years, they didn't see each other. When an aunt died, however, Carol expected Paul to attend the funeral. Kim, who had been on hormones for over a year, was a pallbearer, wearing a man's suit, with only a ponytail to attract comment. Carol said, "It was a funeral. But he looked *so* sad, and I still had no clue. A month later, Paul called and said, 'Did you ever wonder as I was growing up whether I was comfortable with my own sexual identity?' I said, 'I thought you were the golden child.' He said, 'Well, I've been dressing as a woman.'" Carol was bewildered, and she worried about telling Loren.

Kim once said, "When I transitioned, I felt like I had climbed out of a wet suit I had been wearing my entire life. Imagine that magnificent rush, the tactile sensations, as though your body had just woken up. But I also felt like this new person couldn't go home, and I began to dismantle my connections to Montana. At the time I didn't know how thoroughly all of this saddened me, and to compensate for that, I started to turn my hometown into a place that I didn't really need to go back to." That exile continued even after Loren had been told the news; no one else in the family was to know.

Loren had contracted hepatitis in medical school; while Kim was growing into herself, his condition was worsening. He was on a waiting list for a liver transplant, but at sixty-two, he was not given priority. In the summer of 2003, he decided to visit each of his children. Kim had moved to New York, told her parents that she was a lesbian, and started seeing a woman named Claire Jones. Carol and Loren had dinner with Kim and Claire the night they arrived. "I started feeling better about everything," Carol said. "I loved Claire the minute I met her. I was so worried Kim was going to be alone. Claire walked around the corner, and I just breathed a sigh of relief."

Several months later, Loren collapsed and was taken on an emergency flight for treatment in Denver. Kim flew immediately to join her parents. She arrived at the hospital a few hours before her father died, while her brothers were still arranging transport to Colorado. Kim reached Marc on the phone as he was boarding his flight and said, "I've been out of touch. I didn't know how to handle it; but now because of Dad's death, we're all going to be together, and you need to know about me." At the Denver airport, Kim gave Marc her card and said, "Here are my phone numbers. You can call me anytime."

Later that day, Carol, Kim, Marc, and Todd set out for

Montana by car. During the long trip, Kim reaffirmed her connection to Marc and tried to answer his many questions. He was bewildered, but not unkind. Whenever there was cell phone reception across the plains of Wyoming, Kim made calls to uncles, aunts, and cousins. "My father has died," Kim recalled. "They're reeling. They're hearing the news about me. And they respond with, 'We're just glad to have you back.'"

Carol decided to host a tea party for friends in Helena who could help get the word out about Kim, so she wouldn't need to discuss it at the funeral. Kim was at the airport picking up Claire when the tea party took place. Carol had invited nineteen women and the male pastor from her church. She explained Kim's transition in brief, then said, "I'm not responsible *for* my child and who she's become, but I am responsible *to* her, and she is a wonderful person. I love her. I don't know if you need to know anything else, but that's all I need to know." After a moment of silence, somebody said, "Amen." Then Carol said, "I'm telling you this now, and I'm not going to speak about it again the rest of the weekend. I'm concentrating on Loren's service, and celebrating his life." Carol and the rest of the family never encountered the kind of community hatred that I had seen so many other families battle.

Tim O'Leary, who had been Paul's closest friend, was in town for the funeral. Kim was planning to stay away from the viewing at the funeral home. "I've said I'm not going because I want to keep it about my dad, but I'm really chickening out. Before I know it, Tim and all these guys I knew in high school, essentially the football team, open our front door, and they've got cases of beer, and Frank Mayo's saying, 'Yeah, I had this dream that we were all fat, bald, and old, and you were a girl.' Claire's sitting on the couch, knocking back cheap beer, and there's a couple more cases outside in a snowbank to keep them cold. This guy has his arm around Claire, and they're laughing, and I was just like, 'This is going to work out just fine.'"

A few years before I met her, Kim had decided to make a documentary that would begin with her twentieth high school reunion that fall; Marc had been held back a grade in elementary school, so they graduated in the same class, and both planned to attend. *Prodigal Sons* is full of the childhood Kim shared with Marc and Todd, including footage shot by her father when she was still Paul, the quarterback; she finished the film early in our interview process.

Six months after I met her, Kim called me one night, excitedly, with an invitation. The pastor from her church in Helena was organizing a *Prodigal Sons* weekend: a screening on Friday night, seminars on Saturday to discuss issues raised by the film, and a sermon by Kim on Sunday. The night of the screening, Plymouth Congregational was packed, with a long waiting list for tickets. I sat next to Carol in the back row, and she cried through much of the film and had to leave the sanctuary twice. When the film ended, Kim stood at the front of the church, and the audience began to applaud. A few people stood up, then a few more, and then it became a standing ovation. When it ended, Kim invited her mother up; Carol had composed her face into a smile by then, and as she walked briskly down the aisle, everyone stood up again, and when Carol arrived at the altar, she and Kim stood with their arms around each other's shoulders while the audience continued cheering.

At the reception afterward, I told one of the church ladies that Kim had worried about the conversation the film would provoke, and the lady said, "Our hardest conversations aren't with other people; they're with ourselves. Once she had settled who she was in herself, we were ready to have whatever conversations we needed to make sure she knew this was always home."

On Sunday, the pastor told me there were more congregants than she'd seen any time but Christmas and Easter. The entire McKerrow clan was there; some had had to drive many hours from their farms. Kim came forward. Although the parable of the prodigal son is usually interpreted as a story about the father, she said, it is also a story about a son who receives a welcome he would never have dared to expect. She said, "The night before last, when our film was playing in here, I went outside to the columbarium where my father's ashes rest. As I was kneeling there by what I call 'Dad's spot,' I thought of the hours and hours of videotape that he shot lovingly of me during my football games, and how much of the same footage was now being shown inside this sanctuary. Now, it's certainly not the context that any of us expected. But I knew Dad would be proud. And just then, the dusk breeze blew in this waft of sound, and it was strangely familiar to me, and I realized it was the cross-town football game coming from the stadium. The band was playing, and the announcer was bellowing, and all of these old tapes were playing inside here, on the screen, and I knew that new ones were being recorded just a few blocks away. Those recording their new memories to tape should be only so lucky as to be surprised by the last thing that they expected from their loved ones, only so fortunate as to get a chance to welcome them home with radical love. I thought about how all these cycles of lives would continue on, and so many aspects of my life coalesced in that one beautiful, stunning, blessed moment: the past and the present, parent and child, male and female—the pain that life sometimes brings, and the soothing love that welcomes it with open arms, after its exhausting journey into a distant country."

That afternoon after the service, Carol and I went for a long walk. I said, "Do you wish that Paul had just been happy to be Paul, and had stayed that way?" Carol said, "Well, of course I do. It would have been easier for Paul, and for the rest of us. But the key phrase in there is 'happy to be Paul.' He wasn't, and I am just so glad that he had the courage to do something about it. I had somebody say this weekend, 'Carol, Paul died, and I haven't finished mourning that.' I don't feel that. Kim is much more present to people than Paul ever was. Paul was never rude, he just wasn't totally present. We didn't quite have his attention." She laughed, and then said with adoring emphasis, "And look what we got! Kim!" And grace seemed to be both the cause and the consequence of her happiness in that emphatic declaration.

As I worked on this chapter, I kept returning in my mind to Alfred Tennyson's poem in which he wrote about a friend,

> And manhood fused with female grace
> In such a sort, the child would twine
> A trustful hand, unask'd, in thine,
> And find his comfort in thy face.

Our notions of masculinity and femininity are really modern. Though Tennyson's friend was neither trans nor gay, his magnetism existed in this blending of strength and gentleness, boldness and compassion. I remember first reading Tennyson's lines when I was a teenager, thinking that he celebrated this friend for the very qualities that most troubled me in myself. I wanted to be something noble, not just a boy who had failed at real masculinity and was making do. I wanted to emulate what was best in my father and mother, in the life of the mind, to which men often stake first claim, and that of the heart, in which women usually have the upper hand. I saw in Tennyson's bracing words praise not to an androgynous face, but to the intricate nature of beauty. Masculinity and femininity here seemed not to be locked in binary competition, but fused in collaboration.

I have a great life as a man and have made it all work, but I know that at twelve I'd have chosen to be a woman if it had been an easy and complete transformation. Perhaps that is only because being a woman looked more respectable to me than being a gay man, and twelve is a conformist age. I don't regret not being a woman, any more than I regret not being a football hero, or not being born into the British royal family; trans children usually believe they are already members of a different gender, and I never did. Being gay has worked out happily for me in the end, and I don't feel the afflictions I have resolved as permanent losses.

Yet I like to imagine a science fiction future when gender-bending will not entail surgical procedures, hormone injections, and social condemnation—a society in which everyone is able to choose his or her own gender at any time. Without physical trauma, such people would be fully of their affirmed gender, with an entirely functioning reproductive system and mind and heart of the self they believe is rightly theirs. If they wish to linger at the middle of a gender spectrum—physically, psychologically, or both—that, too, would be possible.

At the same time, I know that choice can be burdensome and exhausting and frightening—especially unaccustomed choice. A piece of me thinks people who cannot do a competent job of voting in an electoral democracy, who have a record-high divorce rate, who fail to love children born because they didn't use birth control would collapse if given full leeway to choose their gender. I likewise believe that choice is the only true luxury, that the striving inherent in decision-making gives decisions value. I like to imagine a future in which we would be able to choose everything. I'd quite possibly choose what I have now—and would love it even more for having done so.

But that is not yet the society we live in. Perhaps the immutable error of parenthood is that we give our children what we wanted, whether they want it or not. We heal our wounds with the love we wish we'd received, but are often blind to the wounds we inflict. The longing of a child is to be seen, and once the child is seen, he or she or they wants to be loved for a true self. It is time to focus on the child rather than the gender label.

Father

I STARTED THIS BOOK TO FORGIVE my parents and ended it by becoming a parent. I wanted to find out why I had experienced so much pain in my childhood, to understand what was my doing, what was my parents', and what was the world's; I likewise wanted to figure out my own future. I felt I owed it to both my parents and myself to prove that we had been less than half the problem. In retrospect it seems obvious that my research about parenting was also a means to subdue my anxieties about becoming a parent. But the mind works in mysterious ways, and this secret purpose revealed itself only gradually.

I grew up afraid of illness and disability, inclined to avert my gaze from anyone who was too different—despite all the ways I knew myself to be different. This book helped me kill that bigoted impulse, which I had always known to be ugly. The obvious melancholy in the stories I heard should, perhaps, have made me shy away from paternity, but it had the opposite effect. Parenting had challenged these families, but almost none regretted it; they demonstrated that with enough emotional discipline and will, one could love anyone. I was comforted by this acceptance and the reassurance that difficult love is no less a thing than easy love.

For a long time, children used to make me sad. The absence

of children in the lives of gay people had repeatedly been held up to me as my tragedy. My parents, and even the world, had encouraged me to marry a woman and have a family. I spent years drifting between relationships with men and relationships with women. I loved some of the women with whom I was intimate, but I was with women largely because children were part of the equation. The recognition that I was really gay came only when I understood that gayness was a matter not of behavior, but of identity.

When I was coming of age, that identity and being a father seemed incompatible. The unlikely prospect of being a gay parent troubled me then because I thought that growing up with a gay father would mean my children would be teased and marginalized. As a child, I had been mocked for being different, and I didn't want to foist a version of that experience on anyone else. In the twenty years that followed, social reality changed. Other gay people made the leap to parenthood. When I expressed a wish for biological children, that wish was repeatedly devalued, often by people who reminded me that loads of abandoned children needed good homes. These arguments were often made by people who had produced biological children and had never contemplated adoption. My wish to create a child struck some other people as quaint or self-indulgent.

Since homosexuality does not appear to be transmissible, I was consigning my presumed children to the potential discomfort of coming from a strange place rather than of being a strange thing. Some critics felt this eased the problem; they spoke of how gay people should be allowed to have children because the children are no more likely to be gay than any others. In other words, they accepted my horizontal identity only so long as it never became vertical. I would not have been dissuaded from having children if I had known that they were likely to be gay; nor was I dissuaded by the likelihood that they would be straight.

The right to reproduce should be among the inalienable ones. Yet the prejudice against people with horizontal identities is revealed most clearly when members of those identity groups who have the potential to pass on aberrant traits decide to have their own children—the very issue that does not apply so directly to gay parents, and that has made us seem less threatening. Many people are outraged when a disabled or challenged adult produces a disabled or challenged child.

Newscaster and actress Bree Walker was born with ectrodactyly, or lobster-claw syndrome, which results in deformities of the hands and feet. She bore a child with the syndrome, and when she became pregnant again, she knew that her second child might also inherit the condition. She chose to keep the pregnancy and became the fodder of outrage. Implicit in all the criticisms was that Walker—who has had a successful career and marriage, is telegenic, and has many strengths to pass on—had no right to become pregnant. Her attackers even went so far as to imply that she was morally obligated to abort, no matter how much she wanted her child, or how competent she was to raise it. "I felt that my pregnancy had been terrorized," Walker later said. The talk shows that discussed her situation reduced her children to their disability. Media commentators largely failed to acknowledge that veterans of a condition their children may inherit are uniquely qualified to understand the risks and rewards of life with that condition. Their choices are better-informed than our judgments of them.

Deciding whether to have a child is a loaded question for anyone whose genetics are considered suspect. The disability scholar Adrienne Asch wrote in a 1999 essay, "Chronic illness and disability are not equivalent to acute illness or sudden injury. Most people with spinal bifida, achondroplasia, Down syndrome, and many other mobility and sensory impairments perceive themselves as healthy, not sick, and describe their conditions as givens of their lives—the equipment with which they meet the world." There is truth in what Asch says, but it is not the whole truth. In 2003, I was sent to interview a young woman named Laura Rothenberg about her cystic fibrosis, and we ended up enjoying a brief friendship. Even though both her parents were carriers (CF is a recessive gene), she had a horizontal experience of the illness because neither of them had manifested it. She wrote a poignant memoir, *Breathing for a Living*, in which she praised many things inherent in the identity that CF gave her. Nonetheless, she did not see herself as healthy and would have welcomed a cure—not because she was rejecting this part of herself, but because she wanted to feel good and live long. Her deterioration and death at the age of twenty-two bore little similarity to the experience of a healthy achondroplastic dwarf. Yet, consumed with grief just after her death, her father said to me, "When Laura was conceived, they didn't have an amniocentesis test for CF. But they developed one. If we'd known, Laura would not have been born. I still have the thought, 'My God—she could have been denied life.' What a tragedy that would have been."

It is not a great leap from choosing to keep a pregnancy despite a prenatal diagnosis to selecting for difference. An article in the *Los Angeles Times* pointed out, "Creating made-to-order babies with genetic defects would seem to be an ethical minefield, but to some parents with disabilities—say, deafness or dwarfism—it just means making babies like them." In a survey of nearly two hundred clinics that offer preimplantation genetic diagnosis (PGD), a process that has been available for two decades, 3 percent admitted having used the test to select for an embryo with a disability. Dr. Robert J. Stillman of the Shady Grove Fertility Center, which has offices in Maryland, Virginia, and Pennsylvania, has denied requests to select for deafness and dwarfism. "One of the prime dictates of parenting is to make a better world for our children," he said. "Dwarfism and deafness are not the norm."

By what logic does making a better world have to do with hewing to the norm? The debate about embryo selection pertains to that most elusive and most socially determined of human rights—dignity. In 2008, Britain made selecting an embryo with disability genes illegal. People who chose PGD to avoid Down syndrome, for example, would not be permitted to implant an embryo with any known disability. Deaf activists were horrified. "There is no going around this," wrote one blogger. "We are being devalued, unworthy to be human simply because we are imperfect."

Sharon Duchesneau and Candace McCullough, lesbian Deaf women, wanted a child, and in 2002 they asked a friend who was fifth-generation deaf to be their sperm donor. They produced two deaf children, Gauvin and Jehanne. They decided to share their experience with a reporter from the *Washington Post*, stimulating an onslaught of attacks similar to those on Bree Walker. Fox News ran a story under the headline "Victims from Birth: Engineering Defects in Helpless Children Crosses the Line."

Few people would assert that a Deaf married couple should not procreate because of the risk of producing deaf children. Some would stipulate that the line be drawn between what one accepts and what one seeks, arguing that the deaf children of heterosexual deaf parents occur by "natural" process—but love and rules to do not mix well, and the concept of *natural* is itself a constantly shifting, unnatural idea often used to cover prejudice. Those who objected to Duchesneau's and McCullough's choice may also not have understood the life experience of those two women, who are college-educated, professionally successful, apparently happy, socially active, and in a good relationship. Like many parents, they wanted a child who would be like them.

This is a difficult argument to buck. Sharon said, "It would be nice to have a child who is the same as us." Candy said, "I want to be the same as my child; I want the baby to enjoy what we enjoy." These don't seem like radical statements until you learn they came from deaf people.

Legal scholar John Corvino pointed out that the public rage was rooted in a fundamental metaphysical fallacy. "They could have chosen a different donor," he argued. "Or they could have chosen adoption rather than pregnancy. But neither of those choices would have resulted in Gauvin's having hearing. On the contrary, they would have resulted in his not being born at all." The Deaf activist Patrick Boudreault said, "No one is talking, ever, about deliberately deafening a child born hearing."

William Saletan, national correspondent at *Slate*, wrote, "Old fear: designer babies. New fear: deformer babies." Of course, "deformer" babies are designer babies too; they just don't follow the most popular designs. And designer babies aren't going anywhere; they will undoubtedly become increasingly common as technology advances. In 2006, nearly half of the PGD clinics surveyed by the Genetics and Public Policy Center at Johns Hopkins University offered a gender-selection service. University College London recently announced the birth of one of the first babies selected to be free of a genetic breast-cancer vulnerability. The Fertility Institutes in Los Angeles declared that they were planning to help couples select for gender, hair color, and eye color, though such outrage ensued that they suspended the program. Such choices are inevitably the future. How different are they from standard protocols for sperm and egg donors, which screen donors for undesirable hereditary traits and provide information on physical attractiveness, coloring, height, weight, and college entrance test scores?

Human beings like to fix things; if we learn to control the weather, we will soon be blind to the majesty of hurricanes and intolerant of the silence of the blizzard. In 2005, the journalist Patricia E. Bauer described in the *Washington Post* the pressures she had had to negotiate when she decided to keep a daughter prenatally diagnosed with Down syndrome. She wrote, "Prenatal testing is making your right to abort a disabled child more like your duty to abort a disabled child." No one should be forced to keep a pregnancy she dreads, and no one should be pressured to terminate a pregnancy she desires. Those who are prepared to love children with horizontal qualities give dignity to them, whether or not they have used prenatal testing. With access to reproductive technologies, we are deciding what kind of children will make us happy, and what kind we will make happy. It may be irresponsible to avoid this guesswork, but it is naive to think it is anything more. Imagined love has little in common with love.

Which parents should have children and which children should be born will always be debated. We question the decision of people with HIV to produce kids they might not live to raise; we try to prevent teen pregnancies; we judge whether people with disabilities should pass on those differences. It is possible to sterilize people with disapproval as well as with a scalpel, and it is almost equally cruel. Educating people on the challenges their children may embody is sensible, but preventing them from having children because we think we know the value of those lives smacks of fascism. It is not happenstance that you need a license to get married, but not to have a child.

No one in any of the categories this book explores would have had a better life half a century ago. The dizzying technological advances that threaten many of these identities have coincided with identity politics that are shaping a more tolerant world. We live in an increasingly diverse society, and the lessons in tolerance that come with that diversity have extended even to populations too disenfranchised to make their own claims—a change larger in scope than any that the suffragettes or the civil rights activists envisioned. Disabled people are on television; transgender people hold public office; members of the helping professions are working with criminals, prodigies, and people conceived in rape. Jobs programs exist for people with schizophrenia and autism.

The idea that we live in a shameless time is widely lamented. Why are so many people going on TV to talk about their idiocy, their tragedy, even their cruelty? Why do we embrace rich people who have stolen their fortunes? We may not be ashamed enough of what is authentically reprehensible, but we are likewise increasingly unashamed of what never should have embarrassed us in the first place. The opposite of identity politics is embarrassment. We are closer than ever to the rights of life, liberty, and the pursuit of happiness. Fewer and fewer people are mortified by who they truly are.

Extraordinary is a numbers game. You may argue over whether something extraordinary is good or bad, but you cannot argue about whether it is extraordinary—and yet the term is endlessly subject to false claims. Ordinary people insist that they are unique, while extraordinary people maintain that they are really just like everyone else. Dull people would like to be thought remarkable, while exceptional people hope for the modest comforts of fitting in. We long for and resist difference; we aspire to and fear individuality. A child's most challenging differences from his parents, by definition, manifest in areas that are unfamiliar to them. Our tendency to misrepresent children as more or less original than they are reflects our misgivings about the relationship between individuality and happiness. Acknowledging difference need not threaten love; indeed, it can enrich it.

Ideally, profound acceptance allows children to become most fully themselves. Within his or her own family, someone's dwarfism or autism or prodigiousness or transgenderism may be secondary. Such people are ideally, first and foremost, the children of their parents, fully recognized citizens of the tiny nation that is a family. Parents need not merely love their children despite their defects but may find the surprising rightness in those imperfections. A wise psychiatrist once said to me, "People want to get better, but they don't want to change." But I would propose that only by allowing people born with horizontal identities *not* to change does one allow them to get better. Any of us can be a better version of himself, but none of us can be someone else.

Mainstreaming, inclusion, deinstitutionalization, the disability rights movement, identity politics—all these forces both emphasize and normalize difference. They focus on securing accommodation of unusual needs, while asserting that our most basic needs are all the same. They aspire to change the world so that more people can feel unremarkable in it. Many of the parents and children I interviewed were dedicated to extending the good conditions they had achieved at home into the larger community, and so they had become activists—some as a life's calling, others merely by agreeing to speak on the record. They did so in hopes that a kinder society would help their children and themselves across their life span.

An integrated educational system benefits many people with horizontal identities; it likewise helps those who share a classroom with them. Similarly, building a compassionate society benefits not only those who are newly tolerated, but also those who are newly tolerating. Incorporating exceptional people into the social fabric is expensive and time-consuming. The emotional and logistical exercises can be draining. Yet if parents often end up grateful for their problematic children, and those problematic children end up grateful for their challenges, then so, in the end, can we all be grateful for the courage such people may embody, the generosity they may teach us, even the ways they complicate the world.

I began work on this book at about the same time I met John, who is now my husband. I had always wanted children, had contemplated having a child with an old friend, had dabbled in research on fertility—but the possibility had lingered in abstraction. John gave me more courage to be extraordinary, and more confidence about being ordinary, but from the stories of these hundreds of exceptional families I gradually understood that those were not incompatible goals, that being anomalous does not deprive anyone of the right or ability to be typical. Emily Perl Kingsley helped get children with Down syndrome on television so that no one else would feel as alone as she had. Neurodiversity and Deaf rights activists claimed the acceptance of aberration as their due. Sue Klebold said, "Columbine made me feel more connected to mankind than anything else possibly could have." Their tenor of persuasive wonder resonated deeply with me.

I had struggled for years with childlessness, and just when I had reconciled myself to that sadness, I began to see its inverse hope and started to figure out how I could be fruitful and multiply. I had been unpopular as a child, and children continued to intimidate me. I felt that in their eyes, I was still bad at dodge-ball, with a funny gait, and emotionally awkward—that I had retained all the qualities that had made children shun me in my own childhood, qualities I had eventually understood to be aligned with my sexuality. I was still afraid of being called *gay* by children; my secure identity resonated like an insult when spoken by a child. I avoided children because of how *much* they made me feel. Like any powerful feeling, it was hard to read; what was manifest was its strength rather than its nature. I was usually relieved to leave other people's children after a few hours. Would I feel otherwise if I had my own? I was also afraid of becoming the oppressor of a child who was different from me, as I had at times felt oppressed.

John already had a biological son when I met him. He and the child's biological mother, Laura, had been coworkers, and Laura had observed him for years before she and her partner, Tammy, asked him to help them have a child. He had agreed, and they signed legal documents in which he forswore paternal rights and they forswore claims to support. He had offered to be in the child's life to the extent he was able, if the child and his mothers so wished, but he had remained largely uninvolved. A few months after our relationship began, we ran into Tammy and Laura with their toddler, Oliver, at the 2001 Minnesota State Fair. His mothers had told him to call John *Donor Dad*, a term that seemed to acknowledge the relationship without giving it equal footing to Tammy's and Laura's. Oliver, unable to comprehend *Donor Dad*, called John *Donut Dad*, which made everybody laugh. But then who was I? Eighteen months later, they asked John to be their donor again, and Laura subsequently gave birth to Lucy. I was wary of John's connection to this family, and also fascinated. John had fathered *children*, and I looked at them for clues to who he really was. I didn't really like them yet, but that was irrelevant to this grip of emotion and biology.

I had been considering the possibility of having my own biological children for some years. In 1999, during a business trip to Texas, I attended a dinner that included my college friend Blaine. Blaine had always been magical to me: reflexively kind, with an acute intelligence that she never shows off, and possessed of timeless grace. She had recently divorced and shortly thereafter lost her mother, and she mentioned that the best tribute she could pay to her happy childhood was to become a mother herself. I said, in a lighthearted way at a table full of other people, that I'd be game to be the father to her child. She countered, brightly, that she might just take me up on the offer. When I got home, I wrote her a letter and said I knew she'd probably been joking, but that I thought she would be the best mother in the world, and I hoped she'd have a child with someone.

Four years later, Blaine flew to New York in 2003 for my surprise fortieth birthday party. We went to dinner the following night and realized that we both wanted to follow through with the baby project. I had never been so honored or so alarmed. Our arrangements would be similar to John's with Tammy and Laura in some ways, but different in others; I would be the legal father of a child who would bear my last name. Though our child would live in Texas with Blaine, the relationship would be explicitly paternal.

John was initially against the idea. We talked about it——John and I, Blaine and I. It took three years to iron out the details. Blaine and I created a pregnancy working through an IVF clinic. Blaine, meanwhile, had met her partner, Richard, putting a reasonable, if unusual, balance in place.

The more curious our arrangements became, the more traditional they started to feel. John had previously proposed that we get married, and I decided to honor the idea, though I was still a leery convert to gay marriage. Tammy and Laura and their children came to our marriage ceremony; Oliver served as John's ring-bearer. Blaine, four months pregnant with the child she and I had conceived, came with Richard, and John ventured that we'd had the first gay shotgun wedding.

In October, some complications in the pregnancy emerged, so John and I hurried to Fort Worth a month early for the delivery of little Blaine by Caesarean section on November 5, 2007. I was the first person to hold her. I kept trying on the idea that I was now a father, and I didn't know what to do with it; it was as though I had suddenly been told that I was still myself and also a shooting star. Already deep in my research, I knew that every child has a touch of the horizontal and reshapes his or her parents. I scanned my daughter's little face for clues as to who she was, and for hints of who she would make me become.

I soon realized that I wanted to bring up a child at home with John, to be a pledge between us. John's original arrangement with Tammy and Laura had answered a question; the arrangement with Blaine was more intimate; and the prospect of having a child who would live full-time with the two of us was an explosion of everything we had been taught to expect from life as gay men. I hadn't wanted to get married; then the reality had entranced me. I exacted a child as fair trade, believing John, too, would end up entranced. Because John was less sure about wanting this child than I professed to be, I had to act as cheerleader for the enterprise. I was full of hopeful infatuation with a person who did not yet exist and sure that fatherhood would exalt everything I already cherished about John, but the conversation stalled there. Our love for each other was a prerequisite for a child, but not a reason for one. We could not procreate as a social experiment or as a political statement or to make ourselves whole, and I could not be the sole enthusiast in our decisions. Then John gave me an antique cradle tired up with a bow for my birthday and said, "If it's a boy, can we call him George, after my grandpa?"

A lawyer laid out the advantages of having one woman provide the egg and another the womb, so neither would have a full claim as mother. John had proposed that I be the biological father of this child and said that he might sire the next, if there were one. Like many middle-aged couples with fertility issues, we began the blind-dating egg hunt. I was sorry that I would never see what might come of the mixing of John's genes with my own, but thankful that we could have a child at all.

My research had made me acutely conscious of the quasi-eugenic aspect of the donor search—the ways we were opting for a donor who conformed to our standards of intelligence, character, health, and appearance. For me, these personal decisions had political overtones. I did not want to devalue the extraordinary lives I had come to respect, yet I couldn't deny that I wanted a child who would be familiar enough so that we would know how to soothe him or her. At the same time,

I understood that genetic lineage comes with no guarantees. The catalog of attractive attributes touting each donor made me feel as though we were choosing a car we would be driving for the rest of our lives. Sunroof? Good highway mileage? Red hair? High SAT scores? The whole quest was absurd, depressing, morally troubling. Yet the care of choosing the egg donor seemed like one concrete gesture we could make, an iota of knowledge in this vast mystery.

We told Laura and Tammy about our plan, and Laura said to John, "We couldn't have had Oliver and Lucy without you, and we'll never be able to thank you enough for that, but I could be your surrogate to show how much you and Andrew mean to us." There followed medical screenings, fertility treatments, embryo transfers, and ultrasounds. Like many of the families I had met, mine was touched in equal measure by changes in social norms and changes in technology. Their fortunate concurrence was the precondition of our children.

We got pregnant on our second IVF protocol. Although we had been extremely deliberate in egg selection, we ultimately decided not to have amniocentesis. This decision caught me by surprise when I made it with John and Laura. The risk of having a disabled child (highly unlikely according to less invasive but less conclusive tests) no longer seemed frightening enough to risk a miscarriage. I could have imagined terminating if we had received bad amnio results, but I could no longer have done so with the certain logic that would have guided me before I wrote this book. My research had shattered that clarity.

We drew closer to Laura, Tammy, and the kids. Oliver and Lucy referred to the yet-to-come baby as their brother. I was shy of their enthusiasm at first, but John and I went to Minneapolis for the late stages of the pregnancy and end up staying there for more than a month, seeing the four of them almost every day. When Oliver and Lucy learned that little Blaine called us *Daddy* and *Papa John*, they told their mothers they wanted to call us *Daddy* and *Papa*, too. Having set out to have two children, I was suddenly contemplating four, and now I believed that I could love them all profoundly, even if I loved them differently. John's insistence that we were all one family made it happen. By little Blaine, by the imminent baby, by Oliver and Lucy, and by the extraordinary families I'd come to know, I had been changed, and children no longer made me sad.

The day of George's birth—induced on April 9, 2009—was emotionally charged before it began. I had heard too many stories that started, "The pregnancy seemed to go so well, and then suddenly, when she went into labor . . ." I tried to quell my anxiety, but by the time George's head showed, my palms were damp with fear. Then out popped George, instantly proving the strength of his lungs with a good cry, and wiggling his arms and legs. The obstetrician pronounced him healthy. And then we noticed his umbilical cord, which was knotted.

George had come out at just the right time. If the labor had gone on longer or we had waited a few more days to induce labor, the knot might have tightened, depriving him of oxygen, destroying his brain, and giving Laura a potentially fatal hemorrhage. I cut the umbilical cord below the knot, so that danger could be kept far away from our miraculous baby.

Many photos were taken, and we took off our shirts so he

could be on our skin, and we watched him be weighed and measured, and we saw ointments put on his eyes, and we introduced him to Oliver and Lucy. We called my father and stepmother, my brother, Blaine, and a few others who matter deeply to us. John was instantly enraptured, as I knew he would be, because birth is so mysterious and so much weirder than sorcery or intergalactic warfare that it humbles you instantly. I had felt it with little Blaine and I felt it again here. This person hadn't existed before, and now he did, and I remember thinking what everyone had always thought; that his coming into the world made up for all the previous losses.

The next morning, the pediatrician told us that George had not been drawing his legs up the way that babies are supposed to, and was instead holding them out stiff and straight for up to three minutes at a time. She referred to this as "inappropriately high muscle tone" and said that it might reflect brain damage, and that she wanted to order a CAT scan. I asked whether this was unusual, and she said, simply, that it was not a frequent occurrence at this stage. I felt the inside parts of my body that are usually warm go cold, while the parts exposed to the air suddenly seemed to be on fire. The pediatrician calmly explained that the baby's unusual behavior could signal bleeding in the brain and that such bleeding might resolve itself or might need to be surgically alleviated. She mentioned the knot in the cord and said we needed to be certain that it hadn't had an impact. She noted that his head was unusually large, which could be related to the presence of tumors. She added that he was stiffening one leg more than the other, which might mean that he had asymmetrical brain development or a mass in his brain. She was young, and I could tell that this was the steady, competent manner she had learned for the purpose of being honest with people without alarming them, but there was nothing calm in what she said.

From the time George was conceived until that day, I had kept thinking how ironic it would be if, in the midst of writing about exceptional children, I were to produce such a child. Now, I asked how soon the CAT scan could be done, and the pediatrician said she'd set it up as soon as possible, and in her brisk and pleasant way she left the room. I looked at George and knew I loved him by how hard I suddenly tried not to love him. I remembered all the parents who had described spreading the news about their thriving baby and then picking up the phone a day or two later to report a different tale. I wanted him to be well, but I wanted me to be well, too, and even as I formulated that divide, it collapsed, and I saw that one thing could not be true without the other.

So many parents had told me how the need to deal with such situations upstages the emotions of them, and I was relieved to settle into problem-solving mode. I would do everything right, which would postpone anguish. I remembered parents saying that they don't tell you at the beginning that your child will need thirty major interventions; they tell you he will need one, and then a little later that he will need one more, and then another— that the gradualism deprives you of volition. I was determined to be awake at each choice to what might come next.

The pediatric nurse explained that she had to do an arterial blood draw; she drove a needle deep into his wrist. An arterial blood draw? Had any of the 400 parents I had met mentioned an arterial blood draw? Finally, we were set for the CAT scan. I felt two conflicting guilts: first that I had produced a child who might suffer, and second that despite all the stories I'd heard from parents who found deep meaning in bringing up exceptional children, I didn't want to join their number. What I was experiencing was illness, and like all parents since the dawn of time, I wanted to protect my child from illness. And I wanted also to protect myself. Yet I knew from the work I had done that if our son had any of the things for which we were about to start testing, those conditions would ultimately be his identity, and if they were his identity, they would become my identity too—one we both might come to cherish.

The imaging room was grim, despite touches intended to make it cheerful and friendly. We watched helplessly as George was positioned in the machine. He was more or less asleep and did not stir as his head was locked into place with several blankets wedged next to it and straps fastened across his forehead. They let us stay, wearing big lead aprons, and we tried to comfort George, and I was suddenly aware of how uncomforting I was to someone who had not yet learned to turn to me for comfort.

I think all love is one-third projection and one-third acceptance and never more than one-third knowledge and insight. With my children's births I had projected and accepted so much, so fast. I remembered Sara Hadden wanting to baptize her son when she found out how severely disabled he was, as a way of formalizing her belief that he was nonetheless a person. I realized that George, who had done nothing more admirable than cry and feed, was richly and permanently human to me, possessed of a soul, and no alteration could change that. The tree doesn't grow far from the apple.

Back in our room, we waited for what felt like a very long time. Finally we learned that George was fine. The whole thing was over. But I was permanently changed. I understood the day George was declared well that hope is a squalling, pink thing newly arrived, that there is no other optimism so great as having a child. Our love for our children is almost entirely situational, and yet it is very nearly the strongest emotion we know. This book's stories were to my love for my children much as parables are to faith, the concrete narratives that make the greatest abstractions true. I am the parent I am in the wake of this book's epic narratives of resilience.

When I was born, the common view was that nurture decided almost everything. In the decades that followed, the emphasis shifted to nature. In the last twenty years, people have talked more broadly about the intricate ways that nature and nurture propel each other. I was intellectually persuaded by this nuanced integration, but the experience of having my own children has made me wonder if a third element is involved, some unknowable inflection of spirit or divinity. Most of the parents I interviewed for this book said they would never want other children than the ones they had, which at first seemed surprising given the challenges their children embody. But why does any of us prefer our own children, all of them defective in some regard, to others real or imagined? If some glorious angel descended into my living room and offered to exchange my children for other, better children—brighter, kinder, funnier, more loving, more disciplined, more accomplished—I would clutch the ones I have and, like most parents, pray away the atrocious specter.

After George arrived, the question arose of how the family relationships might constellate. John and I have complete charge of George; Blaine and I had agreed in advance that we would make the major decisions about little Blaine together; Laura and Tammy have separate parental authority, and we do not set the course for Oliver and Lucy, nor Laura and Tammy for George. The three arrangements are different, and in the same ways most parents try to suppress sibling rivalry, we struggle to avoid situational comparisons. Occasional frictions are sparked by conflicting priorities and boundaries, disparate resources, myriad parenting styles—but they are overshadowed by the fact that it all somehow functions. We have fought hard for the familial relationships into which others stumble, and there is a veteran's peace in our mutual devotion.

It must be easier to lead a life in which you are not constantly inventing all the roles, in which there is a script to follow. We have often felt like Christopher Columbus landing for the first time on the wilder shores of love, and while being a pioneer can be thrilling, sometimes one would prefer a place where the roads have already been built and the Internet access is wireless. Most people expect to have children, and there are vulnerabilities attached to that; I had expected not to have children, and the reversal contains stranger vulnerabilities. We have made many careful, thoughtful decisions, but so much of how we've worked it out wasn't actually rooted in choice. Like other parents, I simply lived my life from day to day, until the unusual became quotidian. I have said that parents do not reproduce, but create. In fact, we also discover.

John and I sent out birth announcements that included a picture of us with George. One of John's cousins returned hers with a terse note that began, "Your lifestyle is against our Christian values," and ended with, "We wish to have no further contact." Some people scorn the idea of calling six primary parents and four children in three states a family, or fear that the existence of our family somehow undermines theirs. An old friend said to me over lunch one day, "Isn't it wonderful how your father accepts your children?" I pointed out that my children were his grandchildren, and she said, "Yes, but even so." That kind of surprise can be very taxing, a constant reminder that we are not the norm.

Some people are trapped by the belief that love comes in finite quantities, and that our kind of love exhausts the supply upon which they need to draw. I do not accept competitive models of love, only additive ones. My journeys toward a family and this book have taught me that love is a magnifying phenomenon—that every increase in love strengthens all the other love in the world, that much as loving one's family can be a means of loving God, so the love that exists within any family can fortify the love of all families. The affection my family have found in one another is not a better love, but it is another love, and just as species diversity is crucial to sustain the planet, this diversity strengthens the ecosphere of kindness. Loving one's own strange children is good training for loving other people's strange children. The road less traveled by, as it turns out, leads to pretty much the same place. Now, children make me happy.

A generation ago, this love would have stayed dormant and unrealized. But so, too, would much of the love described in this book, the love of all these parents for children who would once have died young, or been put away, or lived unacknowledged as fully human. My family is radical for a different reason from most of the others I have chronicled, but all of us are exponents of revolutionary love against the odds.

As a parent, for all that I relish glee, I know that attachment happens when things turn dark. Parenting is an exercise in safety, and the perpetual menace of danger is what exalts parental love above affection; without the night terrors, the spiking fevers, the litany of bruises and woes, it would be a second-rate entertainment. It took me some time to understand that attention to one's children's needs is the essence of gratification. From that perspective, it made sense that the difficult loves of these pages are so deep. I want more than anything for my children to be happy, and I love them because they are sad, and the erratic project of kneading that sadness into joy is the engine of my life as a father, as a son, as a friend—and as a writer.

Sometimes, people end up thankful for what they mourned. You cannot achieve this state by seeking tragedy, but you can keep yourself open more to sorrow's richness than to its despair. Insofar as I have written a self-help book, it is a how-to manual for openness: a description of how to tolerate what cannot be cured, and an argument that cures are not always appropriate even when they are possible.

Given how unimaginable my family would have been fifty years ago, I have no choice but to champion progress; change has been good to me, and I am indebted to it. I hope these stories will contribute to the force that is polishing the rough surface of the world. Until the planet grows smooth, however, love will continue to toughen under siege; the very threats to love strengthen it even as they suffuse it with pain. In the harsh moments of loss that are my topic here, love captures a tender heart.

I felt something brilliant and terrifying for my son as he lay in that *Star Trek*–like CAT scanner that I had not yet felt for little Blaine, who had not encountered such adversity, nor for Oliver and Lucy, who were already themselves when I got to know them. It changed my relationship to them all. Children ensnared me the moment I connected fatherhood with loss, but I'm not sure I would have noticed that if I hadn't been immersed in this research. Encountering so much strange love, I fell into its bewitching patterns and saw how splendor can illuminate even the most abject vulnerabilities. I had witnessed and learned the terrifying joy of unbearable responsibility, recognized how it conquers everything else. Sometimes, I had thought the heroic parents in this book were fools, enslaving themselves to a life's journey with their alien children, trying to breed identity out of misery. That day in the hospital with George, I was startled to find that my research had built me a plank, and that I was ready to join them on their ship.

Acknowledgments

A book such as this one is a group enterprise, and I am grateful, first and foremost, to the individuals and families who agreed to be interviewed, in many cases speaking about painful experiences at considerable personal cost. *Far from the Tree* would not exist without them, and neither would the world it documents. I am humbled by their grit, wisdom, generosity, and truthfulness.

The original impetus for this investigation came from an assignment to write about Deaf culture for the *New York Times Magazine*, and I thank Adam Moss and Jack Rosenthal for proposing that topic to me, and Annette Grant for editing my article. I engaged with the question of prodigies when I was assigned to write about Evgeny Kissin for the *New Yorker*, and I am grateful to Tina Brown, Henry Finder, and Charles Michener for encouraging me in that work. Leslie Hawke came to my house one night in 2001 with a screening copy of Lisa Hedley's astonishing film *Dwarfs: Not a Fairy Tale*; from our conversation that night, this book took shape. In 2007, Adam Moss suggested that I write about the neurodiversity movement for *New York*, an assignment that turned out to be pivotal in my evolving understanding of the people I was writing about; Emily Nussbaum was my editor for that story. I thank them both.

I was lucky enough to have guides who helped me enter many of the communities I wished to document. Jackie Roth opened up Deaf culture to me starting in 1994 and arranged many interviews I've included here. Betty Adelson was my chief adviser on dwarfs, and I thank her for reading and correcting drafts of that chapter. Suzanne Elliott Armstrong and Betsy Goodwin were helpful as I worked on Down syndrome. Daniel M. Geschwind, Thomas Insel,

James D. Watson, and Bruce Stillman assisted me incalculably with the science of autism. Jeffrey Lieberman was my tireless guide to the science of schizophrenia, and David Nathan generously spent time discussing the condition and helping me to meet patients. For their tremendous assistance with my schizophrenia research, I thank Colleen Marie Barrett, Bruce M. Cohen, Cathie Cook, and Scott Rauch at McLean Hospital. Kathleen Seidel educated me on many issues around disability and gave me my training in disability rights. I am particularly grateful to Justin Davidson, Siu Li GoGwilt, Charles Hamlen, Sarah Billinghurst Solomon, and Shirley Young for their unflagging support as I worked on the prodigies chapter, and to Susan Ebersole and Robert Sirota for introducing me to students at the Manhattan School of Music. I am grateful to Jesse Dudley for translating for me *Dad's Aspirations Are That High*, by Yuanju Li (2001) (爸爸的心就这么高：钢琴天才郎朗和他的父亲 / *Ba ba de xin jiu zhe mo gao: gang qin tian cai Lang Lang he ta de fu qin)*. I thank Janet Benshoof for sharing her insights from a lifetime devoted to reproductive rights. In connection with the crime chapter, I thank the inspirational Stephen DiMenna, who encouraged me to accompany him to the Hennepin County Home School, where Tom Bezek, Thelma Fricke, Shelley Whelan, and Terry Wise kindly facilitated my interviews with residents and their families. Alex Busansky and Jennifer Trone, of the Commission on Safety and Abuse in America's Prisons, provided terrific background information for that chapter. My work on the trans community relied on the help and support of Matt Foreman, Lisa Mottet, Kim Pearson and her TYFA team, and Rachel Pepper.

I was fortunate to have a sterling research team who obtained and organized vast bodies of information. Over a decade, smart and stalwart

Ian Beilin, witty and compelling Stephen Bitterolf, rigorous and loyal Susan Ciampa, conscientious Jonah Engle, free-thinking Edric Mesmer, scrupulous and astute Kari Milchman, gracious and splendid Deborah Pursch, courageous Jacob Shamberg, and brilliantly imaginative Rachel Trocchio variously brought knowledge, coherence, and discernment to my research. Pat Towers edited a sample chapter. I am very grateful to Susan Kittenplan for her excellent edit of the manuscript when it was at its most cumbersome. I thank Eugene Corey for transcribing the earlier interviews, and Sandra Arroyo, Sonia Houmis, Kathleen Vach, and the rest of the team at TruTranscripts for working on the later ones.

I became something of a residency junky while working on this book. I had one stay at the Rockefeller Foundation Bellagio Center, one at the Ucross Foundation, two at the MacDowell Colony, and four at Yaddo. The serenity these institutions afforded me was critical to the book. I would like particularly to thank Pilar Palacia and Darren Walker at the Rockefeller Foundation; Sharon Dynak and Ruthie Salvatore at Ucross; Michelle Aldredge, Nancy Devine, David Macy, Brendan Tapley, and Cheryl Young at MacDowell; and Cathy Clarke, Elaina Richardson, and Candace Wait at Yaddo.

I remain deeply indebted as always to my wise and loyal agent and friend, Andrew Wylie, who has championed my work now for almost a quarter century and has helped me to become the writer I am. I am grateful also to his able deputies, especially Sarah Chalfant, Alexandra Levenberg, and Jeffrey Posternak. I pay tribute to my beloved editor at Scribner, Nan Graham, who reads with a valiant heart and a kind pencil; her signal mix of empathy, enthusiasm, patience, and insight shaped this book from the time when I was only imagining it to the time when I finally completed it. I thank, also at Scribner, Brian Belfiglio, Steve Boldt, Rex Bonomelli, Daniel Burgess, Roz Lippel,

Kate Lloyd, Susan Moldow, Greg Mortimer, Carolyn Reidy, Kathleen Rizzo, Kara Watson, and Paul Whitlatch. At Chatto & Windus, I thank Alison Samuel, who bought the book, and Clara Farmer, who saw it through production. For their help with the Young Adult edition, I thank my adapter, Laurie Calkhoven; my wonderful editor, Zareen Jaffery, and her able assistant, Mekisha Telfer. I thank managing editor, Katrina Groover; Chloë Foglia, art director; and Moricor and Moricar for the cover embroidery. I am grateful to Andrew Essex, Ben Freda, Jonathan Hills, Trinity Ray, Eric Rayman, Andres Saavedra, and Eric Schwinn for their help with other aspects of publication.

I thank Cheryl Henson and Ed Finn for giving me the jacket image, and Adam Fuss for creating it; I thank Annie Leibovitz for creating and giving me my author photo.

Every book I've written has been corrected by Katherine Keenum, my freshman writing tutor. Her devotion is profoundly heartening, and her close reading, invaluable.

Kathleen Seidel came on board to organize my bibliography, compile citations, and check facts; she took it upon herself to question prejudices related to identity, disability, medicine, and the law. She was a brilliant *diaskeuast*, and this would have been an entirely different book without her meticulous intelligence, bracing precision, passion for accuracy, and sense of justice.

Alice Truax wrestled multiple drafts of this book to the ground. Her understanding of my purpose was so profound that I felt as though she had climbed inside my mind to make repairs. My method is associative; hers, logical. With infinite patience and skill, she chipped away at great blocks of chaos to reveal the coherence trapped inside them.

Many people helped keep my life running while I was writing this book, and I'd like to thank Sergio Avila, Lorilynn Bauer, Juan and Amalia Fernandez, Ildikó Fülöp, Judy Gutow, Christina Harper, Brenda Hernández-Reynoso, Marsha Johnson, Celso, Miguela, and Olga Mancol, Tatiana Martushev, Heather Nedwell, Jacek Niewinski, Mindy Pollack, Kylee Sallak, Eduardo and Elfi de los Santos, Marie Talentowski, Ester Tolete, Danusia Trevino, and Bechir Zouay.

It is impossible to acknowledge everyone who participated in this work; almost daily, someone said something that helped me understand more clearly my underlying topics of identity and love. Among the glorious people who made helpful introductions or discussed ideas that are central to the book or read and commented on sections of it are Cordelia Anderson, Laura Anderson, Anne Applebaum, Lucy Armstrong, Dorothy Arnsten, Jack Barchas, Nesli Basgoz, Frank Bayley, Cris Beam, Bill and Bunny Beekman, Meica and Miguel de Beistegui, Erika Belsey and Alexi Worth, Mary Bisbee-Beek, Richard Bradley, Susan Brody, Hugo Burnand, Elizabeth Burns, Elizabeth and Blake Cabot, Mario and Ariadne Calvo-Platero, S. Talcott Camp, Thomas Caplan, Christian Caryl, Amy Fine Collins, Cathryn Collins, Robert Couturier, Dana B. Cowin and Barclay Palmer, Rebecca Culley and Peter K. Lee, Mary D'Alton, Nana-Ama Danquah, Cecile David-Weill, Justin Davidson and Ariella Budick, Nick Davis and Jane Mendelsohn, Roland Davis and Margot Norris, Miraj Desai, Freddy Eberstadt, Nenna Eberstadt and Alistair Bruton, Nicholas Rollo David Evans, Melissa Feldman, Lorraine Ferguson, Susannah Fiennes, Adam and Olivia Flatto, Bill Foreman and Reg Barton, Cornelia Foss, Richard A. Friedman and Bob Hughes, Richard C. Friedman, Fran Gallacher, Arlyn Gardner, Rhonda Garelick, Kathleen Gerard, Bernard Gersten and Cora Cahan, Icy Gordon, Ann Gottleib, Philip Gourevich and Larissa MacFarquhar, Geordie and Kathryn Greig, Guo Fang, Melanie and Martin Hall, Han Feng, Amy Harmon, John Hart, Ashton Hawkins and Johnnie Moore,

David Hecht, Cheryl Henson and Ed Finn, David Herskovits and Jennifer Egan, Gillie Holme and Camille Massey, Richard Hubbard, Ana Joanes, Lisa Jonas, Maira Kalman, William Kentridge and Anne Stanwix, Terry Kirk, Larry Kramer, Søren Krogh, Mary Krueger and Andreas Saavedra, Roger and Neroli Lacey, Jhumpa Lahiri and Alberto Vourvoulias-Bush, Katherine Lanpher, Paul LeClerc, Michael Lee and Ashutosh Khandekar, Justin Leites, Jeffrey and Rosemarie Lieberman, Jennie Livingston, Betsy de Lotbinière, Ivana Lowell and Howard Blum, Sue Macartney-Snape, John MacPhee, Jamie Marks, Mary E. Marks, Cleopatra Mathis, Tey Meadow, James Meyer, Juliet Mitchell, Isaac Mizrahi, R. Clayton Mulford, Freda and Christian Murck, John and Nancy Novogrod, Rusty O'Kelley III and John Haskins, Ann Olson, Beatrix Ost and Ludwig Kuttner, Mary Alice Palmer, Harriet Paterson and Rick Cockett, Julie Peters, Alice Playten, Francine du Plessix Gray, Charles and Barbara Prideaux, Dièry Prudent and Mariza Scotch, Deborah and David Pursch, Emily K. Rafferty, Kim Reed and Claire Jones, Maggie Robbins, Paul and Susannah Robinson, Marion Lignana Rosenberg, Robert Rosenkranz and Alexandra K. Munroe, Steven Rosoff and Tanis Allen, Ira Sachs, Eric Saltzman, Phillip and Donna Satow, Christina Schmidt, Lisa Schmitz, John Schneeman, Jill Schuker, Alex Shand, Julie Sheehan, Nicola Shulman, Polly Shulman, Michael Silverman, Dee Smith, Doug Smith, Gordon Smith, Calvin, Emmett, and Abigail Solomon, David and Sarah Long Solomon, Cindy Spiegel, Moonhawk River Stone, Kerry J. Sulkowicz and Sandra Leong, Ezra Susser, Claudia Swan, Dean Swanson, András Szántó and Alanna Stang, Dina Temple-Raston, Phyllis Toohey, Tara Tooke, Carll Tucker and Jane Bryant Quinn, Susan Wadsworth, Kathryn Walker, Jim and Liz Watson, Caroline Weber, Helen Whitney, Susan Willard, Hope and Grant Winthrop, Jaime Wolf, Micky Wolfson, Doug Wright and Dave Clement, and Larisa Zvezdochetova.

I thank Laura Scher and Tammy Ward for cheering me on as I wrote and for bringing so much joy into my life.

I am forever indebted to Blaine Smith for her exquisite sympathy, generosity, and wisdom; I am grateful to her also for her insights on this book's design.

My stepmother, Sarah Billinghurst Solomon, talked through *Far from the Tree* with me year in and year out, providing copious insights and encouragement. Additionally, she urged me to stay with my father and her for long periods when I needed to write. The time we all had together was magical, and this book would not exist without it.

My father, Howard Solomon, my most loyal reader, pored over a stupefying number of early fragments and later versions of this book. We talked about every interview and idea, and he never wavered in his conviction that the undertaking would succeed. His lifelong devotion was my first experience of the kind of unstinting parenthood I've chronicled here.

I am grateful to Oliver Scher, Lucy Scher, Blaine Solomon, and George Solomon for their patience when my work kept me from fun and games. This book is a tribute to them, but it required their forbearance.

Finally, I thank my husband, John Habich Solomon, who lived with me when I was working and lived without me when I was working. His editing of the manuscript into precision was a great boon; his editing of my life into happiness is the greatest boon I've ever known.

Notes

To avoid making this book even longer than it is or festooning it with ellipsis marks, further notes can be found online at http://www.andrewsolomon.com/far-from-the-tree-footnotes.

A note on the notes: I allowed everyone I interviewed the choice of being quoted by name or pseudonymously. I have indicated all pseudonyms in the notes. Though I attempted to stay as true as possible to the identities of those who are quoted pseudonymously, I have changed some personal information to protect the privacy of people who wished me to do so.

Further Reading

For further reading on materials that influenced my thinking, as well as a list of sources from which I made direct citations, please visit http://www.andrewsolomon.com/far-from-the-tree-bibliography.

Permissions

Index